Algorithms Unlocked

Algorithms Unlocked

Thomas H. Cormen

The MIT Press
Cambridge, Massachusetts   London, England

MIT Press books may be purchased at special quantity discounts for business or sales promotional use. For information, please email special_sales@mitpress.mit.edu or write to Special Sales Department, The MIT Press, 55 Hayward Street, Cambridge, MA 02142.

This book was set in Times Roman and Mathtime Pro 2 by the author and was printed and bound in the United States of America.

Library of Congress Cataloging-in-Publication Data

Cormen, Thomas H.
Algorithms Unlocked / Thomas H. Cormen.
    p. cm
Includes bibliographical references and index.
ISBN 978-0-262-51880-2 (pbk. : alk. paper)
1. Computer algorithms. I. Title.
QA76.9.A43C685 2013
005.1—dc23

2012036810

10 9 8 7 6 5 4 3 2

Contents

In loving memory of my mother, Renee Cormen.

Preface

How do computers solve problems? How can your little GPS find, out of the gazillions of possible routes, the fastest way to your destination, and do so in mere seconds? When you purchase something on the Internet, how is your credit-card number protected from someone who intercepts it? The answer to these, and a ton of other questions, is ***algorithms***. I wrote this book to unlock the mystery of algorithms for you.

I coauthored the textbook *Introduction to Algorithms*. It's a wonderful book (of course, I'm biased), but it gets pretty technical in spots.

This book is not *Introduction to Algorithms*. It's not even a textbook. It goes neither broadly nor deeply into the field of computer algorithms, it doesn't prescriptively teach techniques for designing computer algorithms, and it contains nary a problem or exercise for the reader to solve.

So just what is this book? It's a place for you to start, if

- you're interested in how computers solve problems,

- you want to know how to evaluate the quality of these solutions,

- you'd like to see how problems in computing and approaches to solving them relate to the non-computer world,

- you can handle a little mathematics, and

- you have not necessarily ever written a computer program (though it doesn't hurt to have programmed).

Some books about computer algorithms are conceptual, with little technical detail. Some are chock full of technical precision. Some are in between. Each type of book has its place. I'd place this book in the in-between category. Yes, it has some math, and it gets rather precise in some places, but I've avoided getting deep into details (except perhaps toward the end of the book, where I just couldn't control myself).

I think of this book as a bit like an antipasto. Suppose you go to an Italian restaurant and order an antipasto, holding off on deciding whether to order the rest of the meal until you've had the antipasto. It arrives, and you eat it. Maybe you don't like the antipasto, and you decide to not order anything else. Maybe you like it, but it fills you up, so that you don't need to order anything else. Or maybe you like the antipasto, it does not fill you up, and you're looking forward to the rest of the meal. Thinking of this book as the antipasto, I'm hoping for one of the latter two outcomes: either you read this book, you're satisfied, and you feel no need to delve deeper into the world of algorithms; or you like what you read here so much that you want to learn more. Each chapter ends with a section titled "Further reading," which will guide you to books and articles that go deeper into the topics.

What will you learn from this book?

I can't tell you what you will learn from this book. Here's what I *intend* for you to learn from this book:

- What computer algorithms are, one way to describe them, and how to evaluate them.

- Simple ways to search for information in a computer.

- Methods to rearrange information in a computer so that it's in a prescribed order. (We call this task "sorting.")

- How to solve basic problems that we can model in a computer with a mathematical structure known as a "graph." Among many applications, graphs are great for modeling road networks (which intersections have direct roads to which other intersections, and how long are these roads?), dependencies among tasks (which task must precede which other tasks?), financial relationships (what are the exchange rates among all world currencies?), or interactions among people (who knows whom? who hates whom? which actor appeared in a movie with which other actor?).

- How to solve problems that ask questions about strings of textual characters. Some of these problems have applications in areas such as biology, where the characters represent base molecules and the strings of characters represent DNA structure.

- The basic principles behind cryptography. Even if you have never encrypted a message yourself, your computer probably has (such as when you purchase goods online).

- Fundamental ideas of data compression, going well beyond "f u cn rd ths u cn gt a gd jb n gd pay."

- That some problems are hard to solve on a computer in any reasonable amount of time, or at least that nobody has ever figured out how to do so.

What do you already need to know to understand the material in this book?

As I said earlier, there's some math in this book. If math scares you, then you can try skipping over it, or you can try a less technical book. But I've done my best to make the math accessible.

I don't assume that you've ever written or even read a computer program. If you can follow instructions in outline format, you should be able to understand how I express the steps that, together, form an algorithm. If you get the following joke, you're already part of the way there:

> Did you hear about the computer scientist who got stuck in the shower? He[1] was washing his hair and following the instructions on the shampoo bottle. They read "Lather. Rinse. Repeat."

I've used a fairly informal writing style in this book, hoping that a personal approach will help make the material accessible. Some chapters depend on material in previous chapters, but such dependencies are few. Some chapters start off in a nontechnical manner and become progressively more technical. Even if you find that you're getting in over your head in one chapter, you can probably benefit from reading at least the beginning of the next chapter.

Reporting errors

If you find an error in this book, please let me know about it by sending email to algorithms-unlocked@mit.edu.

Acknowledgments

Much of the material in this book draws from *Introduction to Algorithms*, and so I owe a great deal to my coauthors on that book, Charles Leiserson, Ron Rivest, and Cliff Stein. You'll find that throughout this

---

[1] Or she. Given the unfortunate gender ratio in computer science, chances are it was he.

book, I shamelessly refer to (read: plug) *Introduction to Algorithms*, known far and wide by the initials CLRS of the four authors. Writing this book on my own makes me realize how much I miss collaborating with Charles, Ron, and Cliff. I also transitively thank everyone we thanked in the preface of CLRS.

I also drew on material from courses that I've taught at Dartmouth, especially Computer Science 1, 5, and 25. Thanks to my students for letting me know, by their insightful questions, which pedagogical approaches worked and, by their stony silence, which did not.

This book came to be at the suggestion of Ada Brunstein, who was our editor at the MIT Press when we prepared the third edition of CLRS. Ada has since moved on, and Jim DeWolf took her place. Originally, this book was slated to be part of the MIT Press "Essential Knowledge" series, but the MIT Press deemed it too technical for the series. (Imagine that—I wrote a book too technical for MIT!) Jim handled this potentially awkward situation smoothly, allowing me to write the book that I wanted to write rather than the book that the MIT Press originally thought I was writing. I also appreciate the support of Ellen Faran and Gita Devi Manaktala of the MIT Press.

Julie Sussman, P.P.A., was our technical copyeditor for the second and third editions of CLRS, and I am once again thrilled to have her copyedit this book. Best. Technical. Copyeditor. Ever. She let me get away with nothing. Here's evidence, in the form of part of an email that Julie sent me about an early draft of Chapter 5:

> Dear Mr. Cormen,
>
> Authorities have apprehended an escaped chapter, which has been found hiding in your book. We are unable to determine what book it has escaped from, but we cannot imagine how it could have been lodging in your book for these many months without your knowledge, so we have no option but to hold you responsible. We hope that you will take on the task of reforming this chapter and will give it an opportunity to become a productive citizen of your book. A report from the arresting officer, Julie Sussman, is appended.

In case you're wondering what "P.P.A." stands for, the first two letters are for "Professional Pain." You can probably guess what the "A" stands for, but I want to point out that Julie takes pride in this title, and rightly so. Thanks a googol, Julie!

I am no cryptographer, and the chapter on principles of cryptography benefited tremendously from comments and suggestions by Ron Rivest, Sean Smith, Rachel Miller, and Huijia Rachel Lin. That chapter has a footnote on baseball signs, and I thank Bob Whalen, the baseball coach at Dartmouth, for patiently explaining to me some of the signing systems in baseball. Ilana Arbisser verified that computational biologists align DNA sequences in the way that I explain in Chapter 7. Jim DeWolf and I went through several iterations of titles for this book, but it was an undergraduate student at Dartmouth, Chander Ramesh, who came up with *Algorithms Unlocked*.

The Dartmouth College Department of Computer Science is an awesome place to work. My colleagues are brilliant and collegial, and our professional staff is second to none. If you're looking for a computer science program at the undergraduate or graduate level, or if you seek a faculty position in computer science, I encourage you to apply to Dartmouth.

Finally, I thank my wife, Nicole Cormen; my parents, Renee and Perry Cormen; my sister, Jane Maslin; and Nicole's parents, Colette and Paul Sage, for their love and support. My father is sure that the figure on page 2 is a 5, not an S.

TOM CORMEN
Hanover, New Hampshire
November 2012

1 What Are Algorithms and Why Should You Care?

Let's start with the question that I'm often asked: "What is an algorithm?"[1]

A broad answer would be "a set of steps to accomplish a task." You have algorithms that you run in your everyday life. You have an algorithm to brush your teeth: open the toothpaste tube, pick up your toothbrush, squeeze toothpaste onto the brush until you have applied enough to the brush, close the tube, put the brush into one quadrant of your mouth, move the brush up and down for N seconds, etc. If you have to commute to a job, you have an algorithm for your commute. And so on.

But this book is about algorithms that run on computers or, more generally, computational devices. Just as algorithms that *you* run affect your everyday life, so do algorithms that run on computers. Do you use your GPS to find a route to travel? It runs what we call a "shortest-path" algorithm to find the route. Do you buy products on the Internet? Then you use (or should be using) a secure website that runs an encryption algorithm. When you buy products on the Internet, are they delivered by a private delivery service? It uses algorithms to assign packages to individual trucks and then to determine the order in which each driver should deliver packages. Algorithms run on computers all over the place—on your laptop, on servers, on your smartphone, on embedded systems (such as in your car, your microwave oven, or climate-control systems)—everywhere!

What distinguishes an algorithm that runs on a computer from an algorithm that you run? You might be able to tolerate it when an algorithm is imprecisely described, but a computer cannot. For example, if you drive to work, your drive-to-work algorithm might say "if traffic is bad, take an alternate route." Although you might know what you mean by "bad traffic," a computer does not.

So a computer algorithm is a set of steps to accomplish a task that is described precisely enough that a computer can run it. If you have

---

[1]Or, as a fellow with whom I used to play hockey would ask, "What's a nalgorithm?"

done even a little computer programming in Java, C, C++, Python, Fortran, Matlab, or the like, then you have some idea of what that level of precision means. If you have never written a computer program, then perhaps you will get a feel for that level of precision from seeing how I describe algorithms in this book.

Let's go to the next question: "What do we want from a computer algorithm?"

Computer algorithms solve computational problems. We want two things from a computer algorithm: given an input to a problem, it should always produce a correct solution to the problem, and it should use computational resources efficiently while doing so. Let's examine these two desiderata in turn.

Correctness

What does it mean to produce a correct solution to a problem? We can usually specify precisely what a correct solution would entail. For example, if your GPS produces a correct solution to finding the best route to travel, it might be the route, out of all possible routes from where you are to your desired destination, that will get you there soonest. Or perhaps the route that has the shortest possible distance. Or the route that will get you there soonest but also avoids tolls. Of course, the information that your GPS uses to determine a route might not match reality. Unless your GPS can access real-time traffic information, it might assume that the time to traverse a road equals the road's distance divided by the road's speed limit. If the road is congested, however, the GPS might give you bad advice if you're looking for the fastest route. We can still say that the routing algorithm that the GPS runs is correct, however, even if the input to the algorithm is not; for the input given to the routing algorithm, the algorithm produces the fastest route.

Now, for some problems, it might be difficult or even impossible to say whether an algorithm produces a correct solution. Take optical character recognition for example. Is this 11×6 pixel image a 5 or an S?

Some people might call it a 5, whereas others might call it an S, so how could we declare that a computer's decision is either correct or incorrect? We won't. In this book, we will focus on computer algorithms that have knowable solutions.

Sometimes, however, we can accept that a computer algorithm might produce an incorrect answer, as long as we can control how often it does so. Encryption provides a good example. The commonly used RSA cryptosystem relies on determining whether large numbers—really large, as in hundreds of digits long—are prime. If you have ever written a computer program, you could probably write one that determines whether a number n is prime. It would test all candidate divisors from 2 through $n - 1$, and if any of these candidates is indeed a divisor of n, then n is composite. If no number between 2 and $n - 1$ is a divisor of n, then n is prime. But if n is hundreds of digits long, that's a lot of candidate divisors, more than even a really fast computer could check in any reasonable amount of time. Of course, you could make some optimizations, such as eliminating all even candidates once you find that 2 is not a divisor, or stopping once you get to $\sqrt{n}$ (since if d is greater than $\sqrt{n}$ and d is a divisor of n, then n/d is less than $\sqrt{n}$ and is also a divisor of n; therefore, if n has a divisor, you will find it by the time you get to $\sqrt{n}$). If n is hundreds of digits long, then although $\sqrt{n}$ has only about half as many digits as n does, it's still a really large number. The good news is that we know of an algorithm that tests quickly whether a number is prime. The bad news is that it can make errors. In particular, if it declares that n is composite, then n is definitely composite, but if it declares that n is prime, then there's a chance that n is actually composite. But the bad news is not all that bad: we can control the error rate to be really low, such as one error in every 2^{50} times. That's rare enough—one error in about every million billion times—for most of us to be comfortable with using this method to determine whether a number is prime for RSA.

Correctness is a tricky issue with another class of algorithms, called approximation algorithms. Approximation algorithms apply to optimization problems, in which we want to find the best solution according to some quantitative measure. Finding the fastest route, as a GPS does, is one example, where the quantitative measure is travel time. For some problems, we have no algorithm that finds an optimal solution in any reasonable amount of time, but we know of an approximation algorithm that, in a reasonable amount of time, can find a solution that is almost optimal. By "almost optimal," we typically mean that the quantitative measure of the solution found by the approximation algorithm is within some known factor of the optimal solution's quantitative measure. As long as we specify what the desired factor is, we can say that a correct solution from an approximation algorithm is any solution that is within that factor of the optimal solution.

Resource usage

What does it mean for an algorithm to use computational resources efficiently? We alluded to one measure of efficiency in the discussion of approximation algorithms: time. An algorithm that gives a correct solution but takes a long time to produce that correct solution might be of little or no value. If your GPS took an hour to determine which driving route it recommends, would you even bother to turn it on? Indeed, time is the primary measure of efficiency that we use to evaluate an algorithm, once we have shown that the algorithm gives a correct solution. But it is not the only measure. We might be concerned with how much computer memory the algorithm requires (its "memory footprint"), since an algorithm has to run within the available memory. Other possible resources that an algorithm might use: network communication, random bits (because algorithms that make random choices need a source of random numbers), or disk operations (for algorithms that are designed to work with disk-resident data).

In this book, as in most of the algorithms literature, we will focus on just one resource: time. How do we judge the time required by an algorithm? Unlike correctness, which does not depend on the particular computer that the algorithm runs on, the actual running time of an algorithm depends on several factors extrinsic to the algorithm itself: the speed of the computer, the programming language in which the algorithm is implemented, the compiler or interpreter that translates the program into code that runs on the computer, the skill of the programmer who writes the program, and other activity taking place on the computer concurrently with the running program. And that all assumes that the algorithm runs on just one computer with all its data in memory.

If we were to evaluate the speed of an algorithm by implementing it in a real programming language, running it on a particular computer with a given input, and measuring the time the algorithm takes, we would know nothing about how fast the algorithm ran on an input of a different size, or possibly even on a different input of the same size. And if we wanted to compare the relative speed of the algorithm with some other algorithm for the same problem, we would have to implement them both and run both of them on various inputs of various sizes. How, then, can we evaluate an algorithm's speed?

The answer is that we do so by a combination of two ideas. First, we determine how long the algorithm takes as a function of the size of its input. In our route-finding example, the input would be some representation of a roadmap, and its size would depend on the number of intersections and the number of roads connecting intersections in the map. (The physical size of the road network would not matter, since we can characterize all distances by numbers and all numbers occupy the same size in the input; the length of a road has no bearing on the input size.) In a simpler example, searching a given list of items to determine whether a particular item is present in the list, the size of the input would be the number of items in the list.

Second, we focus on how fast the function that characterizes the running time grows with the input size—the *rate of growth* of the running time. In Chapter 2, we'll see the notations that we use to characterize an algorithm's running time, but what's most interesting about our approach is that we look at only the dominant term in the running time, and we don't consider coefficients. That is, we focus on the **order of growth** of the running time. For example, suppose we could determine that a specific implementation of a particular algorithm to search a list of n items takes $50n + 125$ machine cycles. The $50n$ term dominates the 125 term once n gets large enough, starting at $n \geq 3$ and increasing in dominance for even larger list sizes. Thus, we don't consider the low-order term 125 when we describe the running time of this hypothetical algorithm. What might surprise you is that we also drop the coefficient 50, thereby characterizing the running time as growing linearly with the input size n. As another example, if an algorithm took $20n^3 + 100n^2 + 300n + 200$ machine cycles, we would say that its running time grows as n^3. Again, the low-order terms—$100n^2$, $300n$, and 200—become less and less significant as the input size n increases.

In practice, the coefficients that we ignore do matter. But they depend so heavily on the extrinsic factors that it's entirely possible that if we were comparing two algorithms, A and B, that have the same order of growth and are run on the same input, then A might run faster than B with a particular combination of machine, programming language, compiler/interpreter, and programmer, while B runs faster than A with some other combination. Of course, if algorithms A and B both produce correct solutions and A always runs twice as fast as B, then, all other things being equal, we prefer to always run A instead of B. From the point of view of comparing algorithms in the abstract, however, we focus on the order of growth, unadorned by coefficients or low-order terms.

The final question that we ask in this chapter: "Why should I care about computer algorithms?" The answer to this question depends on who you are.

Computer algorithms for non-computer people

Even if you don't consider yourself a computer insider, computer algorithms matter to you. After all, unless you're on a wilderness expedition without a GPS, you probably use them every day. Did you search for something on the Internet today? The search engine you used—whether it was Google, Bing, or any other search engine—employed sophisticated algorithms to search the Web and to decide in which order to present its results. Did you drive your car today? Unless you're driving a classic vehicle, its on-board computers made millions of decisions, all based on algorithms, during your trip. I could go on and on.

As an end user of algorithms, you owe it to yourself to learn a little bit about how we design, characterize, and evaluate algorithms. I assume that you have at least a mild interest, since you have picked up this book and read this far. Good for you! Let's see if we can get you up to speed so that you can hold your own at your next cocktail party in which the subject of algorithms comes up.[2]

Computer algorithms for computer people

If you're a computer person, then you had better care about computer algorithms! Not only are they at the heart of, well, everything that goes on inside your computer, but algorithms are just as much a technology as everything else that goes on inside your computer. You can pay a premium for a computer with the latest and greatest processor, but you

---

[2]Yes, I realize that unless you live in Silicon Valley, the subject of algorithms rarely comes up at cocktail parties that you attend, but for some reason, we computer science professors think it important that our students not embarrass us at cocktail parties with their lack of knowledge in particular areas of computer science.

need to run implementations of good algorithms on that computer in order for your money to be well spent.

Here's an example that illustrates how algorithms are indeed a technology. In Chapter 3, we are going to see a few different algorithms that sort a list of n values into ascending order. Some of these algorithms will have running times that grow like n^2, but some will have running times that grow like only $n \lg n$. What is $\lg n$? It is the base-2 logarithm of n, or $\log_2 n$. Computer scientists use base-2 logarithms so frequently that just like mathematicians and scientists who use the shorthand $\ln n$ for the natural logarithm—$\log_e n$—computer scientists use their own shorthand for base-2 logarithms. Now, because the function $\lg n$ is the inverse of an exponential function, it grows very slowly with n. If $n = 2^x$, then $x = \lg n$. For example, $2^{10} = 1024$, and therefore $\lg 1024$ is only 10; similarly $2^{20} = 1,048,576$ and so $\lg 1,048,576$ is only 20; and $2^{30} = 1,073,741,824$ means that $\lg 1,073,741,824$ is only 30. So a growth of $n \lg n$ vs. n^2 trades a factor of n for a factor of only $\lg n$, and that's a deal you should take any day.

Let's make this example more concrete by pitting a faster computer (computer A) running a sorting algorithm whose running time on n values grows like n^2 against a slower computer (computer B) running a sorting algorithm whose running time grows like $n \lg n$. They each must sort an array of 10 million numbers. (Although 10 million numbers might seem like a lot, if the numbers are eight-byte integers, then the input occupies about 80 megabytes, which fits in the memory of even an inexpensive laptop computer many times over.) Suppose that computer A executes 10 billion instructions per second (faster than any single sequential computer at the time of this writing) and computer B executes only 10 million instructions per second, so that computer A is 1000 times faster than computer B in raw computing power. To make the difference even more dramatic, suppose that the world's craftiest programmer codes in machine language for computer A, and the resulting code requires $2n^2$ instructions to sort n numbers. Suppose further that just an average programmer writes for computer B, using a high-level language with an inefficient compiler, with the resulting code taking $50n \lg n$ instructions. To sort 10 million numbers, computer A takes

$$\frac{2 \cdot (10^7)^2 \text{ instructions}}{10^{10} \text{ instructions/second}} = 20{,}000 \text{ seconds} \,,$$

which is more than 5.5 hours, while computer B takes

$$\frac{50 \cdot 10^7 \lg 10^7 \text{ instructions}}{10^7 \text{ instructions/second}} \approx 1163 \text{ seconds} ,$$

which is under 20 minutes. By using an algorithm whose running time grows more slowly, even with a poor compiler, computer B runs more than 17 times faster than computer A! The advantage of the $n \lg n$ algorithm is even more pronounced when we sort 100 million numbers: where the n^2 algorithm on computer A takes more than 23 days, the $n \lg n$ algorithm on computer B takes under four hours. In general, as the problem size increases, so does the relative advantage of the $n \lg n$ algorithm.

Even with the impressive advances we continually see in computer hardware, total system performance depends on choosing efficient algorithms as much as on choosing fast hardware or efficient operating systems. Just as rapid advances are being made in other computer technologies, they are being made in algorithms as well.

Further reading

In my highly biased opinion, the clearest and most useful source on computer algorithms is *Introduction to Algorithms* [CLRS09] by four devilishly handsome fellows. The book is commonly called "CLRS," after the initials of the authors. I've drawn on it for much of the material in this book. It's far more complete than this book, but it assumes that you've done at least a little computer programming, and it pulls no punches on the math. If you find that you're comfortable with the level of mathematics in this book, and you're ready to go deeper into the subject, then you can't do better than CLRS. (In my humble opinion, of course.)

John MacCormick's book *Nine Algorithms That Changed the Future* [Mac12] describes several algorithms and related aspects of computing that affect our everyday lives. MacCormick's treatment is less technical than this book. If you find that my approach in this book is too mathematical, then I recommend that you try reading MacCormick's book. You should be able to follow much of it even if you have a meager mathematical background.

In the unlikely event that you find CLRS too watered down, you can try Donald Knuth's multi-volume set *The Art of Computer Programming* [Knu97, Knu98a, Knu98b, Knu11]. Although the title of the series makes it sound like it might focus on details of writing code, these books contain brilliant, in-depth analyses of algorithms. Be warned, however: the material in *TAOCP* is intense. By the way, if you're wondering where the word "algorithm" comes from, Knuth says that it derives from the name "al-Khowârizmî," a ninth-century Persian mathematician.

In addition to CLRS, several other excellent texts on computer algorithms have been published over the years. The chapter notes for Chapter 1 of CLRS list many such texts. Rather than replicate that list here, I refer you to CLRS.

2 How to Describe and Evaluate Computer Algorithms

In the previous chapter, you got a taste of how we couch the running time of a computer algorithm: by focusing on the running time as a function of the input size, and specifically on the order of growth of the running time. In this chapter, we'll back up a bit and see how we describe computer algorithms. Then we'll see the notations that we use to characterize the running times of algorithms. We'll wrap up this chapter by examining some techniques that we use to design and understand algorithms.

How to describe computer algorithms

We always have the option of describing a computer algorithm as a runnable program in a commonly used programming language, such as Java, C, C++, Python, or Fortran. Indeed, several algorithms textbooks do just that. The problem with using real programming languages to specify algorithms is that you can get bogged down in the details of the language, obscuring the ideas behind the algorithms. Another approach, which we took in *Introduction to Algorithms*, uses "pseudocode," which looks like a mashup of various programming languages with English mixed in. If you've ever used a real programming language, you can figure out pseudocode easily. But if you have not ever programmed, then pseudocode might seem a bit mysterious.

The approach I'm taking in this book is that I'm not trying to describe algorithms to software or hardware, but to "wetware": the gray matter between your ears. I am also going to assume that you have never written a computer program, and so I won't express algorithms using any real programming language or even pseudocode. Instead, I'll describe them in English, using analogies to real-world scenarios whenever I can. In order to indicate what happens when (what we call "flow of control" in programming), I'll use lists and lists within lists. If you want to implement an algorithm in a real programming language, I'll give you credit for being able to translate my description into runnable code.

Although I will try to keep descriptions as nontechnical as possible, this book is about algorithms for computers, and so I will have to use computing terminology. For example, computer programs contain ***procedures*** (also known as functions or methods in real programming languages), which specify how to do something. In order to actually get the procedure to do what it's supposed to do, we ***call*** it. When we call a procedure, we supply it with inputs (usually at least one, but some procedures take no inputs). We specify the inputs as ***parameters*** within parentheses after the name of the procedure. For example, to compute the square root of a number, we might define a procedure SQUARE-ROOT(x); here, the input to the procedure is referred to by the parameter x. The call of a procedure may or may not produce output, depending on how we specified the procedure. If the procedure produces output, we usually consider the output to be something passed back to its caller. In computing parlance we say that the procedure ***returns*** a value.

Many programs and algorithms work with arrays of data. An ***array*** aggregates data of the same type into one entity. You can think of an array as being like a table, where given the ***index*** of an ***entry***, we can talk about the array ***element*** at that index. For example, here is a table of the first five U.S. presidents:

Index	President
1	George Washington
2	John Adams
3	Thomas Jefferson
4	James Madison
5	James Monroe

For example, the element at index 4 in this table is James Madison. We think of this table not as five separate entities, but as one table with five entries. An array is similar. The indices into an array are consecutive numbers that can start anywhere, but we will usually start them at 1.[1] Given the name of an array and an index into the array, we combine them with square brackets to indicate a particular array element. For example, we denote the ith element of an array A by $A[i]$.

---

[1] If you program in Java, C, or C++, you are used to arrays that start at 0. Starting arrays at 0 is nice for computers, but for wetware it's often more intuitive to start at 1.

Arrays in computers have one other important characteristic: it takes equally long to access any element of an array. Once you give the computer an index i into an array, it can access the ith element as quickly as it can access the first element, regardless of the value of i.

Let's see our first algorithm: searching an array for a particular value. That is, we are given an array, and we want to know which entry in the array, if any, holds a given value. To see how we can search an array, let's think of the array as a long bookshelf full of books, and suppose that you want to know where on the shelf you can find a book by Jonathan Swift. Now, the books on the shelf might be organized in some way, perhaps alphabetically by author, alphabetically by title, or, in a library, by call number. Or perhaps the bookshelf is like my bookshelf at home, where I have not organized my books in any particular way.

If you couldn't assume that the books were organized on the shelf, how would you find a book by Jonathan Swift? Here's the algorithm I would follow. I would start at the left end of the shelf and look at the leftmost book. If it's by Swift, I have located the book. Otherwise, I would look at the next book to the right, and if that book is by Swift, I have located the book. If not, I would keep going to the right, examining book after book, until either I find a book by Swift or I run off the right-hand end of the shelf, in which case I can conclude that the bookshelf does not contain any book by Jonathan Swift. (In Chapter 3, we'll see how to search for a book when the books *are* organized on the shelf.)

Here is how we can describe this searching problem in terms of computing. Let's think of the books on the bookshelf as an array of books. The leftmost book is in position 1, the next book to its right is in position 2, and so on. If we have n books on the shelf, then the rightmost book is in position n. We want to find the position number on the shelf of any book by Jonathan Swift.

As a general computing problem, we are given an array A (the entire shelf full of books to search through) of n elements (the individual books), and we want to find whether a value x (a book by Jonathan Swift) is present in the array A. If it is, then we want to determine an index i such that $A[i] = x$ (the ith position on the shelf contains a book by Jonathan Swift). We also need some way to indicate that array A does not contain x (the bookshelf contains no books by Jonathan Swift). We do not assume that x appears at most once in the array (perhaps you have multiple copies of some book), and so if x is present in array A, it may appear multiple times. All we want from a searching algorithm is *any* index at which we'll find x in the array. We'll assume that the indices of this array start at 1, so that its elements are $A[1]$ through $A[n]$.

If we search for a book by Jonathan Swift by starting at the left end of the shelf, checking book by book as we move to the right, we call that technique *linear search*. In terms of an array in a computer, we start at the beginning of the array, examine each array element in turn ($A[1]$, then $A[2]$, then $A[3]$, and so on, up through $A[n]$) and record where we find x, if we find it at all.

The following procedure, LINEAR-SEARCH, takes three parameters, which we separate by commas in the specification.

Procedure LINEAR-SEARCH(A, n, x)

Inputs:
- A: an array.
- n: the number of elements in A to search through.
- x: the value being searched for.

Output: Either an index i for which $A[i] = x$, or the special value NOT-FOUND, which could be any invalid index into the array, such as 0 or any negative integer.

1. Set *answer* to NOT-FOUND.
2. For each index i, going from 1 to n, in order:
   A. If $A[i] = x$, then set *answer* to the value of i.
3. Return the value of *answer* as the output.

In addition to the parameters A, n, and x, the LINEAR-SEARCH procedure uses a *variable* named *answer*. The procedure *assigns* an initial value of NOT-FOUND to *answer* in step 1. Step 2 checks each array entry $A[1]$ through $A[n]$ to see if the entry contains the value x. Whenever entry $A[i]$ equals x, step 2A assigns the current value of i to *answer*. If x appears in the array, then the output value returned in step 3 is the last index in which x appeared. If x does not appear in the array, then the equality test in step 2A never evaluates to true, and the output value returned is NOT-FOUND, as assigned to *answer* back in step 1.

Before we continue discussing linear search, a word about how to specify repeated actions, such as in step 2. It is quite common in algorithms to perform some action for a variable taking values in some range. When we perform repeated actions, we call that a *loop*, and we call each time through the loop an *iteration* of the loop. For the loop of step 2, I wrote "For each index i, going from 1 to n, in order." Instead, from now on, I'll write "For $i = 1$ to n," which is shorter, yet conveys the same structure. Notice that when I write a loop in this way, we have to give the *loop variable* (here, i) an initial value (here, 1), and in each iteration of the loop, we have to test the current value of the loop variable against a limit (here, n). If the current value of the loop variable is less than or equal to the limit, then we do everything in the loop's *body* (here, step 2A). After an iteration executes the loop body, we *increment* the loop variable—adding 1 to it—and go back and compare the loop variable, now with its new value, with the limit. We repeatedly test the loop variable against the limit, execute the loop body, and increment the loop variable, until the loop variable exceeds the limit. Execution then continues from the step immediately following the loop body (here, step 3). A loop of the form "For $i = 1$ to n" performs n iterations and $n + 1$ tests against the limit (because the loop variable exceeds the limit in the $(n + 1)$st test).

I hope that you find it obvious that the LINEAR-SEARCH procedure always returns a correct answer. You might have noticed, however, that this procedure is inefficient: it continues to search the array even after it has found an index i for which $A[i] = x$. Normally, you wouldn't continue searching for a book once you have found it on your bookshelf, would you? Instead, we can design our linear search procedure to stop searching once it finds the value x in the array. We assume that when we say to return a value, the procedure immediately returns the value to its caller, which then takes control.

Procedure BETTER-LINEAR-SEARCH(A, n, x)

Inputs and Output: Same as LINEAR-SEARCH.

1. For $i = 1$ to n:

   A. If $A[i] = x$, then return the value of i as the output.

2. Return NOT-FOUND as the output.

Believe it or not, we can make linear search even more efficient. Observe that each time through the loop of step 1, the BETTER-LINEAR-SEARCH procedure makes two tests: a test in step 1 to determine whether $i \leq n$ (and if so, perform another iteration of the loop) and the equality test in step 1A. In terms of searching a bookshelf, these tests correspond to you having to check two things for each book: have you gone past the end of the shelf and, if not, is the next book by Jonathan Swift? Of course, you don't incur much of a penalty for going past the end of the shelf (unless you keep your face really close to the books as you examine them, there's a wall at the end of the shelf, and you smack your face into the wall), but in a computer program it's usually very bad to try to access array elements past the end of the array. Your program could crash, or it could corrupt data.

You can make it so that you have to perform only one check for every book you examine. What if you knew for sure that your bookshelf contained a book by Jonathan Swift? Then you'd be assured of finding it, and so you'd never have to check for running off the end of the shelf. You could just check each book in turn to see whether it's by Swift.

But perhaps you lent out all your books by Jonathan Swift, or maybe you thought you had books by him but you never did, so you might not be sure that your bookshelf contains any books by him. Here's what you can do. Take an empty box the size of a book and write on its narrow side (where the spine of a book would be) "*Gulliver's Travels* by Jonathan Swift." Replace the rightmost book with this box. Then, as you search from left to right along the bookshelf, you need to check only whether you're looking at something that is by Swift; you can forget about having to check whether you're going past the end of the book-shelf because you *know* that you'll find something by Swift. The only question is whether you really found a book by Swift, or did you find the empty box that you had labeled as though it were by him? If you found the empty box, then you didn't really have a book by Swift. That's easy to check, however, and you need to do that only once, at the end of your search, rather than once for every book on the shelf.

There's one more detail you have to be aware of: what if the only book by Jonathan Swift that you had on your bookshelf was the right-most book? If you replace it by the empty box, your search will terminate at the empty box, and you might conclude that you didn't have the book. So you have to perform one more check for that possibility, but it's just one check, rather than one check for every book on the shelf.

In terms of a computer algorithm, we'll put the value x that we're searching for into the last position, $A[n]$, after saving the contents of $A[n]$ into another variable. Once we find x, we test to see whether we *really* found it. We call the value that we put into the array a **sentinel**, but you can think of it as the empty box.

Procedure SENTINEL-LINEAR-SEARCH(A, n, x)

Inputs and Output: Same as LINEAR-SEARCH.

1. Save $A[n]$ into *last* and then put x into $A[n]$.
2. Set i to 1.
3. While $A[i] \neq x$, do the following:
   A. Increment i.
4. Restore $A[n]$ from *last*.
5. If $i < n$ or $A[n] = x$, then return the value of i as the output.
6. Otherwise, return NOT-FOUND as the output.

Step 3 is a loop, but not one that counts through some loop variable. Instead, the loop iterates as long as a condition holds; here, the condition is that $A[i] \neq x$. The way to interpret such a loop is to perform the test (here, $A[i] \neq x$), and if the test is true, then do everything in the loop's body (here, step 3A, which increments i). Then go back and perform the test, and if the test is true, execute the body. Keep going, performing the test then executing the body, until the test comes up false. Then continue from the next step after the loop body (here, continue from step 4).

The SENTINEL-LINEAR-SEARCH procedure is a bit more complicated than the first two linear search procedures. Because it places x into $A[n]$ in step 1, we are guaranteed that $A[i]$ will equal x for some test in step 3. Once that happens, we drop out of the step-3 loop, and the index i won't change thereafter. Before we do anything else, step 4 restores the original value in $A[n]$. (My mother taught me to put things back when I was done with them.) Then we have to determine whether we really found x in the array. Because we put x into the last element, $A[n]$, we know that if we found x in $A[i]$ where $i < n$, then we really did find x and we want to return the index i. What if we found x in $A[n]$? That means we didn't find x before $A[n]$, and so we need to determine whether $A[n]$ equals x. If it does, then we want to return the index n, which equals i at this point, but if it does not, we want to return NOT-FOUND. Step 5 does these tests and returns the correct index if x was originally in the array. If x was found only because step 1 put it into the array, then step 6 returns NOT-FOUND. Although SENTINEL-LINEAR-SEARCH has to perform two tests after its loop terminates, it performs only one test in each loop iteration, thereby making it more efficient than either LINEAR-SEARCH or BETTER-LINEAR-SEARCH.

How to characterize running times

Let's return to the LINEAR-SEARCH procedure from page 13 and understand its running time. Recall that we want to characterize the running time as a function of the input size. Here, our input is an array A of n elements, along with the number n and the value x that we're searching for. The sizes of n and x are insignificant as the array gets large—after all, n is just a single integer and x is only as large as one of the n array elements—and so we'll say that the input size is n, the number of elements in A.

We have to make some simple assumptions about how long things take. We will assume that each individual operation—whether it's an arithmetic operation (such as addition, subtraction, multiplication, or division), a comparison, assigning to a variable, indexing into an array, or calling or returning from a procedure—takes some fixed amount of time that is independent of the input size.[2] The time might vary from operation to operation, so that division might take longer than addition, but when a step comprises just simple operations, each individual execution of that step takes some constant amount of time. Because the operations executed differ from step to step, and because of the extrinsic factors listed back on page 4, the time to execute a step might vary from step to step. Let's say that each execution of step i takes t_i time, where t_i is some constant that does not depend on n.

Of course, we have to take into account that some steps execute multiple times. Steps 1 and 3 execute just once, but what about step 2? We have to test i against n a total of $n + 1$ times: n times in which $i \leq n$, and once when i equals $n + 1$ so that we drop out of the loop. Step 2A executes exactly n times, once for each value of i from 1 to n. We don't know in advance how many times we set *answer* to the value of i; it could be anywhere from 0 times (if x is not present in the array) to n times (if every value in the array equals x). If we're going to be precise in our accounting—and we won't normally be this precise—we need to

---

[2]If you know a bit about actual computer architecture, you might know that the time to access a given variable or array element is not necessarily fixed, for it could depend on whether the variable or array element is in the cache, in main memory, or out on disk in a virtual-memory system. Some sophisticated models of computers take these issues into account, but it's often good enough to just assume that all variables and array entries are in main memory and that they all take the same amount of time to access.

recognize that step 2 does two different things that execute a different number of times: the test of i against n happens $n + 1$ times, but incrementing i happens only n times. Let's separate the time for line 2 into t_2' for the test and t_2'' for incrementing. Similarly, we'll separate the time for step 2A into t_{2A}' for testing whether $A[i] = x$ and t_{2A}'' for setting *answer* to i. Therefore, the running time of LINEAR-SEARCH is somewhere between

$$t_1 + t_2' \cdot (n + 1) + t_2'' \cdot n + t_{2A}' \cdot n + t_{2A}'' \cdot 0 + t_3$$

and

$$t_1 + t_2' \cdot (n + 1) + t_2'' \cdot n + t_{2A}' \cdot n + t_{2A}'' \cdot n + t_3 \, .$$

Now we rewrite these bounds, collecting terms that multiply by n together, and collecting the rest of the terms, and we see that the running time is somewhere between the ***lower bound***

$$(t_2' + t_2'' + t_{2A}') \cdot n + (t_1 + t_2' + t_3)$$

and the ***upper bound***

$$(t_2' + t_2'' + t_{2A}' + t_{2A}'') \cdot n + (t_1 + t_2' + t_3) \, .$$

Notice that both of these bounds are of the form $c \cdot n + d$, where c and d are constants that do not depend on n. That is, they are both *linear functions* of n. The running time of LINEAR-SEARCH is bounded from below by a linear function of n, and it is bounded from above by a linear function of n.

We use a special notation to indicate that a running time is bounded from above by some linear function of n and from below by some (possibly different) linear function of n. We write that the running time is $\Theta(n)$. That's the Greek letter theta, and we say "theta of n" or just "theta n." As promised in Chapter 1, this notation discards the low-order term $(t_1 + t_2' + t_3)$ and the coefficients of n $(t_2' + t_2'' + t_{2A}'$ for the lower bound and $t_2' + t_2'' + t_{2A}' + t_{2A}''$ for the upper bound). Although we lose precision by characterizing the running time as $\Theta(n)$, we gain the advantages of highlighting the order of growth of the running time and suppressing tedious detail.

This Θ-notation applies to functions in general, not just those that describe running times of algorithms, and it applies to functions other than linear ones. The idea is that if we have two functions, $f(n)$ and $g(n)$, we say that $f(n)$ is $\Theta(g(n))$ if $f(n)$ is within a constant factor of $g(n)$

for sufficiently large n. So we can say that the running time of LINEAR-SEARCH is within a constant factor of n once n gets large enough.

There's an intimidating technical definition of Θ-notation, but fortunately we rarely have to resort to it in order to use Θ-notation. We simply focus on the dominant term, dropping low-order terms and constant factors. For example, the function $n^2/4 + 100n + 50$ is $\Theta(n^2)$; here we drop the low-order terms $100n$ and 50, and we drop the constant factor $1/4$. Although the low-order terms will dominate $n^2/4$ for small values of n, once n goes above 400, the $n^2/4$ term exceeds $100n + 50$. When $n = 1000$, the dominant term $n^2/4$ equals $250{,}000$, while the low-order terms $100n + 50$ amount to only $100{,}050$; for $n = 2000$ the difference becomes $1{,}000{,}000$ vs. $200{,}050$. In the world of algorithms, we abuse notation a little bit and write $f(n) = \Theta(g(n))$, so that we can write $n^2/4 + 100n + 50 = \Theta(n^2)$.

Now let's look at the running time of BETTER-LINEAR-SEARCH from page 14. This one is a little trickier than LINEAR-SEARCH because we don't know in advance how many times the loop will iterate. If $A[1]$ equals x, then it will iterate just once. If x is not present in the array, then the loop will iterate all n times, which is the maximum possible. Each loop iteration takes some constant amount of time, and so we can say that *in the worst case*, BETTER-LINEAR-SEARCH takes $\Theta(n)$ time to search an array of n elements. Why "worst case"? Because we want algorithms to have low running times, the worst case occurs when an algorithm takes the maximum time over any possible input.

In the best case, when $A[1]$ equals x, BETTER-LINEAR-SEARCH takes just a constant amount of time: it sets i to 1, checks that $i \leq n$, the test $A[i] = x$ comes up true, and the procedure returns the value of i, which is 1. This amount of time does not depend on n. We write that the *best-case running time* of BETTER-LINEAR-SEARCH is $\Theta(1)$, because in the best case, its running time is within a constant factor of 1. In other words, the best-case running time is a constant that does not depend on n.

So we see that we cannot use Θ-notation for a blanket statement that covers all cases of the running time of BETTER-LINEAR-SEARCH. We cannot say that the running time is always $\Theta(n)$, because in the best case it's $\Theta(1)$. And we cannot say that the running time is always $\Theta(1)$, because in the worst case it's $\Theta(n)$. We can say that a linear function of n is an *upper bound* in all cases, however, and we have a notation for that: $O(n)$. When we speak this notation, we say "big-oh of n" or just "oh of n." A function $f(n)$ is $O(g(n))$ if, once n becomes sufficiently large, $f(n)$ is bounded from above by some constant times $g(n)$. Again, we abuse notation a little and write $f(n) = O(g(n))$. For BETTER-LINEAR-SEARCH, we can make the blanket statement that its running time in all cases is $O(n)$; although the running time might be better than a linear function of n, it's never worse.

We use O-notation to indicate that a running time is never *worse* than a constant times some function of n, but how about indicating that a running time is never *better* than a constant times some function of n? That's a lower bound, and we use Ω-notation, which mirrors O-notation: a function $f(n)$ is $\Omega(g(n))$ if, once n becomes sufficiently large, $f(n)$ is bounded from below by some constant times $g(n)$. We say that "$f(n)$ is big-omega of $g(n)$" or just "$f(n)$ is omega of $g(n)$," and we can write $f(n) = \Omega(g(n))$. Since O-notation gives an upper bound, Ω-notation gives a lower bound, and Θ-notation gives both upper and lower bounds, we can conclude that a function $f(n)$ is $\Theta(g(n))$ if and only if $f(n)$ is both $O(g(n))$ and $\Omega(g(n))$.

We can make a blanket statement about a lower bound for the running time of BETTER-LINEAR-SEARCH: in all cases it's $\Omega(1)$. Of course, that's a pathetically weak statement, since we'd expect any algorithm on any input to take at least constant time. We won't use Ω-notation much, but it will occasionally come in handy.

The catch-all term for Θ-notation, O-notation, and Ω-notation is ***asymptotic notation***. That's because these notations capture the growth of a function as its argument asymptotically approaches infinity. All of these asymptotic notations give us the luxury of dropping low-order terms and constant factors so that we can ignore tedious details and focus on what's important: how the function grows with n.

Now let's turn to SENTINEL-LINEAR-SEARCH from page 16. Just like BETTER-LINEAR-SEARCH, each iteration of its loop takes a constant amount of time, and there may be anywhere from 1 to n iterations. The key difference between SENTINEL-LINEAR-SEARCH and BETTER-LINEAR-SEARCH is that the time per iteration of SENTINEL-LINEAR-SEARCH is less than the time per iteration of BETTER-LINEAR-SEARCH. Both take a linear amount of time in the worst case, but the constant factor for SENTINEL-LINEAR-SEARCH is better. Although we'd expect SENTINEL-LINEAR-SEARCH to be faster in practice, it would be by only a constant factor. When we express the running times of BETTER-LINEAR-SEARCH and SENTINEL-LINEAR-SEARCH using asymptotic notation, they are equivalent: $\Theta(n)$ in the worst case, $\Theta(1)$ in the best case, and $O(n)$ in all cases.

Loop invariants

For our three flavors of linear search, it was easy to see that each one gives a correct answer. Sometimes it's a bit harder. There's a wide range of techniques, more than I can cover here.

One common method of showing correctness uses a *loop invariant*: an assertion that we demonstrate to be true each time we start a loop iteration. For a loop invariant to help us argue correctness, we have to show three things about it:

Initialization: It is true before the first iteration of the loop.

Maintenance: If it is true before an iteration of the loop, it remains true before the next iteration.

Termination: The loop terminates, and when it does, the loop invariant, along with the reason that the loop terminated, gives us a useful property.

As an example, here's a loop invariant for BETTER-LINEAR-SEARCH:

At the start of each iteration of step 1, if x is present in the array A, then it is present in the *subarray* (a contiguous portion of an array) from $A[i]$ through $A[n]$.

We don't even need this loop invariant to show that if the procedure returns an index other than NOT-FOUND, then the index returned is correct: the only way that the procedure can return an index i in step 1A is because x equals $A[i]$. Instead, we will use this loop invariant to show that if the procedure returns NOT-FOUND in step 2, then x is not anywhere in the array:

Initialization: Initially, $i = 1$ so that the subarray in the loop invariant is $A[1]$ through $A[n]$, which is the entire array.

Maintenance: Assume that at the start of an iteration for a value of i, if x is present in the array A, then it is present in the subarray from $A[i]$ through $A[n]$. If we get through this iteration without returning, we know that $A[i] \neq x$, and therefore we can safely say that if x is present in the array A, then it is present in the subarray from $A[i+1]$ through $A[n]$. Because i is incremented before the next iteration, the loop invariant will hold before the next iteration.

Termination: This loop must terminate, either because the procedure returns in step 1A or because $i > n$. We have already handled the case where the loop terminates because the procedure returns in step 1A.

To handle the case where the loop terminates because $i > n$, we rely on the contrapositive of the loop invariant. The ***contrapositive*** of the statement "if A then B" is "if not B then not A." The contrapositive of a statement is true if and only if the statement is true. The contrapositive of the loop invariant is "if x is not present in the subarray from $A[i]$ through $A[n]$, then it is not present in the array A."

Now, when $i > n$, the subarray from $A[i]$ through $A[n]$ is empty, and so this subarray cannot hold x. By the contrapositive of the loop invariant, therefore, x is not present anywhere in the array A, and so it is appropriate to return NOT-FOUND in step 2.

Wow, that's a lot of reasoning for what's really just a simple loop! Do we have to go through all that every time we write a loop? I don't, but there are a few computer scientists who insist on such rigorous reasoning for every single loop. When I'm writing real code, I find that most of the time that I write a loop, I have a loop invariant somewhere in the back of my mind. It might be so far back in my mind that I don't even realize that I have it, but I could state it if I had to. Although most of us would agree that a loop invariant is overkill for understanding the simple loop in BETTER-LINEAR-SEARCH, loop invariants can be quite handy when we want to understand why more complex loops do the right thing.

Recursion

With the technique of ***recursion***, we solve a problem by solving smaller instances of the same problem. Here's my favorite canonical example of recursion: computing $n!$ ("n-factorial"), which is defined for nonnegative values of n as $n! = 1$ if $n = 0$, and

$$n! = n \cdot (n-1) \cdot (n-2) \cdot (n-3) \cdots 3 \cdot 2 \cdot 1$$

if $n \geq 1$. For example, $5! = 5 \cdot 4 \cdot 3 \cdot 2 \cdot 1 = 120$. Observe that

$$(n-1)! = (n-1) \cdot (n-2) \cdot (n-3) \cdots 3 \cdot 2 \cdot 1 ,$$

and so

$n! = n \cdot (n - 1)!$

for $n \geq 1$. We have defined $n!$ in terms of a "smaller" problem, namely $(n-1)!$. We could write a recursive procedure to compute $n!$ as follows:

Procedure FACTORIAL(n)

Input: An integer $n \geq 0$.

Output: The value of $n!$.

1. If $n = 0$, then return 1 as the output.
2. Otherwise, return n times the value returned by recursively calling FACTORIAL($n - 1$).

The way I wrote step 2 is pretty cumbersome. I could instead just write "Otherwise, return $n \cdot$ FACTORIAL($n - 1$)," using the recursive call's return value within a larger arithmetic expression.

For recursion to work, two properties must hold. First, there must be one or more **base cases**, where we compute the solution directly without recursion. Second, each recursive call of the procedure must be on a *smaller instance* of *the same problem* that will eventually reach a base case. For the FACTORIAL procedure, the base case occurs when n equals 0, and each recursive call is on an instance in which the value of n is reduced by 1. As long as the original value of n is nonnegative, the recursive calls will eventually get down to the base case.

Arguing that a recursive algorithm works might feel overly simple at first. The key is to believe that each recursive call produces the correct result. As long as we are willing to believe that recursive calls do the right thing, arguing correctness is often easy. Here is how we could argue that the FACTORIAL procedure returns the correct answer. Clearly, when $n = 0$, the value returned, 1, equals $n!$. We assume that when $n \geq 1$, the recursive call FACTORIAL($n - 1$) does the right thing: it returns the value of $(n - 1)!$. The procedure then multiplies this value by n, thereby computing the value of $n!$, which it returns.

Here's an example where the recursive calls are not on smaller instances of the same problem, even though the mathematics is correct. It is indeed true that if $n \geq 0$, then $n! = (n + 1)!/(n + 1)$. But the following recursive procedure, which takes advantage of this formula, would fail to ever give an answer when $n \geq 1$:

Procedure BAD-FACTORIAL(n)

Input and Output: Same as FACTORIAL.

1. If $n = 0$, then return 1 as the output.
2. Otherwise, return BAD-FACTORIAL($n + 1$)$/(n + 1)$.

If we were to call BAD-FACTORIAL(1), it would generate a recursive call of BAD-FACTORIAL(2), which would generate a recursive call of BAD-FACTORIAL(3), and so on, never getting down to the base case when n equals 0. If you were to implement this procedure in a real programming language and run it on an actual computer, you would quickly see something like a "stack overflow error."

We can often rewrite algorithms that use a loop in a recursive style. Here is linear search, without a sentinel, written recursively:

Procedure RECURSIVE-LINEAR-SEARCH(A, n, i, x)

Inputs: Same as LINEAR-SEARCH, but with an added parameter i.

Output: The index of an element equaling x in the subarray from $A[i]$ through $A[n]$, or NOT-FOUND if x does not appear in this subarray.

1. If $i > n$, then return NOT-FOUND.
2. Otherwise ($i \leq n$), if $A[i] = x$, then return i.
3. Otherwise ($i \leq n$ and $A[i] \neq x$), return
   RECURSIVE-LINEAR-SEARCH($A, n, i + 1, x$).

Here, the subproblem is to search for x in the subarray going from $A[i]$ through $A[n]$. The base case occurs in step 1 when this subarray is empty, that is, when $i > n$. Because the value of i increases in each of step 3's recursive calls, if no recursive call ever returns a value of i in step 2, then eventually i becomes greater than n and we reach the base case.

Further reading

Chapters 2 and 3 of CLRS [CLRS09] cover much of the material in this chapter. An early algorithms textbook by Aho, Hopcroft, and Ullman [AHU74] influenced the field to use asymptotic notation to analyze algorithms. There has been quite a bit of work in proving programs correct; if you would like to delve into this area, try the books by Gries [Gri81] and Mitchell [Mit96].

3 Algorithms for Sorting and Searching

In Chapter 2, we saw three variations on linear search of an array. Can we do any better? The answer: it depends. If we know nothing about the order of the elements in the array, then no, we cannot do better. In the worst case, we have to look through all n elements because if we don't find the value we're looking for in the first $n - 1$ elements, it might be in that last, nth, element. Therefore, we cannot achieve a better worst-case running time than $\Theta(n)$ if we know nothing about the order of the elements in the array.

Suppose, however, that the array is sorted into nondecreasing order: each element is less than or equal to its successor in the array, according to some definition of "less than." In this chapter, we shall see that if an array is sorted, then we can use a simple technique known as binary search to search an n-element array in only $O(\lg n)$ time. As we saw in Chapter 1, the value of $\lg n$ grows very slowly compared with n, and so binary search beats linear search in the worst case.[1]

What does it mean for one element to be less than another? When the elements are numbers, it's obvious. When the elements are strings of text characters, we can think of a *lexicographic ordering*: one element is less than another if it would come before the other element in a dictionary. When elements are some other form of data, then we have to define what "less than" means. As long as we have some clear notion of "less than," we can determine whether an array is sorted.

Recalling the example of books on a bookshelf from Chapter 2, we could sort the books alphabetically by author, alphabetically by title, or, if in a library, by call number. In this chapter, we'll say that the books are sorted on the shelf if they appear in alphabetical order by author, reading from left to right. The bookshelf might contain more than one book by the same author, however; perhaps you have several works by William Shakespeare. If we want to search for not just any book by

---

[1] If you are a non-computer person who skipped the section "Computer algorithms for computer people" in Chapter 1, you ought to read the material about logarithms on page 7.

Shakespeare, but a specific book by Shakespeare, then we would say that if two books have the same author, then the one whose title is first alphabetically should go on the left. Alternatively, we could say that all we care about is the author's name, so that when we search, anything by Shakespeare will do. We call the information that we are matching on the *key*. In our bookshelf example, the key is just the author's name, rather than a combination based first on the author's name and then the title in case of two works by the same author.

How, then, do we get the array to be sorted in the first place? In this chapter, we'll see four algorithms—selection sort, insertion sort, merge sort, and quicksort—to sort an array, applying each of these algorithms to our bookshelf example. Each sorting algorithm will have its advantages and its disadvantages, and at the end of the chapter we'll review and compare these sorting algorithms. All of the sorting algorithms that we'll see in this chapter take either $\Theta(n^2)$ or $\Theta(n \lg n)$ time in the worst case. Therefore, if you were going to perform only a few searches, you'd be better off just running linear search. But if you were going to search many times, you might be better off first sorting the array and then searching by running binary search.

Sorting is an important problem in its own right, not just as a pre-processing step for binary search. Think of all the data that must be sorted, such as entries in a phone book, by name; checks in a monthly bank statement, by check numbers and/or the dates that the checks were processed by the bank; or even results from a Web-search engine, by relevance to the query. Furthermore, sorting is often a step in some other algorithm. For example, in computer graphics, objects are often layered on top of each other. A program that renders objects on the screen might have to sort the objects according to an "above" relation so that it can draw these objects from bottom to top.

Before we proceed, a word about what it is that we sort. In addition to the key (which we'll call a *sort key* when we're sorting), the elements that we sort usually include as well what we call *satellite data*. Although satellite data could come from a satellite, it usually does not. Satellite data is the information that is associated with the sort key and should travel with it when elements are moved around. In our bookshelf example, the sort key is the author's name and the satellite data is the book itself.

I explain satellite data to my students in a way that they are sure to understand. I keep a spreadsheet with student grades, with rows sorted alphabetically by student name. To determine final course grades at the end of the term, I sort the rows, with the sort key being the column containing the percentage of points obtained in the course, and the rest of the columns, including the student names, as the satellite data. I sort into decreasing order by percentage, so that rows at the top correspond to A's and rows at the bottom to D's and E's.[2] Suppose that I were to rearrange only the column containing the percentages and not move the entire row containing the percentage. That would leave the student names in alphabetical order regardless of percentages. Then the students whose names appear early in the alphabet would be happy while the students with names at the end of the alphabet—not so much.

Here are some other examples of sort keys and satellite data. In a phone book, the sort key would be the name and the satellite data would be the address and phone number. In a bank statement, the sort key would be the check number and the satellite data would include the amount of the check and the date it cleared. In a search engine, the sort key would be the measure of relevance to the query and the satellite data would be the URL of the Web page, plus whatever other data the search engine stores about the page.

When we work with arrays in this chapter, we will act as though each element contains only a sort key. If you were implementing any of the sorting algorithms here, you would have to make sure that you move the satellite data associated with each element, or at least a pointer to the satellite data, whenever you move the sort key.

In order for the bookshelf analogy to apply to arrays in a computer, we need to assume that the bookshelf and its books have two additional features, which I admit are not terribly realistic. First, all books on the bookshelf are the same size, because in a computer array, all array entries are the same size. Second, we can number the positions of the books on the bookshelf from 1 to n, and we will call each position a *slot*. Slot 1 is the leftmost slot, and slot n is the rightmost. As you have probably guessed, each slot on the bookshelf corresponds to an array entry.

I also want to address the word "sorting." In common speech, sorting can mean something different from how we use it in computing.

---

[2]Dartmouth uses E, not F, to indicate a failing grade. I don't know why for sure, but I would guess that it simplified the computer program that converts letter grades to numeric grades on a 4.0 scale.

My Mac's online dictionary defines "sort" by "arrange systematically in groups; separate according to type, class, etc.": the way that you might "sort" clothing for example, with shirts in one place, pants in another place, and so on. In the world of computer algorithms, sorting means to put into some well-defined order, and "arranging systematically in groups" is called "bucketing," "bucketizing," or "binning."

Binary search

Before we see some sorting algorithms, let's visit binary search, which requires the array being searched to be already sorted. Binary search has the advantage that it takes only $O(\lg n)$ time to search an n-element array.

In our bookshelf example, we start with the books already sorted by author name, left to right on the shelf. We'll use the author name as the key, and let's search for any book by Jonathan Swift. Now, you might figure that because the author's last name starts with "S," which is the 19th letter of the alphabet, you could go about three-quarters of the way over on the shelf (since 19/26 is close to 3/4) and look in the slot there. But if you have all of Shakespeare's works, then you have several books by an author whose last name comes before Swift, which could push books by Swift farther to the right than you expected.

Instead, here's how you could apply binary search to finding a book by Jonathan Swift. Go to the slot exactly halfway over on the shelf, find the book there, and examine the author's name. Let's say that you've found a book by Jack London. Not only is that not the book you're searching for, but because you know that the books are sorted alphabetically by author, you know that all books to the left of the book by London can't be what you're searching for. By looking at just one book, you have eliminated half of the books on the shelf from consideration! Any books by Swift must be on the right-hand half of the shelf. So now you find the slot at the halfway point of just the right-hand half and look at the book there. Suppose that it's by Leo Tolstoy. Again, that's not the book you're searching for, but you know that you can eliminate all books to the right of this one: half of the books that remained as possibilities. At this point, you know that if your bookshelf contains any books by Swift, then they are in the quarter of the books that are to the right of the book by London and to the left of the book by Tolstoy. Next, you find the book in the slot at the midpoint within this quarter under consideration. If it's by Swift, you are done. Otherwise, you can again eliminate half of the remaining books. Eventually, you either find a book by Swift or you get to the point at which no slots remain as possibilities. In the latter case, you conclude that the bookshelf contains no books by Jonathan Swift.

In a computer, we perform binary search on an array. At any point, we are considering only a subarray, that is, the portion of the array between and including two indices; let's call them p and r. Initially, $p = 1$ and $r = n$, so that the subarray starts out as the entire array. We repeatedly halve the size of the subarray that we are considering until one of two things happens: we either find the value that we're searching for or the subarray is empty (that is, p becomes greater than r). The repeated halving of the subarray size is what gives rise to the $O(\lg n)$ running time.

In a little more detail, here's how binary search works. Let's say that we're searching for the value x in array A. In each step, we are considering only the subarray starting at $A[p]$ and ending at $A[r]$. Because we will be working with subarrays quite a bit, let's denote this subarray by $A[p..r]$. At each step, we compute the midpoint q of the subarray under consideration by taking the average of p and r and then dropping the fractional part, if any: $q = \lfloor (p + r)/2 \rfloor$. (Here, we use the "floor" operation, $\lfloor \ \rfloor$, to drop the fractional part. If you were implementing this operation in a language such as Java, C, or C++, you could just use integer division to drop the fractional part.) We check to see whether $A[q]$ equals x; if it does, we are done, because we can just return q as an index where array A contains x.

If instead, we find that $A[q] \neq x$, then we take advantage of the assumption that array A is already sorted. Since $A[q] \neq x$, there are two possibilities: either $A[q] > x$ or $A[q] < x$. We first handle the case where $A[q] > x$. Because the array is sorted, we know that not only is $A[q]$ greater than x, but also—thinking of the array as laid out from left to right—that every array element to the right of $A[q]$ is greater than x. Therefore, we can eliminate from consideration all elements at or to the right of $A[q]$. We will start our next step with p unchanged, but with r set to $q - 1$:

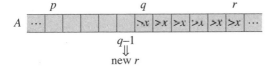

If instead we find that $A[q] < x$, we know that every array element at or to the left of $A[q]$ is less than x, and so we can eliminate these elements from consideration. We will start our next step with r unchanged, but with p set to $q + 1$:

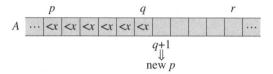

Here is the exact procedure for binary search:

Procedure BINARY-SEARCH(A, n, x)

Inputs and Output: Same as LINEAR-SEARCH.

1. Set p to 1, and set r to n.
2. While $p \leq r$, do the following:
   A. Set q to $\lfloor (p + r)/2 \rfloor$.
   B. If $A[q] = x$, then return q.
   C. Otherwise $(A[q] \neq x)$, if $A[q] > x$, then set r to $q - 1$.
   D. Otherwise $(A[q] < x)$, set p to $q + 1$.
3. Return NOT-FOUND.

The loop in step 2 does not necessarily terminate because p becomes greater than r. It can terminate in step 2B because it finds that $A[q]$ equals x and returns q as an index in A where x occurs.

In order to show that the BINARY-SEARCH procedure works correctly, we just need to show that x is not present anywhere in the array if BINARY-SEARCH returns NOT-FOUND in step 3. We use the following loop invariant:

> At the start of each iteration of the loop of step 2, if x is anywhere in the array A, then it is somewhere in the subarray $A[p \mathinner{.\,.} r]$.

And a brief argument using the loop invariant:

Initialization: Step 1 initializes the indices p and r to 1 and n, respectively, and so the loop invariant is true when the procedure first enters the loop.

Maintenance: We argued above that steps 2C and 2D adjust either p or r correctly.

Termination: If x is not in the array, then eventually the procedure gets to the point where p and r are equal. When that happens, step 2A computes q to be the same as p and r. If step 2C sets r to $q - 1$, then at the start of the next iteration, r will equal $p - 1$, so that p will be greater than r. If step 2D sets p to $q + 1$, then at the start of the next iteration, p will equal $r + 1$, and again p will be greater than r. Either way, the loop test in step 2 will come up false, and the loop will terminate. Because $p > r$, the subarray $A[p..r]$ will be empty, and so the value x cannot be present in it. Taking the contrapositive of the loop invariant (see page 22) gives us that if x is not present in the subarray $A[p..r]$, then it is not present anywhere in array A. Therefore, the procedure is correct in returning NOT-FOUND in step 3.

We can also write binary search as a recursive procedure:

Procedure RECURSIVE-BINARY-SEARCH(A, p, r, x)

Inputs and Output: Inputs A and x are the same as LINEAR-SEARCH, as is the output. The inputs p and r delineate the subarray $A[p..r]$ under consideration.

1. If $p > r$, then return NOT-FOUND.
2. Otherwise ($p \leq r$), do the following:
   A. Set q to $\lfloor (p + r)/2 \rfloor$.
   B. If $A[q] = x$, then return q.
   C. Otherwise ($A[q] \neq x$), if $A[q] > x$, then return
      RECURSIVE-BINARY-SEARCH($A, p, q - 1, x$).
   D. Otherwise ($A[q] < x$), return
      RECURSIVE-BINARY-SEARCH($A, q + 1, r, x$).

The initial call is RECURSIVE-BINARY-SEARCH($A, 1, n, x$).

Now let's see how it is that binary search takes $O(\lg n)$ time on an n-element array. The key observation is that the size $r - p + 1$ of the subarray under consideration is approximately halved in each iteration of the loop (or in each recursive call of the recursive version, but let's focus on the iterative version in BINARY-SEARCH). If you try all the cases, you'll find that if an iteration starts with a subarray of s elements, the next iteration will have either $\lfloor s/2 \rfloor$ or $s/2 - 1$ elements, depending on whether s is even or odd and whether $A[q]$ is greater than or less than x. We have already seen that once the subarray size gets down to 1, the procedure will finish by the next iteration. So we can ask, how many iterations of the loop do we need to repeatedly halve a subarray from its original size n down to a size of 1? That would be the same as the number of times that, starting with a subarray of size 1, we would need to double its size to reach a size of n. But that's just exponentiation: repeatedly multiplying by 2. In other words, for what value of x does 2^x reach n? If n were an exact power of 2, then we've already seen on page 7 that the answer is $\lg n$. Of course, n might not be an exact power of 2, in which case the answer will be within 1 of $\lg n$. Finally, we note that each iteration of the loop takes a constant amount of time, that is, the time for a single iteration does not depend on the size n of the original array or on the size of the subarray under consideration. Let's use asymptotic notation to suppress the constant factors and low-order term. (Is the number of loop iterations $\lg n$ or $\lfloor \lg n \rfloor + 1$? Who cares?) We get that the running time of binary search is $O(\lg n)$.

I used O-notation here because I wanted to make a blanket statement that covers all cases. In the worst case, when the value x is not present in the array, we halved and halved and halved until the subarray under consideration was empty, yielding a running time of $\Theta(\lg n)$. In the best case, when x is found in the first iteration of the loop, the running time is $\Theta(1)$. No Θ-notation covers all cases, but a running time of $O(\lg n)$ is always correct for binary search—as long as the array is already sorted.

It is possible to beat $\Theta(\lg n)$ worst-case time for searching, but only if we organize data in more elaborate ways and make certain assumptions about the keys.

Selection sort

We now turn our attention to *sorting*: rearranging the elements of the array—also known as *permuting* the array—so that each element is less than or equal to its successor. The first sorting algorithm we'll see, selection sort, is the one I consider the simplest, because it's the one I came up with when I first needed to design a sorting algorithm. It is far from the fastest.

Here is how selection sort would work for sorting books on a bookshelf according to author names. Go through the entire shelf and find the book whose author's name comes earliest in the alphabet. Let's say that it's by Louisa May Alcott. (If the shelf contains two or more books by this author, choose any one of them.) Swap the location of this book with the book in slot 1. The book in slot 1 is now a book by an author whose name comes first alphabetically. Now go through the bookshelf, left to right, starting with the book in slot 2 to find the book in slots 2 through n whose author name comes earliest in the alphabet. Suppose that it's by Jane Austen. Swap the location of this book with the book in slot 2, so that now slots 1 and 2 have the first and second books in the overall alphabetical ordering. Then do the same for slot 3, and so on. Once we have put the correct book into slot $n - 1$ (perhaps it's by H. G. Wells), we are done, because there's only one book left (say, a book by Oscar Wilde), and it's in slot n where it belongs.

To turn this approach into a computer algorithm, change the bookshelf to an array and the books to array elements. Here's the result:

Procedure SELECTION-SORT(A, n)

Inputs:
- A: an array.
- n: the number of elements in A to sort.

Result: The elements of A are sorted into nondecreasing order.

1. For $i = 1$ to $n - 1$:
   A. Set *smallest* to the index of the smallest element in the subarray $A[i .. n]$.
   B. Swap $A[i]$ with $A[smallest]$.

Finding the smallest element in $A[i .. n]$ is a variant on linear search. First declare $A[i]$ to be the smallest element seen in the subarray so far, and then go through the rest of the subarray, updating the index of the smallest element every time we find an element less than the current smallest. Here's the refined procedure:

Procedure SELECTION-SORT(A, n)

Inputs and Result: Same as before.

1. For $i = 1$ to $n - 1$:
   A. Set *smallest* to i.
   B. For $j = i + 1$ to n:
      i. If $A[j] < A[smallest]$, then set *smallest* to j.
   C. Swap $A[i]$ with $A[smallest]$.

This procedure has "nested" loops, with the loop of step 1B nested within the loop of step 1. The inner loop performs all of its iterations for each individual iteration of the outer loop. Notice that the starting value of j in the inner loop depends on the current value of i in the outer loop. This illustration shows how selection sort works on an array of six elements:

The initial array appears in the upper left, and each step shows the array after an iteration of the outer loop. The darker shaded elements hold the subarray that is known to be sorted.

If you wanted to use a loop invariant to argue that the SELECTION-SORT procedure sorts the array correctly, you would need one for each of the loops. This procedure is simple enough that we won't go through the full loop-invariant arguments, but here are the loop invariants:

> At the start of each iteration of the loop of step 1, the subarray $A[1 .. i-1]$ holds the $i-1$ smallest elements of the entire array A, and they are in sorted order.

> At the start of each iteration of the loop of step 1B, $A[smallest]$ is the smallest element in the subarray $A[i .. j - 1]$.

What is the running time of SELECTION-SORT? We'll show that it is $\Theta(n^2)$. The key is to analyze how many iterations the inner loop makes, noting that each iteration takes $\Theta(1)$ time. (Here, the constant factors in the lower and upper bounds in the Θ-notation may differ, because the assignment to *smallest* may or may not occur in a given iteration.) Let's count the number of iterations, based on the value of the loop variable i in the outer loop. When i equals 1, the inner loop iterates for j running from 2 to n, or $n - 1$ times. When i equals 2, the inner loop iterates for j running from 3 to n, or $n - 2$ times. Each time the outer loop increments i, the inner loop runs one time less. In general, the inner loop runs $n - i$ times. In the last iteration of the outer loop, when i equals $n - 1$, the inner loop iterates just one time. Therefore, the total number of inner-loop iterations is

$$(n - 1) + (n - 2) + (n - 3) + \cdots + 2 + 1 .$$

This summation is known as an ***arithmetic series***, and here's a basic fact about arithmetic series: for any nonnegative integer k,

$$k + (k - 1) + (k - 2) + \cdots + 2 + 1 = \frac{k(k + 1)}{2}.$$

Substituting $n - 1$ for k, we see that the total number of inner-loop iterations is $(n - 1)n/2$, or $(n^2 - n)/2$. Let's use asymptotic notation to get rid of the low-order term $(-n)$ and the constant factor $(1/2)$. Then we can say that the total number of inner-loop iterations is $\Theta(n^2)$. Therefore, the running time of SELECTION-SORT is $\Theta(n^2)$. Notice that this running time is a blanket statement that covers all cases. Regardless of the actual element values, the inner loop runs $\Theta(n^2)$ times.

Here's another way to see that the running time is $\Theta(n^2)$, without using the arithmetic series. We'll show separately that the running time is both $O(n^2)$ and $\Omega(n^2)$; putting the asymptotic upper and lower bounds together gives us $\Theta(n^2)$. To see that the running time is $O(n^2)$, observe that each iteration of the outer loop runs the inner loop at most $n - 1$ times, which is $O(n)$ because each iteration of the inner loop takes a constant amount of time. Since the outer loop iterates $n - 1$ times, which is also $O(n)$, the total time spent in the inner loop is $O(n)$ times $O(n)$, or $O(n^2)$. To see that the running time is $\Omega(n^2)$, observe that in each of the first $n/2$ iterations of the outer loop, we run the inner loop at least $n/2$ times, for a total of at least $n/2$ times $n/2$, or $n^2/4$ times. Since each inner-loop iteration takes a constant amount of time, we see that the running time is at least a constant times $n^2/4$, or $\Omega(n^2)$.

Two final thoughts about selection sort. First, we'll see that its asymptotic running time of $\Theta(n^2)$ is the worst of the sorting algorithms that we'll examine. Second, if you carefully examine how selection sort operates, you'll see that the $\Theta(n^2)$ running time comes from the comparisons in step 1Bi. But the number of times that it *moves* array elements is only $\Theta(n)$, because step 1C runs only $n - 1$ times. If moving array elements is particularly time-consuming—perhaps because they are large or stored on a slow device such as a disk—then selection sort might be a reasonable algorithm to use.

Insertion sort

Insertion sort differs a bit from selection sort, though it has a similar flavor. In selection sort, when we decided which book to put into the ith slot, the books in the first i slots were the first i books *overall*, sorted alphabetically by author name. In insertion sort, the books in the first i slots will be the same books *that were originally in the first i slots*, but now sorted by author name.

For example, let's suppose that the books in the first four slots are already sorted by author name, and that, in order, they are books by Charles Dickens, Herman Melville, Jonathan Swift, and Leo Tolstoy. Let's say that the book that starts in slot 5 is by Sir Walter Scott. With insertion sort, we shift the books by Swift and Tolstoy by one slot to the right, moving them from slots 3 and 4 to slots 4 and 5, and then we put the book by Scott into the vacated slot 3. At the time that we work with the book by Scott, we don't care what books are to its right (the books by Jack London and Gustave Flaubert in the figure below); we deal with them later on.

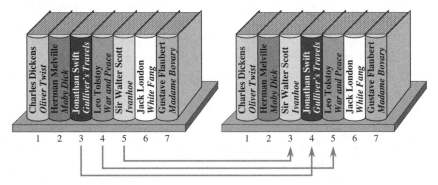

To shift the books by Swift and Tolstoy, we first compare the author name Tolstoy with Scott. Finding that Tolstoy comes after Scott, we shift the book by Tolstoy one slot to the right, from slot 4 to slot 5. Then we compare the author name Swift with Scott. Finding that Swift comes after Scott, we shift the book by Swift one slot to the right, from slot 3 to slot 4, which was vacated when we shifted the book by Tolstoy. Next we compare the author name Herman Melville with Scott. This time, we find that Melville does *not* come after Scott. At this point, we stop comparing author names, because we have found that the book by Scott should be to the right of the book by Melville and to the left of the book by Swift. We can put the book by Scott into slot 3, which was vacated when we shifted the book by Swift.

To translate this idea to sorting an array with insertion sort, the sub-array $A[1 .. i - 1]$ will hold only the elements originally in the first $i - 1$ positions of the array, and they will be in sorted order. To determine where the element originally in $A[i]$ goes, insertion sort marches through $A[1 .. i-1]$, starting at $A[i-1]$ and going toward the left, shifting each element greater than this one by one position to the right. Once we find an element that is not greater than $A[i]$ or we hit the left end of the array, we drop the element originally in $A[i]$ into its new position in the array.

Procedure INSERTION-SORT(A, n)

Inputs and Result: Same as SELECTION-SORT.

1. For $i = 2$ to n:
   A. Set *key* to $A[i]$, and set j to $i - 1$.
   B. While $j > 0$ and $A[j] > key$, do the following:
      i. Set $A[j + 1]$ to $A[j]$.
      ii. Decrement j (i.e., set j to $j - 1$).
   C. Set $A[j + 1]$ to *key*.

The test in step 1B relies on the "and" operator being ***short circuiting***: if the expression on the left, $j > 0$, is false, then it does not evaluate the expression on the right, $A[j] > key$. If it did attempt to access $A[j]$ when $j \leq 0$, an array indexing error would occur.

Here is how insertion sort works on the same array as we saw on page 34 for selection sort:

Once again, the initial array appears in the upper left, and each step shows the array after an iteration of the outer loop of step 1. The darker shaded elements hold the subarray that is known to be sorted. The loop invariant for the outer loop (again, we won't prove it) is the following:

> At the start of each iteration of the loop of step 1, the subarray $A[1 .. i-1]$ consists of the elements originally in $A[1 .. i-1]$, but in sorted order.

The next illustration demonstrates how the inner loop of step 1B works in the above example when i equals 4. We assume that the subarray $A[1 .. 3]$ contains the elements originally in the first three array positions, but now they are sorted. To determine where to place the element originally in $A[4]$, we save it in a variable named *key*, and then shift each element in $A[1 . . 3]$ that is greater than *key* by one position to the right:

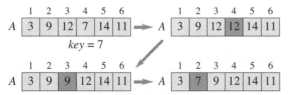

The darker shaded positions show where elements move to. In the last step shown, the value of $A[1]$, 3, is not greater than the value of *key*, 7, and so the inner loop terminates. The value of *key* drops into the position just to the right of $A[1]$, as the last step shows. Of course, we have to save the value originally in $A[i]$ into *key* in step 1A, because the first iteration of the inner loop overwrites $A[i]$.

It is also possible that the inner loop terminates because the test $j > 0$ comes up false. This situation occurs if *key* is less than all the elements in $A[1 . . i - 1]$. When j becomes 0, each element in $A[1 . . i - 1]$ has been shifted to the right, and so step 1C drops *key* into $A[1]$, right where we want it.

When we analyze the running time of INSERTION-SORT, it becomes a bit trickier than SELECTION-SORT. The number of times that the inner loop iterates in the SELECTION-SORT procedure depends only on the index i of the outer loop and not at all on the elements themselves. For the INSERTION-SORT procedure, however, the number of times that the inner loop iterates depends on both the index i of the outer loop *and* the values in the array elements.

The best case of INSERTION-SORT occurs when the inner loop makes zero iterations every time. For that to happen, the test $A[j] > key$ must come up false the first time for each value of i. In other words, we must have $A[i - 1] \leq A[i]$ every time that step 1B executes. How can this situation occur? Only if the array A is already sorted when the procedure starts. In this case, the outer loop iterates $n - 1$ times, and each iteration of the outer loop takes a constant amount of time, so that INSERTION-SORT takes only $\Theta(n)$ time.

The worst case occurs when the inner loop makes the maximum possible number of iterations every time. Now the test $A[j] > key$ must always come up true, and the loop must terminate because the test $j > 0$ comes up false. Each element $A[i]$ must travel all the way to the left of the array. How can this situation happen? Only if the array A starts in reverse sorted order, that is, sorted into *nonincreasing* order. In this case, for each time the outer loop iterates, the inner loop iterates $i - 1$ times. Since the outer loop runs with i going from 2 up to n, the number of inner-loop iterations forms an arithmetic series:

$$1 + 2 + 3 + \cdots + (n - 2) + (n - 1),$$

which, as we saw for selection sort, is $\Theta(n^2)$. Since each inner-loop iteration takes constant time, the worst-case running time of insertion sort is $\Theta(n^2)$. In the worst case, therefore, selection sort and insertion sort have running times that are asymptotically the same.

Would it make sense to try to understand what happens on average with insertion sort? That depends on what an "average" input looks like. If the ordering of elements in the input array were truly random, we would expect each element to be larger than about half the elements preceding it and smaller than about half the elements preceding it, so that each time the inner loop runs, it would make approximately $(i - 1)/2$ iterations. That would cut the running time in half, compared with the worst case. But $1/2$ is just a constant factor, and so, asymptotically, it would be no different from the worst-case running time: still $\Theta(n^2)$.

Insertion sort is an excellent choice when the array starts out as "almost sorted." Suppose that each array element starts out within k positions of where it ends up in the sorted array. Then the total number of times that a given element is shifted, over all iterations of the inner loop, is at most k. Therefore, the total number of times that all elements are shifted, over all inner-loop iterations, is at most kn, which in turn tells us that the total number of inner-loop iterations is at most kn (since each inner-loop iteration shifts exactly one element by one position). If k is a constant, then the total running time of insertion sort would be only $\Theta(n)$, because the Θ-notation subsumes the constant factor k. In fact, we can even tolerate some elements moving a long distance in the array, as long as there are not too many such elements. In particular, if l elements can move anywhere in the array (so that each of these elements can move by up to $n - 1$ positions), and the remaining $n - l$ elements can move at most k positions, then the total number of shifts is at most $l(n - 1) + (n - l)k = (k + l)n - (k + 1)l$, which is $\Theta(n)$ if both k and l are constants.

If we compare the asymptotic running times of insertion sort and selection sort, we see that in the worst case, they are the same. Insertion sort is better if the array is almost sorted. Selection sort has one advantage over insertion sort, however: selection sort moves elements $\Theta(n)$ times no matter what, but insertion sort could move elements up to $\Theta(n^2)$ times, since each execution of step 1Bi of INSERTION-SORT moves an element. As we noted on page 35 for selection sort, if moving an element is particularly time-consuming and you have no reason to expect that insertion sort's input approaches the best-case situation, then you might be better off running selection sort instead of insertion sort.

Merge sort

Our next sorting algorithm, merge sort, has a running time of only $\Theta(n \lg n)$ in all cases. When we compare its running time with the $\Theta(n^2)$ worst-case running times of selection sort and insertion sort, we are trading a factor of n for a factor of only $\lg n$. As we noted on page 7 back in Chapter 1, that's a trade you should take any day.

Merge sort does have a couple of disadvantages compared with the other two sorting algorithms we have seen. First, the constant factor that we hide in the asymptotic notation is higher than for the other two algorithms. Of course, once the array size n gets large enough, that doesn't really matter. Second, merge sort does not work *in place*: it has to make complete copies of the entire input array. Contrast this feature with selection sort and insertion sort, which at any time keep an extra copy of only one array entry rather than copies of all the array entries. If space is at a premium, you might not want to use merge sort.

We employ a common algorithmic paradigm known as ***divide-and-conquer*** in merge sort. In divide-and-conquer, we break the problem into subproblems that are similar to the original problem, solve the subproblems recursively, and then combine the solutions to the subproblems to solve the original problem. Recall from Chapter 2 that in order for recursion to work, each recursive call must be on a smaller instance of the same problem that will eventually hit a base case. Here's a general outline of a divide-and-conquer algorithm:

1. ***Divide*** the problem into a number of subproblems that are smaller instances of the same problem.

2. ***Conquer*** the subproblems by solving them recursively. If they are small enough, solve the subproblems as base cases.

3. ***Combine*** the solutions to the subproblems into the solution for the original problem.

When we sort the books on our bookshelf with merge sort, each sub-problem consists of sorting the books in consecutive slots on the shelf. Initially, we want to sort all n books, in slots 1 through n, but in a general subproblem, we will want to sort all the books in slots p through r. Here's how we apply divide-and-conquer:

1. ***Divide*** by finding the number q of the slot midway between p and r. We do so in the same way that we found the midpoint in binary search: add p and q, divide by 2, and take the floor.

2. ***Conquer*** by recursively sorting the books in each of the two sub-problems created by the divide step: recursively sort the books that are in slots p through q, and recursively sort the books that are in slots $q + 1$ through r.

3. ***Combine*** by merging the sorted books that are in slots p through q and slots $q + 1$ through r, so that all the books in slots p through r are sorted. We'll see how to merge books in a moment.

The base case occurs when fewer than two books need to be sorted (that is, when $p \geq r$), since a set of books with no books or one book is already trivially sorted.

To convert this idea to sorting an array, the books in slots p through r correspond to the subarray $A[p..r]$. Here is the merge sort procedure, which calls a procedure MERGE(A, p, q, r) to merge the sorted subarrays $A[p..q]$ and $A[q + 1..r]$ into the single sorted subarray $A[p..r]$:

Procedure MERGE-SORT(A, p, r)

Inputs:
* A: an array.
* p, r: starting and ending indices of a subarray of A.

Result: The elements of the subarray $A[p..r]$ are sorted into nondecreasing order.

1. If $p \geq r$, then the subarray $A[p..r]$ has at most one element, and so it is already sorted. Just return without doing anything.
2. Otherwise, do the following:
   A. Set q to $\lfloor (p + r)/2 \rfloor$.
   B. Recursively call MERGE-SORT(A, p, q).
   C. Recursively call MERGE-SORT($A, q + 1, r$).
   D. Call MERGE(A, p, q, r).

Although we have yet to see how the MERGE procedure works, we can look at an example of how the MERGE-SORT procedure operates. Let's start with this array:

1	2	3	4	5	6	7	8	9	10
12	9	3	7	14	11	6	2	10	5

The initial call is MERGE-SORT$(A, 1, 10)$. Step 2A computes q to be 5, so that the recursive calls in steps 2B and 2C are MERGE-SORT$(A, 1, 5)$ and MERGE-SORT$(A, 6, 10)$:

1	2	3	4	5
12	9	3	7	14

6	7	8	9	10
11	6	2	10	5

After the two recursive calls return, these two subarrays are sorted:

1	2	3	4	5
3	7	9	12	14

6	7	8	9	10
2	5	6	10	11

Finally, the call MERGE$(A, 1, 5, 10)$ in step 2D merges the two sorted subarrays into a single sorted subarray, which is the entire array in this case:

1	2	3	4	5	6	7	8	9	10
2	3	5	6	7	9	10	11	12	14

If we unfold the recursion, we get the figure on the next page. Diverging arrows indicate divide steps, and converging arrows indicate merge steps. The variables p, q, and r appearing above each subarray are located at the indices to which they correspond in each recursive call. The italicized numbers give the order in which the procedure calls occur after the initial call MERGE-SORT$(A, 1, 10)$. For example, the call MERGE$(A, 1, 3, 5)$ is the 13th procedure call after the initial call, and the call MERGE-SORT$(A, 6, 7)$ is the 16th call.

The real work happens in the MERGE procedure. Therefore, not only must the MERGE procedure work correctly, but it must also be fast. If we are merging a total of n elements, the best we can hope for is $\Theta(n)$ time, since each element has to be merged into its proper place, and indeed we can achieve linear-time merging.

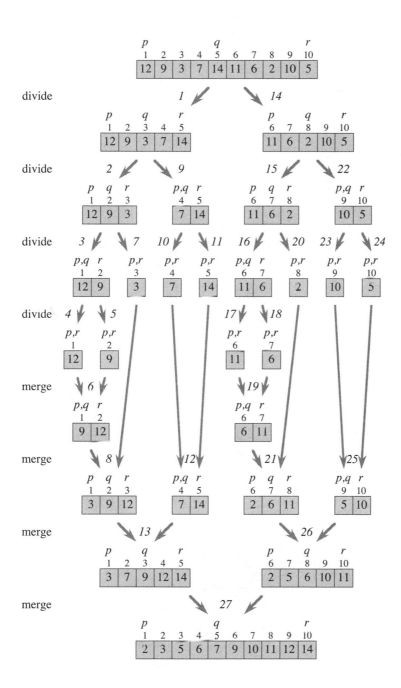

divide

divide

divide

divide

divide

merge

merge

merge

merge

Returning to our book example, let's look at just the portion of the bookshelf from slot 9 through slot 14. Suppose that we have sorted the books in slots 9–11 and that we have sorted the books in slots 12–14:

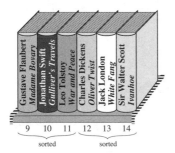

We pull out the books in slots 9–11 and make a pile of them, with the book whose author is alphabetically first on top, and we do the same with the books in slots 12–14, making a separate pile:

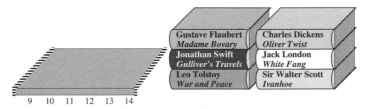

Because the two piles are already sorted, the book that should go back into slot 9 must be one of the books atop its pile: either the book by Gustave Flaubert or the book by Charles Dickens. Indeed, we see that the book by Dickens comes before the book by Flaubert, and so we move it into slot 9:

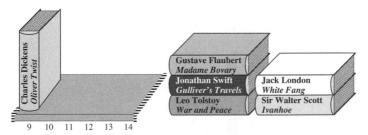

After we move the book by Dickens into slot 9, the book that should go into slot 10 must be either the book still atop the first pile, by Flaubert, or the book now atop the second pile, by Jack London. We move the Flaubert book into slot 10:

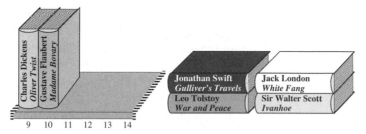

Next, we compare the books now atop their piles, which are by Jonathan Swift and London, and we move the book by London into slot 11. That leaves the book by Sir Walter Scott atop the right pile, and when we compare it with the book by Swift, we move the book by Scott into slot 12. At this point, the right pile is empty:

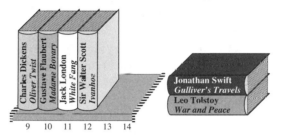

All that remains is to move the books in the left pile into the remaining slots, in order. Now all books in slots 9–14 are sorted:

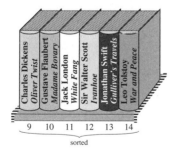

How efficient is this merge procedure? We move each book exactly twice: once to pull it off the shelf and put it into a pile, and once to move it from the top of a pile back onto the shelf. Furthermore, whenever we are deciding which book to put back onto the shelf, we need to compare only two books: those atop their piles. To merge n books, therefore, we move books $2n$ times and compare pairs of books at most n times.

Why pull the books off the shelf? What if we had left the books on the shelf and just kept track of which books we had put into their correct slots on the shelf and which books we hadn't? That could turn out to be a lot more work. For example, suppose that every book in the right half should come before every book in the left half. Before we could move the first book from the right half into the first slot of the left half, we would have to shift every book that started in the left half to the right by one slot in order to make room. And then we'd have to do the same to put the next book that started in the right half into the second slot of the left half. And the same for all the other books that started in the right half. We would have to shift half the books—all the books that started in the left half—each time we wanted to put a book that started in the right half into its correct slot.

That argument explains why we do not merge in place.[3] Returning to how we merge the sorted subarrays $A[p \mathinner{.\,.} q]$ and $A[q + 1 \mathinner{.\,.} r]$ into the subarray $A[p \mathinner{.\,.} r]$, we start by copying the elements to be merged from array A into temporary arrays and then merge them back into A. Let $n_1 = q - p + 1$ be the number of elements in $A[p \mathinner{.\,.} q]$ and $n_2 = r - q$ be the number of elements in $A[q + 1 \mathinner{.\,.} r]$. We create temporary arrays B with n_1 elements and C with n_2 elements, and we copy the elements in $A[p \mathinner{.\,.} q]$, in order, into B, and likewise the elements in $A[q + 1 \mathinner{.\,.} r]$, in order, into C. Now we can merge these elements back into $A[p \mathinner{.\,.} q]$ without fear of overwriting our only copies of them.

We merge the array elements the same way we merge books. We copy elements from the arrays B and C back into the subarray $A[p \mathinner{.\,.} r]$, maintaining indices to keep track of the smallest element not yet copied back in both B and C, and copying back the smaller of the two. In constant time, we can determine which element is smaller, copy it back into the correct position of $A[p \mathinner{.\,.} r]$, and update indices into the arrays.

Eventually, one of the two arrays will have all its elements copied back to $A[p \mathinner{.\,.} r]$. This moment corresponds to the moment when only one pile of books remains. But we use a trick to avoid having to check each time whether one of the arrays has been exhausted: we place at the right end of each of the arrays B and C an extra element that is greater than any other element. Do you recall the sentinel trick that we used in SENTINEL-LINEAR-SEARCH in Chapter 2? This idea is similar. Here, we use ∞ (infinity) as the sentinel's sort key, so that whenever an ele-

---

[3] Actually, it is possible to merge in place in linear time, but the procedure to do so is pretty complicated.

ment with a sort key of ∞ is the smallest remaining element in its array, it is guaranteed to "lose" the contest to see which array has the smaller remaining element.[4] Once all elements from both arrays B and C have been copied back, both arrays have their sentinels as their smallest remaining element. But there's no need to compare the sentinels at this point, because by then we have copied all the "real" elements (the non-sentinels) back to $A[p..r]$. Since we know in advance that we'll be copying elements back into $A[p]$ through $A[r]$, we can stop once we have copied an element back into $A[r]$. We can just run a loop with an index into A running from p to r.

Here is the MERGE procedure. It looks long, but it just follows the method above.

Procedure MERGE(A, p, q, r)

Inputs:
- A: an array.
- p, q, r: indices into A. Each of the subarrays $A[p..q]$ and $A[q+1..r]$ is assumed to be already sorted.

Result: The subarray $A[p..r]$ contains the elements originally in $A[p..q]$ and $A[q+1..r]$, but now the entire subarray $A[p..r]$ is sorted.

1. Set n_1 to $q - p + 1$, and set n_2 to $r - q$.
2. Let $B[1..n_1 + 1]$ and $C[1..n_2 + 1]$ be new arrays.
3. Copy $A[p..q]$ into $B[1..n_1]$, and copy $A[q+1..r]$ into $C[1..n_2]$.
4. Set both $B[n_1 + 1]$ and $C[n_2 + 1]$ to ∞.
5. Set both i and j to 1.
6. For $k = p$ to r:
   A. If $B[i] \leq C[j]$, then set $A[k]$ to $B[i]$ and increment i.
   B. Otherwise ($B[i] > C[j]$), set $A[k]$ to $C[j]$ and increment j.

After steps 1–4 allocate the arrays B and C, copy $A[p..q]$ into B and $A[q+1..r]$ into C, and insert the sentinels into these arrays, each

---

[4] In practice, we represent ∞ by a value that compares as greater than any sort key. For example, if the sort keys are author names, ∞ could be ZZZZ—assuming, of course, that no real author has that name.

iteration of the main loop in step 6 copies back the smallest remaining element to the next position in $A[p..r]$, terminating once it has copied back all the elements in B and C. In this loop, i indexes the smallest remaining element in B, j indexes the smallest remaining element in C, and k indexes the location in A where the element will be copied back into.

If we are merging n elements altogether (so that $n = n_1 + n_2$), it takes $\Theta(n)$ time to copy the elements into arrays B and C, and constant time per element to copy it back into $A[p..r]$, for a total merging time of only $\Theta(n)$.

We claimed earlier that the entire merge-sort algorithm takes time $\Theta(n \lg n)$. We will make the simplifying assumption that the array size n is a power of 2, so that every time we divide the array, the sub-array sizes are equal. (In general, n might not be a power of 2 and so the subarray sizes might not be equal in a given recursive call. A rigorous analysis can take care of this technicality, but let's not concern ourselves with it.)

Here is how we analyze merge sort. Let's say that sorting a sub-array of n elements takes time $T(n)$, which is a function that increases with n (since, presumably, it takes longer to sort more elements). The time $T(n)$ comes from the three components of the divide-and-conquer paradigm, whose times we add together:

1. Dividing takes constant time, because it amounts to just computing the index q.

2. Conquering consists of the two recursive calls on subarrays, each with $n/2$ elements. By how we defined the time to sort a subarray, each of the two recursive calls takes time $T(n/2)$.

3. Combining the results of the two recursive calls by merging the sorted subarrays takes $\Theta(n)$ time.

Because the constant time for dividing is a low-order term compared with the $\Theta(n)$ time for combining, we can absorb the dividing time into the combining time and say that dividing and combining, together, take $\Theta(n)$ time. The conquer step costs $T(n/2) + T(n/2)$, or $2T(n/2)$. Now we can write an equation for $T(n)$:

$$T(n) = 2T(n/2) + f(n),$$

where $f(n)$ represents the time for dividing and combining which, as we just noted, is $\Theta(n)$. A common practice in the study of algorithms is to just put the asymptotic notation right into the equation and let it stand for some function that we don't care to give a name to, and so we rewrite this equation as

$$T(n) = 2T(n/2) + \Theta(n) .$$

Wait! There seems to be something amiss here. We have defined the function T that describes the running time of merge sort in terms of the very same function! We call such an equation a ***recurrence equation***, or just a ***recurrence***. The problem is that we want to express $T(n)$ in a non-recursive manner, that is, not in terms of itself. It can be a real pain in the neck to convert a function expressed as a recurrence into non-recursive form, but for a broad class of recurrence equations we can apply a cookbook method known as the "master method." The master method applies to many (but not all) recurrences of the form $T(n) = aT(n/b) + f(n)$, where a and b are positive integer constants. Fortunately, it applies to our merge-sort recurrence, and it gives the result that $T(n)$ is $\Theta(n \lg n)$.

This $\Theta(n \lg n)$ running time applies to all cases of merge sort—best case, worst case, and all cases in between. Each element is copied $\Theta(n \lg n)$ times. As you can see from examining the MERGE method, when it is called with $p = 1$ and $r = n$, it makes copies of all n elements, and so merge sort definitely does not run in place.

Quicksort

Like merge sort, quicksort uses the divide-and-conquer paradigm (and hence uses recursion). Quicksort uses divide-and-conquer in a slightly different way than merge sort, however. It has a couple of other significant differences from merge sort:

- Quicksort works in place.
- Quicksort's asymptotic running time differs between the worst case and the average case. In particular, quicksort's worst-case running time is $\Theta(n^2)$, but its average-case running time is better: $\Theta(n \lg n)$.

Quicksort also has good constant factors (better than merge sort's), and it is often a good sorting algorithm to use in practice.

Here is how quicksort uses divide-and-conquer. Again let us think about sorting books on a bookshelf. As with merge sort, we initially want to sort all n books in slots 1 through n, and we'll consider the general problem of sorting books in slots p through r.

1. **Divide** by first choosing any one book that is in slots p through r. Call this book the **pivot**. Rearrange the books on the shelf so that all other books with author names that come before the pivot's author or are written by the same author are to the left of the pivot, and all books with author names that come after the pivot's author are to the right of the pivot.

   In this example, we choose the rightmost book, by Jack London, as the pivot when rearranging the books in slots 9 through 15:

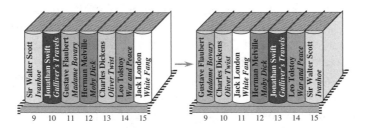

   After rearranging—which we call **partitioning** in quicksort—the books by Flaubert and Dickens, who come before London alphabetically, are to the left of the book by London, and all other books, by authors who come after London alphabetically, are to the right. Notice that after partitioning, the books to the left of the book by London are in no particular order, and the same is true for the books to the right.

2. **Conquer** by recursively sorting the books to the left of the pivot and to the right of the pivot. That is, if the divide step moves the pivot to slot q (slot 11 in the above example), then recursively sort the books in slots p through $q - 1$ and recursively sort the books in slots $q + 1$ through r.

3. **Combine**—by doing nothing! Once the conquer step recursively sorts, we are done. Why? All the books to the left of the pivot (in slots p through $q - 1$) come before the pivot or have the same author as the pivot and are sorted, and all the books to the right of the pivot (in slots $q + 1$ through r) come after the pivot and are sorted. The books in slots p through r can't help but be sorted!

   If you change the bookshelf to the array and the books to array elements, you have the strategy for quicksort. Like merge sort, the base case occurs when the subarray to be sorted has fewer than two elements.

The procedure for quicksort assumes that we can call a procedure PARTITION(A, p, r) that partitions the subarray $A[p \mathinner{\ldotp\ldotp} r]$, returning the index q where it has placed the pivot.

Procedure QUICKSORT(A, p, r)

Inputs and Result: Same as MERGE-SORT.

1. If $p \geq r$, then just return without doing anything.
2. Otherwise, do the following:

    A. Call PARTITION(A, p, r), and set q to its result.
    B. Recursively call QUICKSORT($A, p, q - 1$).
    C. Recursively call QUICKSORT($A, q + 1, r$).

The initial call is QUICKSORT($A, 1, n$), similar to the MERGE-SORT procedure. Here's an example of how the recursion unfolds, with the indices p, q, and r shown for each subarray in which $p \leq r$:

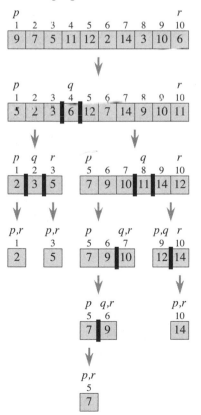

The bottommost value in each array position gives the final element stored there. When you read the array from left to right, looking at the bottommost value in each position, you see that the array is indeed sorted.

The key to quicksort is partitioning. Just as we were able to merge n elements in $\Theta(n)$ time, we can partition n elements in $\Theta(n)$ time. Here's how we'll partition the books that are in slots p through r on the shelf. We choose the rightmost book of the set—the book in slot r—as the pivot. At any time, each book will be in exactly one of four groups, and these groups will be in slots p through r, from left to right:

- group L (left group): books with authors known to come before the pivot's author alphabetically or written by the pivot's author, followed by

- group R (right group): books with authors known to come after the pivot's author alphabetically, followed by

- group U (unknown group): books that we have not yet examined, so we don't know how their authors compare with the pivot's author, followed by

- group P (pivot): just one book, the pivot.

We go through the books in group U from left to right, comparing each with the pivot and moving it into either group L or group R, stopping once we get to the pivot. The book we compare with the pivot is always the leftmost book in group U.

- If the book's author comes after the pivot's author, then the book becomes the rightmost book in group R. Since the book was the leftmost book in group U, and group U immediately follows group R, we just have to move the dividing line between groups R and U one slot to the right, without moving any books:

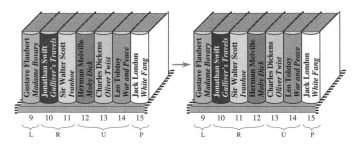

- If the book's author comes before the pivot's author or is the pivot's author, then we will make this book the rightmost book in group L. We swap it with the leftmost book in group R and move the dividing lines between groups L and R and between groups R and U one slot to the right:

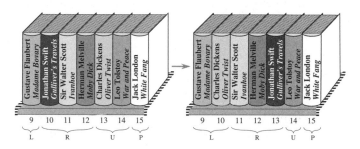

Once we get to the pivot, we swap it with the leftmost book in group R. In our example, we end up with the arrangement of books shown on page 50.

We compare each book with the pivot once, and each book whose author comes before the pivot's author or is the pivot's author causes one swap to occur. To partition n books, therefore, we make at most $n - 1$ comparisons (since we don't have to compare the pivot with itself) and at most n swaps. Notice that, unlike merging, we can partition the books without removing them all from the shelf. That is, we can partition in place.

To convert how we partition books to how we partition a subarray $A[p \mathrel{..} r]$, we first choose $A[r]$ (the rightmost element) as the pivot. Then we go through the subarray from left to right, comparing each element with the pivot. We maintain indices q and u into the subarray that divide it up as follows:

- The subarray $A[p \mathrel{..} q - 1]$ corresponds to group L: each element is less than or equal to the pivot.

- The subarray $A[q \mathrel{..} u - 1]$ corresponds to group R: each element is greater than the pivot.

- The subarray $A[u \mathrel{..} r - 1]$ corresponds to group U: we don't yet know how they compare with the pivot.

- The element $A[r]$ corresponds to group P: it holds the pivot.

These divisions, in fact, are loop invariants. (But we won't prove them.)

At each step, we compare $A[u]$, the leftmost element in group U, with the pivot. If $A[u]$ is greater than the pivot, then we increment u to move the dividing line between groups R and U to the right. If instead $A[u]$ is less than or equal to the pivot, then we swap the elements in $A[q]$ (the leftmost element in group R) and $A[u]$ and then increment both q and u to move the dividing lines between groups L and R and groups R and U to the right. Here's the PARTITION procedure:

Procedure PARTITION(A, p, r)

Inputs: Same as MERGE-SORT.

Result: Rearranges the elements of $A[p \mathbin{..} r]$ so that every element in $A[p \mathbin{..} q - 1]$ is less than or equal to $A[q]$ and every element in $A[q + 1 \mathbin{..} r]$ is greater than q. Returns the index q to the caller.

1. Set q to p.
2. For $u = p$ to $r - 1$ do:
   A. If $A[u] \leq A[r]$, then swap $A[q]$ with $A[u]$ and then increment q.
3. Swap $A[q]$ with $A[r]$ and then return q.

By starting both of the indices q and u at p, groups L ($A[p \mathbin{..} q - 1]$) and R ($A[q \mathbin{..} u - 1]$) are initially empty and group U ($A[u \mathbin{..} r - 1]$) contains every element except the pivot. In some instances, such as if $A[p] \leq A[r]$, an element might be swapped with itself, resulting in no change to the array. Step 3 finishes up by swapping the pivot element with the leftmost element in group R, thereby moving the pivot into its correct place in the partitioned array, and then returning the pivot's new index q.

Here is how the PARTITION procedure operates, step by step, on the subarray $A[5 \mathbin{..} 10]$ created by the first partitioning in the quicksort example on page 52. Group U is shown in white, group L has light shading, group R has darker shading, and the darkest element is the pivot, group P. The first part of the figure shows the initial array and indices, the next five parts show the array and indices after each iteration of the loop of step 2 (including incrementing index u at the end of each iteration), and the last part shows the final partitioned array:

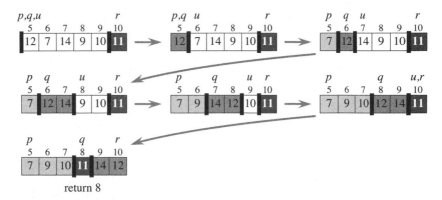

return 8

As when we partitioned books, we compare each element with the pivot once and perform at most one swap for each element that we compare with the pivot. Since each comparison takes constant time and each swap takes constant time, the total time for PARTITION on an n-element subarray is $\Theta(n)$.

So how long does the QUICKSORT procedure take? As with merge sort, let's say that sorting a subarray of n elements takes time $T(n)$, a function that increases with n. Dividing, done by the PARTITION procedure, takes $\Theta(n)$ time. But the time for QUICKSORT depends on how even the partitioning turns out to be.

In the worst case, the partition sizes are really unbalanced. If every element other than the pivot is less than it, then PARTITION ends up leaving the pivot in $A[r]$ and returns the index r to QUICKSORT, which QUICKSORT stores in the variable q. In this case, the partition $A[q + 1 .. r]$ is empty and the partition $A[p .. q - 1]$ is only one element smaller than $A[p .. r]$. The recursive call on the empty subarray takes $\Theta(1)$ time (the time to make the call and determine that the subarray is empty in step 1). We can just roll this $\Theta(1)$ into the $\Theta(n)$ time for partitioning. But if $A[p .. r]$ has n elements, then $A[p .. q - 1]$ has $n - 1$ elements, and so the recursive call on $A[p .. q - 1]$ takes $T(n - 1)$ time. We get the recurrence

$$T(n) = T(n - 1) + \Theta(n) .$$

We can't solve this recurrence using the master method, but it has the solution that $T(n)$ is $\Theta(n^2)$. That's no better than selection sort! How can we get such an uneven split? If every pivot is greater than all other elements, then the array must have started out already sorted. It also turns out that we get an uneven split every time if the array starts out in reverse sorted order.

On the other hand, if we got an even split every time, each of the subarrays would have at most $n/2$ elements. The recurrence would be the same as the recurrence on page 49 for merge sort,

$$T(n) = 2T(n/2) + \Theta(n) ,$$

with the same solution, $T(n)$ is $\Theta(n \lg n)$. Of course, we'd have to be really lucky, or the input array would have to be contrived, to get a perfectly even split every time.

The usual case is somewhere between the best and worst cases. The technical analysis is messy and I won't put you through it, but if the elements of the input array come in a random order, then on average we get splits that are close enough to even that QUICKSORT takes $\Theta(n \lg n)$ time.

Now let's get paranoid. Suppose that your worst enemy has given you an array to sort, knowing that you always pick the last element in each subarray as the pivot, and has arranged the array so that you always get the worst-case split. How can you foil your enemy? You could first check to see whether the array starts out sorted or reverse sorted, and do something special in these cases. Then again, your enemy could contrive the array so that the splits are always bad, but not maximally bad. You wouldn't want to check for every possible bad case.

Fortunately, there's a much simpler solution: don't always pick the last element as the pivot. But then the lovely PARTITION procedure won't work, because the groups aren't where they're supposed to be. That's not a problem, either: before running the PARTITION procedure, swap $A[r]$ with a randomly chosen element in $A[p .. r]$. Now you've chosen your pivot randomly *and* you can run the PARTITION procedure.

In fact, with a little more effort, you can improve your chance of getting a split that's close to even. Instead of choosing one element in $A[p .. r]$ at random, choose three elements at random and swap the median of the three with $A[r]$. By the median of the three, we mean the one whose value is between the other two. (If two or more of the randomly chosen elements are equal, break ties arbitrarily.) Again, I won't make you endure the analysis, but you would have to be really unlucky in how you chose the random elements each time in order for QUICKSORT to take longer than $\Theta(n \lg n)$ time. Moreover, unless your enemy had access to your random number generator, your enemy would have no control over how even the splits turn out to be.

How many times does QUICKSORT swap elements? That depends on whether you count "swapping" an element to the same position it started in as a swap. You could certainly check to see whether this is the case and avoid the swap if it is. So let's call it a swap only when an element really moves in the array as a result of swapping, that is, when $q \neq u$ in step 2A or when $q \neq r$ in step 3 of PARTITION. The best case for minimizing swaps is also one of the worst cases for asymptotic running time: when the array is already sorted. Then no swaps occur. The most swaps occur when n is even and the input array looks like $n, n-2, n-4, \ldots, 4, 2, 1, 3, 5, \ldots, n-3, n-1$. Then $n^2/4$ swaps occur, and the asymptotic running time is still the worst case $\Theta(n^2)$.

Recap

In this chapter and the previous one, we have seen four algorithms for searching and four for sorting. Let's summarize their properties in a couple of tables. Because the three searching algorithms from Chapter 2 were just variations on a theme, we can consider either BETTER-LINEAR-SEARCH or SENTINEL-LINEAR-SEARCH as the representatives for linear search.

Searching algorithms

Algorithm	Worst-case running time	Best-case running time	Requires sorted array?
Linear search	$\Theta(n)$	$\Theta(1)$	no
Binary search	$\Theta(\lg n)$	$\Theta(1)$	yes

Sorting algorithms

Algorithm	Worst-case running time	Best-case running time	Worst-case swaps	In-place?
Selection sort	$\Theta(n^2)$	$\Theta(n^2)$	$\Theta(n)$	yes
Insertion sort	$\Theta(n^2)$	$\Theta(n)$	$\Theta(n^2)$	yes
Merge sort	$\Theta(n \lg n)$	$\Theta(n \lg n)$	$\Theta(n \lg n)$	no
Quicksort	$\Theta(n^2)$	$\Theta(n \lg n)$	$\Theta(n^2)$	yes

These tables do not show average-case running times, because with the notable exception of quicksort, they match the worst-case running times. As we saw, quicksort's average-case running time, assuming that the array starts in a random order, is only $\Theta(n \lg n)$.

How do these sorting algorithms compare in practice? I coded them up in C++ and ran them on arrays of 4-byte integers on two different machines: my MacBook Pro (on which I wrote this book), with a 2.4-GHz Intel Core 2 Duo processor and 4 GB of RAM running Mac OS 10.6.8, and a Dell PC (my website server) with a 3.2-GHz Intel Pentium 4 processor and 1 GB of RAM running Linux version 2.6.22.14. I compiled the code with g++ and optimization level -O3. I ran each algorithm on array sizes ranging up to 50,000, with each array initially in reverse sorted order. I averaged the running times for 20 runs of each algorithm on each array size.

By starting each array in reverse sorted order, I elicited the worst-case asymptotic running times of both insertion sort and quicksort. Therefore, I ran two versions of quicksort: "regular" quicksort, which always chooses the pivot as the last element $A[r]$ of the subarray $A[p \mathrel{..} r]$ being partitioned, and randomized quicksort, which swaps a randomly chosen element in $A[p \mathrel{..} r]$ with $A[r]$ before partitioning. (I did not run the median-of-three method.) The "regular" version of quicksort is also known as *deterministic* because it does not randomize; everything it does is predetermined once it's given an input array to sort.

Randomized quicksort was the champion for $n \geq 64$ on both computers. Here are the ratios of the running times of the other algorithms to randomized quicksort's running times on various input sizes.

MacBook Pro

Algorithm	50	100	500	1000	5000	10,000	50,000
Selection sort	1.34	2.13	8.04	13.31	59.07	114.24	537.42
Insertion sort	1.08	2.02	6.15	11.35	51.86	100.38	474.29
Merge sort	7.58	7.64	6.93	6.87	6.35	6.20	6.27
Deterministic quicksort	1.02	1.63	6.09	11.51	52.02	100.57	475.34

Dell PC

Algorithm	50	100	500	1000	5000	10,000	50,000
Selection sort	0.76	1.60	5.46	12.23	52.03	100.79	496.94
Insertion sort	1.01	1.66	7.68	13.90	68.34	136.20	626.44
Merge sort	3.21	3.38	3.57	3.33	3.36	3.37	3.15
Deterministic quicksort	1.12	1.37	6.52	9.30	47.60	97.45	466.83

Randomized quicksort looks pretty good, but we can beat it. Recall that insertion sort works well when no element has to move very far in the array. Well, once the subproblem sizes in the recursive algorithms get down to some size k, no element has to move more than $k - 1$ positions. Instead of continuing to recursively call randomized quicksort once the subproblem sizes become small, what happens if we instead run insertion sort, suitably modified to sort a subarray rather than the entire array? Indeed, with such a hybrid method, we can sort even faster than randomized quicksort. I found that on my MacBook Pro, a subarray size of 22 was the optimal crossover point, and a subarray size of 17 was the optimal crossover point on my PC. Here are ratios of running times of the hybrid algorithm to randomized quicksort on both machines, for the same problem sizes:

				n			
Machine	50	100	500	1000	5000	10,000	50,000
MacBook Pro	0.55	0.56	0.60	0.60	0.62	0.63	0.66
PC	0.53	0.58	0.60	0.58	0.60	0.64	0.64

Is it possible to beat $\Theta(n \lg n)$ time for sorting? It depends. We'll see in Chapter 4 that if the only way that we can determine where to place elements is by comparing elements, doing different things based on the results of the comparisons, then no, we cannot beat $\Theta(n \lg n)$ time. If we know something about the elements that we can take advantage of, however, we can do better.

Further reading

CLRS [CLRS09] covers insertion sort, merge sort, and both deterministic and randomized quicksort. But the granddaddy of books about sorting and searching remains Volume 3 of Knuth's *The Art of Computer Programming* [Knu98b]; the advice from Chapter 1 applies—*TAOCP* is deep and intense.

4 A Lower Bound for Sorting and How to Beat It

In the previous chapter, we saw four algorithms for sorting n elements in an array. Two of them, selection sort and insertion sort, have worst-case running times of $\Theta(n^2)$, which is not very good. One of them, quicksort, also has a worst-case running time of $\Theta(n^2)$, but takes only $\Theta(n \lg n)$ time on average. Merge sort takes $\Theta(n \lg n)$ time in all cases. In practice, quicksort is the fastest of the four, but if you absolutely had to guard against bad worst-case behavior, you would choose merge sort.

Is $\Theta(n \lg n)$ as good as it gets? Is it possible to devise a sorting algorithm that beats $\Theta(n \lg n)$ time in the worst case? The answer depends on the rules of the game: how is the sorting algorithm allowed to use the sort keys when determining the sorted order?

In this chapter, we'll see that under a certain set of rules, we cannot beat $\Theta(n \lg n)$. Then we'll see two sorting algorithms, counting sort and radix sort, that bend the rules and in so doing manage to sort in only $\Theta(n)$ time.

Rules for sorting

If you examine how the four algorithms from the previous chapter use the sort keys, you'll see that they determine the sorted order based only on comparing pairs of sort keys. All decisions they make are of the form "if this element's sort key is less than this other element's sort key, then do something, and otherwise either do something else or do nothing else." You might be thinking that a sorting algorithm could make *only* decisions of this form; what other kinds of decisions could a sorting algorithm possibly make?

To see what other kinds of decisions are possible, let's take a really simple situation. Suppose that we know two things about the elements we are sorting: each sort key is either 1 or 2, and the elements consist of only sort keys—no satellite data. In this simple situation, we can sort n elements in only $\Theta(n)$ time, beating the $\Theta(n \lg n)$ algorithms from the previous chapter. How? First, go through every element and count how many of them are 1s; let's say that k elements have the value 1. Then we can go through the array, filling the value 1 into the first k positions and then filling the value 2 into the last $n - k$ positions. Here's a procedure:

Procedure REALLY-SIMPLE-SORT (A, n)

Inputs:
* A: an array in which each element is either 1 or 2.
* n: the number of elements in A to sort.

Result: The elements of A are sorted into nondecreasing order.

1. Set k to 0.
2. For $i = 1$ to n:

    A. If $A[i] = 1$, then increment k.
3. For $i = 1$ to k:

    A. Set $A[i]$ to 1.
4. For $i = k + 1$ to n:

    A. Set $A[i]$ to 2.

Steps 1 and 2 count up the number of 1s, incrementing the count k for every element $A[i]$ that equals 1. Step 3 fills $A[1 .. k]$ with 1s, and step 4 fills the remaining positions, $A[k + 1 .. n]$, with 2s. It's pretty easy to see that this procedure runs in $\Theta(n)$ time: the first loop iterates n times, the last two loops, together, iterate n times, and each iteration of each loop takes constant time.

Notice that REALLY-SIMPLE-SORT never compares two array elements *with each other*. It compares each array element with the value 1, but never with another array element. So you see that in this restricted situation, we can sort without comparing pairs of sort keys.

The lower bound on comparison sorting

Now that you have some idea about how the rules of the game may vary, let's see a lower bound on how fast we can sort.

We define a ***comparison sort*** as any sorting algorithm that determines the sorted order only by comparing pairs of elements. The four sorting algorithms from the previous chapter are comparison sorts, but REALLY-SIMPLE-SORT is not.

Here's the lower bound:

In the worst case, any comparison sorting algorithm for n elements requires $\Omega(n \lg n)$ comparisons between pairs of elements.

Recall that Ω-notation gives a lower bound, so that what we're saying is "for sufficiently large n, any comparison sorting algorithm requires at least $cn \lg n$ comparisons in the worst case, for some constant c." Since each comparison takes at least constant time, that gives us an $\Omega(n \lg n)$ lower bound on the time to sort n elements, assuming that we are using a comparison sorting algorithm.

It's important to understand a couple of things about this lower bound. First, it's saying something only about the worst case. You can always make a sorting algorithm run in linear time in the best case: declare that the best case is when the array is already sorted and just check that each element (except for the last one) is less than or equal to its successor in the array. That's easy to do in $\Theta(n)$ time, and if you find that each element is less than or equal to its successor, then you're done. In the *worst case*, however, $\Omega(n \lg n)$ comparisons are necessary. We call this lower bound an ***existential*** lower bound because it says that there exists an input that requires $\Omega(n \lg n)$ comparisons. Another type of lower bound is a ***universal*** lower bound, which applies to all inputs. For sorting, the only universal lower bound we have is $\Omega(n)$, since we have to look at each element at least once. Note that in the previous sentence, I didn't say $\Omega(n)$ *what*. Did I mean $\Omega(n)$ comparisons or $\Omega(n)$ time? I meant $\Omega(n)$ time, since it makes sense that we have to examine each element, even if we're not comparing pairs of elements.

The second important thing is truly remarkable: this lower bound does not depend on the particular algorithm, as long as it's a comparison sorting algorithm. The lower bound applies to *every* comparison sorting algorithm, no matter how simple or complex. The lower bound applies to comparison sorting algorithms that have already been invented or will be invented in the future. It even applies to comparison sorting algorithms that will never be discovered by mankind!

Beating the lower bound with counting sort

We've already seen how to beat the lower bound in a highly restricted setting: there are only two possible values for the sort keys, and each element consists of only a sort key, with no satellite data. In this restricted case, we can sort n elements in only $\Theta(n)$ time without comparing pairs of elements.

We can generalize the method of REALLY-SIMPLE-SORT to handle m different possible values for the sort keys, as long as they are integers in a range of m consecutive integers, say, 0 to $m - 1$, and we can also allow the elements to have satellite data.

Here's the idea. Suppose we know that the sort keys are integers in the range 0 to $m - 1$, and let's suppose further that we know that exactly three elements have sort keys equal to 5 and that exactly six elements have sort keys less than 5 (that is, in the range 0 to 4). Then we know that, in the sorted array, the elements with sort keys equal to 5 should occupy positions 7, 8, and 9. Generalizing, if we know that k elements have sort keys equal to x and that l elements have sort keys less than x, then we know that the elements with sort keys equal to x should occupy positions $l + 1$ through $l + k$ in the sorted array. Therefore, we want to compute, for each possible sort-key value, how many elements have sort keys less than that value and how many elements have sort keys equal to that value.

We can compute how many elements have sort keys less than each possible sort-key value by first computing how many elements have sort keys equal to that value, so let's start with that:

Procedure COUNT-KEYS-EQUAL(A, n, m)

Inputs:
- A: an array of integers in the range 0 to $m - 1$.
- n: the number of elements in A.
- m: defines the range of the values in A.

Output: An array *equal*$[0 .. m - 1]$ such that *equal*$[j]$ contains the number of elements of A that equal j, for $j = 0, 1, 2, \ldots, m - 1$.

1. Let *equal*$[0 .. m - 1]$ be a new array.
2. Set all values in *equal* to 0.
3. For $i = 1$ to n:
   A. Set *key* to $A[i]$.
   B. Increment *equal*$[key]$.
4. Return the *equal* array.

Notice that COUNT-KEYS-EQUAL never compares sort keys with each other. It uses sort keys only to index into the *equal* array. Since the first loop (implicit in step 2) makes m iterations, the second loop (step 3) makes n iterations, and each iteration of each loop takes constant time, COUNT-KEYS-EQUAL takes $\Theta(m + n)$ time. If m is a constant, then COUNT-KEYS-EQUAL takes $\Theta(n)$ time.

Now we can use the *equal* array to compute a running sum to find out how many elements have sort keys less than each value:

Procedure COUNT-KEYS-LESS (*equal*, *m*)

Inputs:
- *equal*: the array returned by COUNT-KEYS-EQUAL.
- *m*: defines the index range of *equal*: 0 to $m - 1$.

Output: An array *less*$[0 .. m - 1]$ such that for $j = 0, 1, 2, \ldots, m - 1$, *less*$[j]$ contains the sum *equal*$[0] + equal[1] + \cdots + equal[j - 1]$.

1. Let *less*$[0 .. m - 1]$ be a new array.
2. Set *less*$[0]$ to 0.
3. For $j = 1$ to $m - 1$:
   A. Set *less*$[j]$ to *less*$[j - 1] + equal[j - 1]$.
4. Return the *less* array.

Assuming that the *equal*$[j]$ gives an accurate count of how many sort keys equal j, for $j = 0, 1, \ldots, m - 1$, you could use the following loop invariant to show that when COUNT-KEYS-LESS returns, *less*$[j]$ says how many sort keys are less than j:

> At the start of each iteration of the loop of step 3, *less*$[j - 1]$ equals the number of sort keys less than $j - 1$.

I'll leave it to you to fill in the initialization, maintenance, and termination parts. You can see easily that the COUNT-KEYS-LESS procedure runs in $\Theta(m)$ time. And it certainly doesn't compare sort keys with each other.

Let's see an example. Suppose that $m = 7$, so that all sort keys are integers in the range 0 to 6, and we have the following array A with $n = 10$ elements: $A = \langle 4, 1, 5, 0, 1, 6, 5, 1, 5, 3 \rangle$. Then *equal* $= \langle 1, 3, 0, 1, 1, 3, 1 \rangle$ and *less* $= \langle 0, 1, 4, 4, 5, 6, 9 \rangle$. Because *less*$[5] = 6$ and *equal*$[5] = 3$ (remember that we index the arrays *less* and *equal* starting from 0, not 1), when we are done sorting, positions 1 through 6 should contain key values less than 5, and positions 7, 8, and 9 should contain the key value 5.

Once we have the *less* array, we can create a sorted array, though not in place:

Procedure REARRANGE($A, less, n, m$)

Inputs:
- A: an array of integers in the range 0 to $m - 1$.
- *less*: the array returned by COUNT-KEYS-LESS.
- n: the number of elements in A.
- m: defines the range of the values in A.

Output: An array B containing the elements of A, sorted.

1. Let $B[1 .. n]$ and $next[0 .. m - 1]$ be new arrays.
2. For $j = 0$ to $m - 1$:
   A. Set $next[j]$ to $less[j] + 1$.
3. For $i = 1$ to n:
   A. Set *key* to $A[i]$.
   B. Set *index* to $next[key]$.
   C. Set $B[index]$ to $A[i]$.
   D. Increment $next[key]$.
4. Return the B array.

The figure on the next page illustrates how REARRANGE moves elements from array A into array B so that they end up in sorted order in B. The top part shows the arrays *less*, *next*, A, and B before the first iteration of the loop of step 3, and each subsequent part shows *next*, A, and B after each iteration. Elements in A are grayed as they are copied into B.

The idea is that, as we go through the array A from start to end, $next[j]$ gives the index in the array B of where the next element of A whose key is j should go. Recall from earlier that if l elements have sort keys less than x, then the k elements whose sort keys equal x should occupy positions $l + 1$ through $l + k$. The loop of step 2 sets up the array *next* so that, at first, $next[j] = l + 1$, where $l = less[j]$. The loop of step 3 goes through array A from start to end. For each element $A[i]$, step 3A stores $A[i]$ into *key*, step 3B computes *index* as the index in array B where $A[i]$ should go, and step 3C moves $A[i]$ into this position in B. Because the next element in array A that has the same sort key as $A[i]$ (if there is one) should go into the next position of B, step 3D increments $next[key]$.

	0	1	2	3	4	5	6
less	0	1	4	4	5	6	9
next	1	2	5	5	6	7	10

	1	2	3	4	5	6	7	8	9	10
A	4	1	5	0	1	6	5	1	5	3
B										

↓

	0	1	2	3	4	5	6
next	1	2	5	5	7	7	10

	1	2	3	4	5	6	7	8	9	10
A	4	1	5	0	1	6	5	1	5	3
B						4				

↓

	0	1	2	3	4	5	6
next	1	3	5	5	7	7	10

	1	2	3	4	5	6	7	8	9	10
A	4	1	5	0	1	6	5	1	5	3
B		1				4				

↓

	0	1	2	3	4	5	6
next	1	3	5	5	7	8	10

	1	2	3	4	5	6	7	8	9	10
A	4	1	5	0	1	6	5	1	5	3
B		1				4	5			

↓

	0	1	2	3	4	5	6
next	2	3	5	5	7	8	10

	1	2	3	4	5	6	7	8	9	10
A	4	1	5	0	1	6	5	1	5	3
B	0	1				4	5			

↓

	0	1	2	3	4	5	6
next	2	4	5	5	7	8	10

	1	2	3	4	5	6	7	8	9	10
A	4	1	5	0	1	6	5	1	5	3
B	0	1	1			4	5			

↓

	0	1	2	3	4	5	6
next	2	4	5	5	7	8	11

	1	2	3	4	5	6	7	8	9	10
A	4	1	5	0	1	6	5	1	5	3
B	0	1	1			4	5			6

↓

	0	1	2	3	4	5	6
next	2	4	5	5	7	9	11

	1	2	3	4	5	6	7	8	9	10
A	4	1	5	0	1	6	5	1	5	3
B	0	1	1			4	5	5		6

↓

	0	1	2	3	4	5	6
next	2	5	5	5	7	9	11

	1	2	3	4	5	6	7	8	9	10
A	4	1	5	0	1	6	5	1	5	3
B	0	1	1	1		4	5	5		6

↓

	0	1	2	3	4	5	6
next	2	5	5	5	7	10	11

	1	2	3	4	5	6	7	8	9	10
A	4	1	5	0	1	6	5	1	5	3
B	0	1	1	1		4	5	5	5	6

↓

	0	1	2	3	4	5	6
next	2	5	5	6	7	10	11

	1	2	3	4	5	6	7	8	9	10
A	4	1	5	0	1	6	5	1	5	3
B	0	1	1	1	3	4	5	5	5	6

How long does REARRANGE take? The loop of step 2 runs in $\Theta(m)$ time, and the loop of step 3 runs in $\Theta(n)$ time. Like COUNT-KEYS-EQUAL, therefore, REARRANGE runs in $\Theta(m + n)$ time, which is $\Theta(n)$ if m is a constant.

Now we can put the three procedures together to create *counting sort*:

Procedure COUNTING-SORT(A, n, m)

Inputs:
- A: an array of integers in the range 0 to $m - 1$.
- n: the number of elements in A.
- m: defines the range of the values in A.

Output: An array B containing the elements of A, sorted.

1. Call COUNT-KEYS-EQUAL(A, n, m), and assign its result to *equal*.
2. Call COUNT-KEYS-LESS(*equal, m*) and assign its result to *less*.
3. Call REARRANGE($A, less, n, m$) and assign its result to B.
4. Return the B array.

From the running times of COUNT-KEYS-EQUAL ($\Theta(m+n)$), COUNT-KEYS-LESS ($\Theta(m)$), and REARRANGE ($\Theta(m + n)$), you can see that COUNTING-SORT runs in time $\Theta(m+n)$, or $\Theta(n)$ when m is a constant. Counting sort beats the lower bound of $\Omega(n \lg n)$ for comparison sorting because it never compares sort keys against each other. Instead, it uses sort keys to index into arrays, which it can do because the sort keys are small integers. If the sort keys were real numbers with fractional parts, or they were character strings, then we could not use counting sort.

You might notice that the procedure assumes that the elements contain only sort keys and not any satellite data. Yet, I promised that, unlike REALLY-SIMPLE-SORT, COUNTING-SORT allows satellite data. And it does, as long as you modify step 3C of REARRANGE to copy the entire element, and not just the sort key.

You might also have noticed that the procedures I've provided are a bit inefficient in how they use arrays. You can combine the *equal, less,* and *next* arrays into one array, but I'll leave that for you to pursue.

I keep mentioning that the running time is $\Theta(n)$ if m is a constant. When would m be a constant? One example would be if I were sorting exams by grade. The grades range from 0 to 100, but the number of students varies. I could use counting sort to sort the exams of n students in $\Theta(n)$ time, since $m = 101$ (remember that the range being sorted is 0 to $m - 1$) is a constant.

In practice, however, counting sort turns out to be useful as part of yet another sorting algorithm, radix sort. In addition to running in linear time when m is a constant, counting sort has another important property: it is **stable**. In a stable sort, elements with the same sort key appear in the output array in the same order as they do in the input array. In other words, a stable sort breaks ties between two elements with equal sort keys by placing first in the output array whichever element appears first in the input array. You can see why counting sort is stable by looking at the loop of step 3 of REARRANGE. If two elements of A have the same sort key, say *key*, then the procedure increases *next[key]* immediately after moving into B the element that occurs earlier in A; that way, by the time it moves the element that occurs later in A, that element will appear later in B.

Radix sort

Suppose that you had to sort strings of characters of some fixed length. For example, I am writing this paragraph on an airplane, and when I made my reservation, I was given the confirmation code XI7FS6. The airline designs all confirmation codes as strings of six characters, where each character is either a letter or a digit. Each character can take 36 values (26 letters plus 10 digits), and so there are $36^6 = 2{,}176{,}782{,}336$ possible confirmation codes. Although that's a constant, it's a pretty large constant, and so the airline would probably rather not rely on counting sort to sort confirmation codes.

For the sake of being concrete, let's say that we can translate each of the 36 characters into a numeric code running from 0 to 35. The code for a digit is the digit itself (so that the code for the digit 5 is 5), and the codes for letters start at 10 for A and run through 35 for Z.

Now let's make things a little simpler and suppose that each confirmation code comprises only two characters. (Not to worry: we'll go back to six characters soon.) Although we could run counting sort with $m = 36^2 = 1296$, we'll instead run it *twice* with $m = 36$. We run it the first time using the *rightmost* character as the sort key. Then we take the result of running counting sort the first time and run it a second time, but now using the *leftmost* character as the sort key. We choose counting sort because it works well when m is relatively small and because it is stable.

For example, suppose that we have the two-character confirmation codes $\langle$F6, E5, R6, X6, X2, T5, F2, T3$\rangle$. After running counting sort on the rightmost character, we get the sorted order $\langle$X2, F2, T3, E5, T5, F6, R6, X6$\rangle$. Notice that because counting sort is stable and X2 comes before F2 in the original order, X2 comes before F2 after sorting on just the rightmost character. Now we sort the result on the leftmost character, again using counting sort, getting the desired result $\langle$E5, F2, F6, R6, T3, T5, X2, X6$\rangle$.

What would have happened if we had sorted on the leftmost character first? After running counting sort on the leftmost character, we'd have $\langle$E5, F6, F2, R6, T5, T3, X6, X2$\rangle$, and then after running counting sort on the rightmost character of the result, we'd get $\langle$F2, X2, T3, E5, T5, F6, R6, X6$\rangle$, which is incorrect.

Why does working from right to left give a correct result? Using a stable sorting method is important; it could be counting sort or any other stable sorting method. Let's suppose that we're working on the ith character position, and assume that if we look at the rightmost $i - 1$ character positions, the array is sorted. Consider any two sort keys. If they differ in the ith character position, then it doesn't matter what's in the $i - 1$ positions to the right: the stable sorting algorithm that sorts on the ith position will put them into the correct order. If, on the other hand, they have the same character in the ith position, then the one that comes first in the $i - 1$ rightmost character positions should come first, and by using a stable sorting method, we guarantee that this is exactly what happens.

So let's return to 6-character confirmation codes, and we'll see how to sort confirmation codes that start out in the order $\langle$XI7FS6, PL4ZQ2, JI8FR9, XL8FQ6, PY2ZR5, KV7WS9, JL2ZV3, KI4WR2$\rangle$. Let's number the characters from right to left as 1 to 6. Then here are the results after running a stable sort on the ith character, working right to left:

i	Resulting order
1	$\langle$PL4ZQ2, KI4WR2, JL2ZV3, PY2ZR5, XI7FS6, XL8FQ6, JI8FR9, KV7WS9$\rangle$
2	$\langle$PL4ZQ2, XL8FQ6, KI4WR2, PY2ZR5, JI8FR9, XI7FS6, KV7WS9, JL2ZV3$\rangle$
3	$\langle$XL8FQ6, JI8FR9, XI7FS6, KI4WR2, KV7WS9, PL4ZQ2, PY2ZR5, JL2ZV3$\rangle$
4	$\langle$PY2ZR5, JL2ZV3, KI4WR2, PL4ZQ2, XI7FS6, KV7WS9, XL8FQ6, JI8FR9$\rangle$
5	$\langle$KI4WR2, XI7FS6, JI8FR9, JL2ZV3, PL4ZQ2, XL8FQ6, KV7WS9, PY2ZR5$\rangle$
6	$\langle$JI8FR9, JL2ZV3, KI4WR2, KV7WS9, PL4ZQ2, PY2ZR5, XI7FS6, XL8FQ6$\rangle$

To generalize, in the ***radix sort*** algorithm, we assume that we can think of each sort key as a d-digit number, where each digit is in the range 0 to $m - 1$. We run a stable sort on each digit, going from right to left. If we use counting sort as the stable sort, then the time to sort on one digit is $\Theta(m + n)$, and the time to sort all d digits is $\Theta(d(m + n))$. If m is a constant (such as 36 in the confirmation code example), then the time for radix sort is $\Theta(dn)$. If d is also a constant (such as 6 for confirmation codes), then the time for radix sort is only $\Theta(n)$.

When radix sort uses counting sort to sort on each digit, it never compares two sort keys against each other. It uses the individual digits to index into arrays within counting sort. That is why radix sort, like counting sort, beats the lower bound of $\Omega(n \lg n)$ for comparison sorting.

Further reading

Chapter 8 of CLRS [CLRS09] expands on all the material in this chapter.

5 Directed Acyclic Graphs

Recall the footnote on page 1, where I revealed that I used to play hockey. For several years, I was a goalie, but eventually my game deteriorated to the point that I couldn't stand watching myself play. It seemed as though every shot found its way to the back of the net. Then, after a hiatus of over seven years, I got back between the pipes (that is, I resumed playing goal) for a couple of games.

My biggest concern wasn't whether I'd be any good—I knew I was going to be terrible—but rather whether I'd remember how to put on all the goalie equipment. In ice hockey, goalies wear a lot of gear (35 to 40 pounds of it), and when dressing for a game, I have to put it on in the right order. For example, because I am right-handed, I wear on my left hand an oversized mitt for catching pucks; it's called a catch glove. Once I've got the catch glove on, my left hand has no dexterity, and I cannot get an upper-body garment of any sort over it.

When I was preparing to don the goalie gear, I made myself a diagram showing which items had to be put on before other items. The diagram appears on the next page. An arrow from item A to item B indicates a constraint that A must be put on before B. For example, I have to put on the chest pad before the sweater. Of course, the "must be put on before" constraint is *transitive*: if item A must be put on before item B, and item B must be put on before item C, then item A must be put on before item C. Therefore, I must put on the chest pad before the sweater, mask, catch glove, and blocker.

For some pairs of items, however, it doesn't matter in which order I put them on. I can put socks on either before or after the chest pad, for example.

I needed to determine an order in which to get dressed. Once I had my diagram, I had to come up with a list containing all the items I had to don, in a single order that did not violate any of the "must be put on before" constraints. I found that several orders worked; below the diagram are three of them.

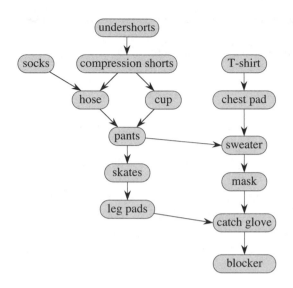

Order #1	Order #2	Order #3
undershorts	undershorts	socks
compression shorts	T-shirt	T-shirt
cup	compression shorts	undershorts
socks	cup	chest pad
hose	chest pad	compression shorts
pants	socks	hose
skates	hose	cup
leg pads	pants	pants
T-shirt	sweater	skates
chest pad	mask	leg pads
sweater	skates	sweater
mask	leg pads	mask
catch glove	catch glove	catch glove
blocker	blocker	blocker

How did I arrive at these orders? Here's how I came up with order #2. I looked for an item that had no incoming arrows, because such an item need not be put on after any other item. I chose undershorts to be the first item in the order, and then, having (conceptually) put on the undershorts, I removed them from the diagram, resulting in the diagram at the top of the next page.

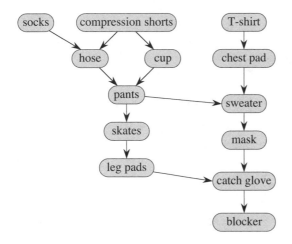

Then, again, I chose an item with no incoming arrows, this time T-shirt. I added it to the end of the order and removed it from the diagram, resulting in this diagram:

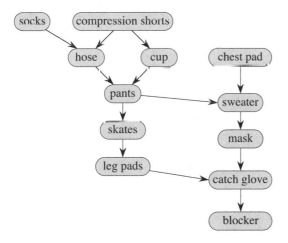

Once again, I chose an item with no incoming arrows—compression shorts—and then I added it to the end of the order and removed it from the diagram, resulting in the diagram at the top of the next page.

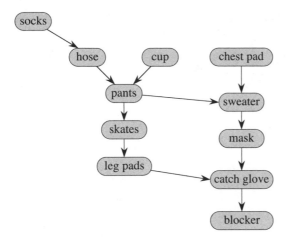

Next, I chose cup:

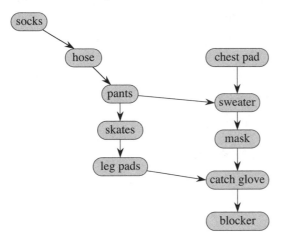

I kept going in this way—choosing an item with no incoming arrows, adding it to the end of the order, and removing the item from the diagram—until no items remained. The three orders shown on page 72 result from making various choices for the item with no incoming arrows, starting from the diagram on page 72.

Directed acyclic graphs

These diagrams are specific examples of ***directed graphs***, which are made of ***vertices*** (singular: ***vertex***), corresponding to the items of goalie equipment, and ***directed edges***, shown by arrows. Each directed edge is an ordered pair of the form (u, v), where u and v are vertices. For example, the leftmost edge in the directed graph on page 72 is (socks, hose). When a directed graph contains a directed edge (u, v), we say that v is **adjacent** to u and that (u, v) **leaves** u and **enters** v, so that the vertex labeled hose is adjacent to the vertex labeled socks and the edge (socks, hose) leaves the vertex labeled socks and enters the vertex labeled hose.

The directed graphs that we have seen have another property: there is no way to get from a vertex back to itself by following a sequence of one or more edges. We call such a directed graph a **directed acyclic graph**, or **dag**. It's acyclic because there is no way to "cycle" from a vertex back to itself. (We'll see a more formal definition of a cycle later in this chapter.)

Dags are great for modeling dependencies where one task must occur before another. Another use for dags arises when planning projects, such as building a house: for example, the framing must be in place before the roof goes on. Or, in cooking, certain steps must occur in certain orders, but for some steps it doesn't matter in which order they happen; we'll see an example of a dag for cooking later in this chapter.

Topological sorting

When I needed to determine a single, linear order in which to put on the goalie equipment, I needed to perform a "topological sort." Put more precisely, a **topological sort** of a dag produces a linear order such that if (u, v) is an edge in the dag, then u appears before v in the linear order. Topological sorting differs from sorting in the sense that we used in Chapters 3 and 4.

The linear order produced by a topological sort is not necessarily unique. But you know that already, since each of the three orders for donning goalie equipment on page 72 could be produced by a topological sort.

Another use for topological sorting occurred at a programming job I had a long time ago. We were creating computer-aided design systems, and our systems could maintain a library of parts. Parts could contain other parts, but no circular dependencies were allowed: a part could not eventually contain itself. We needed to write out the part designs to tape (I *said* that the job was a long time ago) so that each part preceded any other parts that contained it. If each part is a vertex and an edge (u, v) indicates that part v contains part u, then we needed to write the parts according to a topologically sorted linear order.

What vertex would be a good candidate to be the first one in the linear order? Any vertex with no entering edges would do. The number of edges entering a vertex is the vertex's *in-degree*, and so we could start with any vertex whose in-degree is 0. Fortunately, every dag must have at least one vertex with in-degree 0 and at least one vertex with *out-degree* 0 (no edges leaving the vertex), for otherwise there would be a cycle.

So suppose we choose any vertex with in-degree 0—let's call it vertex u—and put it at the beginning of the linear order. Because we have taken care of vertex u first, all other vertices will be placed after u in the linear order. In particular, any vertex v that is adjacent to u must appear somewhere after u in the linear order. Therefore, we can safely remove u and all edges leaving u from the dag, knowing that we've taken care of the dependencies that these edges define. When we remove a vertex and the edges that leave it from a dag, what are we left with? Another dag! After all, we cannot create a cycle by removing a vertex and edges. And so we can repeat the process with the dag that remains, finding some vertex with in-degree 0, placing it after vertex u in the linear order, removing edges, and so on.

The procedure on the next page for topological sorting uses this idea, but instead of actually removing vertices and edges from the dag, it just keeps track of the in-degree of each vertex, decrementing the in-degree for each entering edge that we conceptually remove. Since array indices are integers, let's assume that we identify each vertex by a unique integer in the range 1 to n. Because the procedure needs to quickly identify some vertex with in-degree 0, it maintains the in-degree of each vertex in an array *in-degree* indexed by the vertices, and it maintains a list *next* of all the vertices with in-degree 0. Steps 1–3 initialize the *in-degree* array, step 4 initializes *next*, and step 5 updates *in-degree* and *next* as vertices and edges are conceptually removed. The procedure can choose any vertex in *next* as the next one to put into the linear order.

Let's see how the first few iterations of step 5 work on the dag for putting on goalie equipment. In order to run the TOPOLOGICAL-SORT procedure on this dag, we need to number the vertices, as shown on page 78. Only vertices $1, 2$, and 9 have in-degree 0, and so as we enter the loop of step 5, the list *next* contains only these three vertices. To get order #1 on page 72, the order of the vertices in *next* would be 1, 2, 9. Then, in the first iteration of step 5's loop, we choose vertex 1 (undershorts) as vertex u, delete it from *next*, add this vertex to the

Procedure TOPOLOGICAL-SORT(G)

Input: G: a directed acyclic graph with vertices numbered 1 to n.

Output: A linear order of the vertices such that u appears before v in the linear order if (u, v) is an edge in the graph.

1. Let *in-degree*$[1 .. n]$ be a new array, and create an empty linear order of vertices.
2. Set all values in *in-degree* to 0.
3. For each vertex u:
   A. For each vertex v adjacent to u:
      i. Increment *in-degree*$[v]$.
4. Make a list *next* consisting of all vertices u such that *in-degree*$[u] = 0$.
5. While *next* is not empty, do the following:
   A. Delete a vertex from *next*, and call it vertex u.
   B. Add u to the end of the linear order.
   C. For each vertex v adjacent to u:
      i. Decrement *in-degree*$[v]$.
      ii. If *in-degree*$[v] = 0$, then insert v into the *next* list.
6. Return the linear order.

end of the initially empty linear order, and then decrement *in-degree*$[3]$ (compression shorts). Because that operation takes *in-degree*$[3]$ down to 0, we insert vertex 3 into *next*. Let's assume that when we insert a vertex into *next*, we insert it as the first vertex on the list. Such a list, where we always insert and delete at the same end, is known as a **stack**, because it's like a stack of plates, where you always take a plate from the top and place a new plate at the top. (We call this order **last in, first out**, or **LIFO**.) Under this assumption, *next* becomes 3, 2, 9 and in the next loop iteration, we choose vertex 3 as vertex u. We delete it from *next*, add it to the end of the linear order, so that the linear order now reads "undershorts, compression shorts," and we decrement *in-degree*$[4]$ (from 2 down to 1) and *in-degree*$[5]$ (from 1 down to 0). We insert vertex 5 (cup) into *next*, resulting in *next* becoming 5, 2, 9. In the next iteration, we choose vertex 5 as vertex u, delete it from *next*, add it to the end of the linear order (now "undershorts, compression

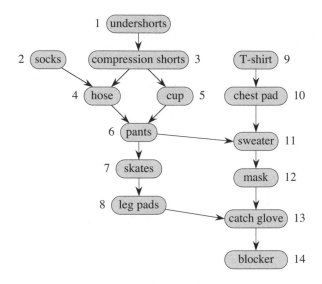

shorts, cup"), and decrement *in-degree*[6], taking it down from 2 to 1. No vertices are added to *next* this time, and so in the next iteration, we choose vertex 2 as vertex u, and so on.

In order to analyze the TOPOLOGICAL-SORT procedure, we first have to understand how to represent a directed graph and a list such as *next*. When representing a graph, we won't require it to be acyclic, because the absence or presence of cycles has no effect on how we represent a graph.

How to represent a directed graph

In a computer, we can represent a directed graph in a few ways. Our convention will be that a graph has n vertices and m edges. We continue to assume that each vertex has its own number from 1 to n, so that we can use a vertex as an index into an array, or even as the row or column number of a matrix.

For now, we just want to know which vertices and edges are present. (Later on, we'll also associate a numeric value with each edge.) We could use an $n \times n$ *adjacency matrix* in which each row and each column corresponds to one vertex, and the entry in the row for vertex u and the column for vertex v is either 1 if the edge (u, v) is present or 0 if the graph does not contain edge (u, v). Since an adjacency matrix has n^2 entries, it must be true that $m \leq n^2$. Alternatively, we could just keep a list of all m edges in the graph in no particular order. As a hybrid between an adjacency matrix and an unordered list, we have the ***adjacency-list representation***, with an n-element array indexed by the vertices in which the array entry for each vertex u is a list of all the vertices adjacent to u. Altogether, the lists have m vertices, since there's one list item for each of the m edges. Here are the adjacency-matrix and adjacency-list representations for the directed graph on page 78:

	1	2	3	4	5	6	7	8	9	10	11	12	13	14
1	0	0	1	0	0	0	0	0	0	0	0	0	0	0
2	0	0	0	1	0	0	0	0	0	0	0	0	0	0
3	0	0	0	1	1	0	0	0	0	0	0	0	0	0
4	0	0	0	0	0	1	0	0	0	0	0	0	0	0
5	0	0	0	0	0	1	0	0	0	0	0	0	0	0
6	0	0	0	0	0	0	1	0	0	0	1	0	0	0
7	0	0	0	0	0	0	0	1	0	0	0	0	0	0
8	0	0	0	0	0	0	0	0	0	0	0	0	1	0
9	0	0	0	0	0	0	0	0	0	1	0	0	0	0
10	0	0	0	0	0	0	0	0	0	0	1	0	0	0
11	0	0	0	0	0	0	0	0	0	0	0	1	0	0
12	0	0	0	0	0	0	0	0	0	0	0	0	1	0
13	0	0	0	0	0	0	0	0	0	0	0	0	0	1
14	0	0	0	0	0	0	0	0	0	0	0	0	0	0

Adjacency matrix (left) — Adjacency lists (right):

1	3
2	4
3	4, 5
4	6
5	6
6	7, 11
7	8
8	13
9	10
10	11
11	12
12	13
13	14
14	(none)

The unordered list of edges and the adjacency-list representation lead to the question of how to represent a list. The best way to represent a list depends on what types of operations we need to perform on the list. For unordered edge lists and adjacency lists, we know in advance how many edges will be in each list, and the contents of the lists won't change, and so we can store each list in an array. We can also use an array to store a list even if the list's contents change over time, as long as we know the maximum number of items that will ever be in the list at any one time. If we don't need to insert an item into the middle of the list or delete an item from the middle of the list, representing a list by an array is as efficient as any other means.

If we do need to insert into the middle of the list, then we can use a ***linked list***, in which each list item includes the location of its successor item in the list, making it simple to splice in a new item after a given item. If we also need to delete from the middle of the list, then each item in the linked list should also include the location of its predecessor item, so that we can quickly splice out an item. From now on, we will assume that we can insert into or delete from a linked list in constant time. A linked list that has only successor links is a *singly linked list*. Adding predecessor links makes a *doubly linked list*.

Running time of topological sorting

If we assume that the dag uses the adjacency-list representation and the *next* list is a linked list, then we can show that the TOPOLOGICAL-SORT procedure takes $\Theta(n+m)$ time. Since *next* is a linked list, we can insert into it or delete from it in constant time. Step 1 takes constant time, and because the *in-degree* array has n elements, step 2 initializes the array to all 0s in $\Theta(n)$ time. Step 3 takes $\Theta(n+m)$ time. The $\Theta(n)$ term in step 3 arises because the outer loop examines each of the n vertices, and the $\Theta(m)$ term is because the inner loop of step 3A visits each of the m edges exactly once over all iterations of the outer loop. Step 4 takes $O(n)$ time, since the *next* list starts with at most n vertices. Most of the work occurs in step 5. Because each vertex is inserted into *next* exactly once, the main loop iterates n times. Steps 5A and 5B take constant time in each iteration. Like step 3A, the loop of step 5C iterates m times altogether, once per edge. Steps 5Ci and 5Cii take constant time per iteration, so that all iterations together of step 5C take $\Theta(m)$ time, and therefore the loop of step 5 takes $\Theta(n+m)$ time. Of course, step 6 takes constant time, and so when we add up the time for all the steps, we get $\Theta(n+m)$.

Critical path in a PERT chart

I like to relax after a day at work by cooking, and I always enjoy cooking and eating kung pao chicken. I have to prepare the chicken, chop vegetables, mix a marinade and cooking sauce, and cook the dish. Just as when I put on goalie equipment, some steps must occur before others, and so I can use a dag to model the procedure for cooking kung pao chicken. The dag appears on the next page.

Next to each vertex in the dag appears a number, indicating how many minutes I need to perform the task corresponding to the vertex. For example, I take four minutes to chop the garlic (because I peel each clove first, and I use a *lot* of garlic). If you add up the times for all the tasks, you can see that if I were to perform them in sequence, it would take me an hour to make kung pao chicken.

If I had help, however, we could perform several of the tasks simultaneously. For example, one person could mix the marinade while some-

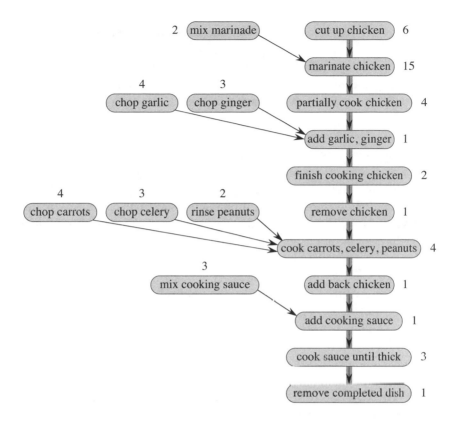

one else cut up the chicken. Given enough people helping, and sufficient space, knives, cutting boards, and bowls, we could perform many of the tasks simultaneously. If you look at any two tasks in the dag and find that there is no way to follow arrows to get from one to the other, then I could assign each of the tasks to a different person and have them done simultaneously.

Given unlimited resources (people, space, cooking equipment) to perform tasks simultaneously, how quickly can we make kung pao chicken? The dag is an example of a ***PERT chart***, an acronym for "program evaluation and review technique." The time to complete the entire job, even with as many tasks performed simultaneously as possible, is given by the "critical path" in the PERT chart. To understand what a critical path is, we first have to understand what a path is, and then we can define a critical path.

A ***path*** in a graph is a sequence of vertices and edges that allow you to get from one vertex to another (or back to itself); we say that the path contains both the vertices on it and the edges traversed. For example, one path in the dag for kung pao chicken has, in order, the vertices labeled "chop garlic," "add garlic, ginger," "finish cooking chicken," and "remove chicken," along with the edges connecting these vertices. A path from a vertex back to itself is a *cycle*, but of course dags do not have cycles.

A *critical path* in a PERT chart is a path for which the sum of the task times is maximum over all paths. The sum of the task times along a critical path gives the minimum possible time for the entire job, no matter how many tasks are performed simultaneously. I shaded the critical path in the PERT chart for cooking kung pao chicken. If you add up the task times along the critical path, you'll see that no matter how much help I have, it takes me at least 39 minutes to make kung pao chicken.[1]

Assuming that all task times are positive, a critical path in a PERT chart must start at some vertex with in-degree 0 and end at some vertex with out-degree 0. Rather than checking paths between all pairs of vertices in which one has in-degree 0 and one has out-degree 0, we can just add two "dummy" vertices, "start" and "finish," as in the figure on the next page. Because these are dummy vertices, we give them task times of 0. We add an edge from start to each vertex with in-degree 0 in the PERT chart, and we add an edge from each vertex with out-degree 0 to finish. Now the only vertex with in-degree 0 is start, and the only vertex with out-degree 0 is finish. A path from start to finish with the maximum sum of task times on its vertices (shaded) gives a critical path in the PERT chart—minus the dummy vertices start and finish, of course.

Once we have added the dummy vertices, we find a critical path by finding a shortest path from start to finish, based on the task times. At this point, you might think I made an error in the previous sentence, because a critical path should correspond to a longest path, not a shortest path. Indeed, it does, but because a PERT chart has no cycles, we can alter the task times so that a shortest path gives us a critical path. In particular, we negate each task time and find a path from start to finish with the *minimum* sum of task times.

Why negate task times and find a path with the minimum sum of task times? Because solving this problem is a special case of finding short-

---

[1] If you're wondering why Chinese restaurants can turn out an order of kung pao chicken in much less time, it's because they prepare many of the ingredients in advance, and their commercial stoves can cook faster than my residential-grade stove.

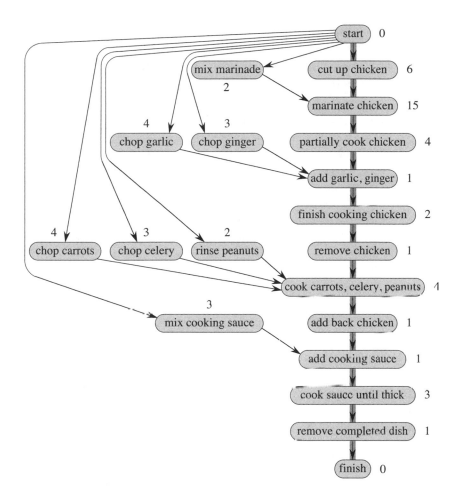

est paths, and we have plenty of algorithms for finding shortest paths. When we talk about shortest paths, however, the values that determine path lengths are associated with edges, not with vertices. We call the value that we associate with each edge its ***weight***. A directed graph with edge weights is a ***weighted directed graph***. "Weight" is a generic term for values associated with edges. If a weighted directed graph represents a road network, each edge represents one direction of a road between two intersections, and the weight of an edge could represent the road's length, the time required to travel the road, or the toll a vehicle pays to use the road. The ***weight of a path*** is the sum of the weights of the edges on the path, so that if edge weights represent road distances, the weight of a path might indicate the total distance traveled along the roads on the path. A ***shortest path*** from vertex u to vertex v is a path whose sum of edge weights is minimum over all paths from u to v. Shortest paths are not necessarily unique, as a directed graph from u to v could contain multiple paths whose weights achieve the minimum.

To convert a PERT chart with negated task times into a weighted directed graph, we push the negated task time for each vertex onto each of its entering edges. That is, if vertex v has a (non-negated) task time of t, we set the weight of each edge (u, v) entering v to be $-t$. Here's the dag we get, with edge weights appearing next to their edges:

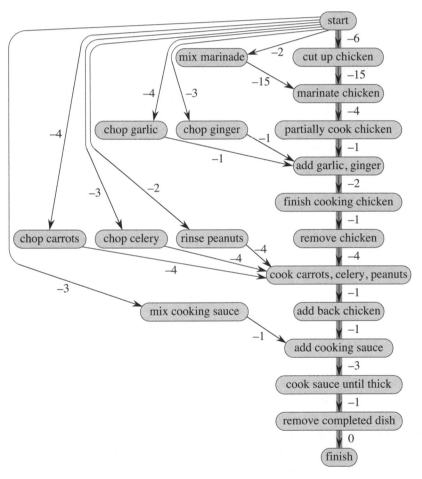

Now we just have to find a shortest path (shaded) from start to finish in this dag, based on these edge weights. A critical path in the original

PERT chart will correspond to the vertices on the shortest path we find, minus start and finish. So let's see how to find a shortest path in a dag.

Shortest path in a directed acyclic graph

There is another advantage to learning how to find a shortest path in a dag: we'll lay the foundations for finding shortest paths in arbitrary directed graphs that may have cycles. We'll examine this more general problem in Chapter 6. As we did for topologically sorting a dag, we'll assume that the dag is stored with the adjacency-list representation, and that with each edge (u, v) we have also stored its weight as $weight(u, v)$.

In a dag that we derive from a PERT chart, we want a shortest path from the **source vertex**, which we call "start," to a specific **target vertex**, "finish." Here, we'll solve the more general problem of finding **single-source shortest paths**, where we find shortest paths from a source vertex to *all* other vertices. By convention, we will name the source vertex s, and we want to compute two things for each vertex v. First, the weight of a shortest path from s to v, which we denote by $sp(s, v)$. Second, the **predecessor** of v on a shortest path from s to v: a vertex u such that a shortest path from s to v is a path from s to u and then a single edge (u, v). We will number the n vertices from 1 to n, so that our algorithms for shortest paths here and in Chapter 6 can store these results in arrays $shortest[1 .. n]$ and $pred[1 .. n]$, respectively. As the algorithms unfold, the values in $shortest[v]$ and $pred[v]$ might not be their correct final values, but when the algorithms are done, they will be.

We need to handle a couple of cases that can arise. First, what if there is no path at all from s to v? Then we define $sp(s, v) = \infty$, so that $shortest[v]$ should come out to ∞. Since v would have no predecessor on a shortest path from s, we also say that $pred[v]$ should be the special value NULL. Moreover, all shortest paths from s start with s, and so s has no predecessor, either; thus we say that $pred[s]$ should also be NULL. The other case arises only in graphs that have both cycles and negative edge weights: what if the weight of a cycle is negative? Then we could go around the cycle forever, decreasing the path weight each time around. If we can get from s to a negative-weight cycle and then to v, then $sp(s, v)$ is undefined. For now, however, we're concerned only with acyclic graphs, and so there are no cycles, much less negative-weight cycles, to worry about.

To compute shortest paths from a source vertex s, we start off with $shortest[s] = 0$ (since we don't have to go anywhere to get from a vertex to itself), *shortest*[v] $= \infty$ for all other vertices v (since we don't know in advance which vertices can be reached from s), and *pred*[v] = NULL for all vertices v. Then we apply a series of ***relaxation steps*** to the edges of the graph:

Procedure RELAX(u, v)

Inputs: u, v: vertices such that there is an edge (u, v).

Result: The value of *shortest*[v] might decrease, and if it does, then *pred*[v] becomes u.

1. If *shortest*[u] $+ weight(u, v) <$ *shortest*[v], then set *shortest*[v] to *shortest*[u] $+ weight(u, v)$ and set *pred*[v] to u.

When we call RELAX(u, v), we are determining whether we can improve upon the current shortest path from s to v by taking (u, v) as the last edge. We compare the weight of the current shortest path to u plus the weight of edge (u, v) with the weight of the current shortest path to v. If it's better to take edge (u, v), then we update *shortest*[v] to this new weight and we set v's predecessor on a shortest path to be u.

If we relax edges along a shortest path, in order, we get the right results. You might wonder how we can be assured of relaxing the edges in order along a shortest path when we don't even know what the path is—after all, that's what we're trying to find out—but it will turn out to be easy for a dag. We're going to relax all the edges in the dag, and the edges of each shortest path will be interspersed, in order, as we go through all the edges and relax each one.

Here's a more precise statement of how relaxing edges along a shortest path works, and it applies to any directed graph, with or without cycles:

Start with *shortest*[u] $= \infty$ and *pred*[u] = NULL for all vertices, except that *shortest*[s] $= 0$ for the source vertex s.

Then relax the edges along a shortest path from s to any vertex v, *in order, starting from the edge leaving s and ending with the edge entering v*. Relaxations of other edges may be interspersed freely with the relaxations along this shortest path, but only relaxations may change any *shortest* or *pred* values.

After the edges have been relaxed, v's *shortest* and *pred* values are correct: *shortest*[v] $= sp(s, v)$ and *pred*[v] is the vertex preceding v on some shortest path from s.

It's pretty easy to see why relaxing the edges along a shortest path, in order, works. Suppose that a shortest path from s to v visits the vertices $s, v_1, v_2, v_3, \ldots, v_k, v$, in that order. After edge (s, v_1) has been relaxed, *shortest*$[v_1]$ must have the correct shortest-path weight for v_1, and *pred*$[v_1]$ must be s. After (v_1, v_2) has been relaxed, *shortest*$[v_2]$ and *pred*$[v_2]$ must be correct. And so on, up through relaxing (v_k, v), after which *shortest*$[v]$ and *pred*$[v]$ have their correct values.

This is great news. In a dag, it's really easy to relax each edge exactly once yet relax the edges along *every* shortest path, in order. How? First, topologically sort the dag. Then consider each vertex, taken in the topologically sorted linear order, and relax all the edges leaving the vertex. Since every edge must leave a vertex earlier in the linear order and enter a vertex later in the order, every path in the dag must visit vertices in an order consistent with the linear order.

Procedure DAG-SHORTEST-PATHS (G, s)

Inputs:
- G: a weighted directed acyclic graph containing a set V of n vertices and a set E of m directed edges.
- s: a source vertex in V.

Result: For each non-source vertex v in V, *shortest*$[v]$ is the weight $sp(s, v)$ of a shortest path from s to v and *pred*$[v]$ is the vertex preceding v on some shortest path. For the source vertex s, *shortest*$[s] = 0$ and *pred*$[s] =$ NULL. If there is no path from s to v, then *shortest*$[v] = \infty$ and *pred*$[v] =$ NULL.

1. Call TOPOLOGICAL-SORT(G) and set l to be the linear order of vertices returned by the call.
2. Set *shortest*$[v]$ to ∞ for each vertex v except s, set *shortest*$[s]$ to 0, and set *pred*$[v]$ to NULL for each vertex v.
3. For each vertex u, taken in the order given by l:
   A. For each vertex v adjacent to u:
      i. Call RELAX(u, v).

The next page shows a dag with weights appearing next to the edges. The *shortest* values from running DAG-SHORTEST-PATHS from source vertex s appear inside the vertices, and shaded edges indicate the *pred* values. The vertices are laid out left to right in the linear order returned by the topological sort, so that all edges go from left to right. If an

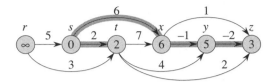

edge (u, v) is shaded, then $pred[v]$ is u and $shortest[v] = shortest[u] + weight(u, v)$; for example, since (x, y) is shaded, $pred[y] = x$ and $shortest[y]$ (which is 5) equals $shortest[x]$ (which is 6) + $weight(x, y)$ (which is -1). There is no path from s to r, and so $shortest[r] = \infty$ and $pred[r] = $ NULL (no shaded edges enter r).

The first iteration of the loop of step 3 relaxes edges (r, s) and (r, t) leaving r, but because $shortest[r] = \infty$, these relaxations do not change anything. The next iteration of the loop relaxes edges (s, t) and (s, x) leaving s, causing $shortest[t]$ to be set to 2, $shortest[x]$ to be set to 6, and both $pred[t]$ and $pred[x]$ to be set to s. The following iteration relaxes edges (t, x), (t, y), and (t, z) leaving t. The value of $shortest[x]$ does not change, since $shortest[t] + weight(t, x)$, which is $2 + 7 = 9$, is greater than $shortest[x]$, which is 6; but $shortest[y]$ becomes 6, $shortest[z]$ becomes 4, and both $pred[y]$ and $pred[z]$ are set to t. The next iteration relaxes edges (x, y) and (x, z) leaving x, causing $shortest[y]$ to become 5 and $pred[y]$ to be set to x; $shortest[z]$ and $pred[z]$ remain unchanged. The final iteration relaxes edge (y, z) leaving y, causing $shortest[z]$ to become 3 and $pred[z]$ to be set to y.

You can easily see how DAG-SHORTEST-PATHS runs in $\Theta(n + m)$ time. As we saw, step 1 takes $\Theta(n + m)$ time, and of course step 2 initializes two values for each vertex and therefore takes $\Theta(n)$ time. As we've seen before, the outer loop of step 3 examines each vertex exactly once, and the inner loop of step 3A examines each edge exactly once over all iterations. Because each call of RELAX in step 3Ai takes constant time, step 3 takes $\Theta(n + m)$ time. Adding up the running times for the steps gives us the $\Theta(n + m)$ for the procedure.

Going back to PERT charts, it's now easy to see that finding a critical path takes $\Theta(n + m)$ time, where the PERT chart has n vertices and m edges. We add the two vertices, start and finish, and we add at most m edges leaving start and at most m edges entering finish, for a total of at most $3m$ edges in the dag. Negating the weights and pushing them from the vertices to the edges takes $\Theta(m)$ time, and then finding a shortest path through the resulting dag takes $\Theta(n + m)$ time.

Further reading

Chapter 22 of CLRS [CLRS09] presents a different algorithm for topologically sorting a dag from the one in this chapter, which appears in
Volume 1 of Knuth's *The Art of Computer Programming* [Knu97]. The
method in CLRS is a bit simpler on the surface, but it's less intuitive
than the approach in this chapter, and it relies on a technique of visit-
ing vertices in a graph known as "depth-first search." The algorithm for
finding single-source shortest paths in a dag appears in Chapter 24 of
CLRS.

You can read more about PERT charts, which have been in use since
the 1950s, in any one of a number of books about project management.

6 Shortest Paths

In Chapter 5, we saw how to find single-source shortest paths in a directed acyclic graph. The algorithm to do so relied on the graph being acyclic—no cycles—so that we could first topologically sort the graph's vertices.

Most graphs that model real-life situations have cycles, however. For example, in a graph that models a road network, each vertex represents an intersection and each directed edge represents a road that you can travel in one direction between intersections. (Two-way roads would be represented by two distinct edges, going in opposite directions.) Such graphs must have cycles, for otherwise once you left an intersection, you would have no way to return to it. Therefore, when your GPS is calculating the shortest or fastest route to a destination, the graph it works with has cycles, and plenty of them.

When your GPS finds the fastest route from your current location to a specific destination, it is solving the ***single-pair shortest path*** problem. To do so, it probably uses an algorithm that finds all shortest paths from a single source, but the GPS pays attention only to the shortest path that it finds to the specific destination.

Your GPS works with a weighted directed graph, where the edge weights represent either distance or travel time. Because you can't drive a negative distance or arrive before you've departed, all edge weights in your GPS's graph are positive. I suppose that some of them could be 0 for some weird reason, so let's say that the edge weights are nonnegative. When all edge weights are nonnegative, we don't have to worry about negative-weight cycles, and all shortest paths are well defined.

For another example of single-source shortest paths, consider the "six degrees of Kevin Bacon" game, in which players try to connect movie actors to Kevin Bacon. In a graph, each vertex represents an actor, and the graph contains edges (u, v) and (v, u) if the actors represented by vertices u and v have ever appeared in the same film. Given some actor, a player tries to find the shortest path from the vertex for that actor to the vertex for Kevin Bacon. The number of edges in the shortest path (in other words, the shortest-path weight when each edge weight is 1) is the actor's "Kevin Bacon number." As an example, Renée Adorée was in a film with Bessie Love, who was in a movie with Eli Wallach, who made a film with Kevin Bacon, and so Renée Adorée's Kevin Bacon number is 3. Mathematicians have a similar concept in the Erdős number, which gives the shortest path from the great Paul Erdős to any other mathematician by a chain of coauthor relationships.[1]

What about graphs with negative-weight edges? How do they relate to the real world? We'll see that we can couch the problem of determining whether an arbitrage opportunity exists in currency trading as determining whether a graph that may have negative-weight edges has a negative-weight cycle.

In terms of algorithms, first we'll explore Dijkstra's algorithm for finding shortest paths from a single source vertex to all other vertices. Dijkstra's algorithm works on graphs that have two important differences from the graphs we saw in Chapter 5: all edge weights must be nonnegative, and the graph may contain cycles. It is at the core of how your GPS finds routes. We'll also examine some choices that we can make when implementing Dijkstra's algorithm. Then, we'll see the Bellman-Ford algorithm, a remarkably simple method for finding single-source shortest paths even when negative-weight edges are present. We can use the result of the Bellman-Ford algorithm to determine whether the graph contains a negative-weight cycle and, if it does, to identify the vertices and edges on the cycle. Both Dijkstra's algorithm and the Bellman-Ford algorithm date back to the late 1950s, so they've stood the test of time. We'll wrap up with the Floyd-Warshall algorithm for the all-pairs problem, where we want to find a shortest path between every pair of vertices.

Just as we did in Chapter 5 for finding shortest paths in a dag, we'll assume that we are given a source vertex s and the weight $weight(u, v)$ of each edge (u, v), and that we want to calculate, for each vertex v, the shortest-path weight $sp(s, v)$ from s to v and the vertex preceding v on some shortest path from s. We'll store the results in $shortest[v]$ and $pred[v]$, respectively.

---

[1]Believe it or not, there's even such a thing as an Erdős-Bacon number, which is the sum of the Erdős and Bacon numbers, and a handful of people have finite Erdős-Bacon numbers, including Paul Erdős himself!

Dijkstra's algorithm

I like to think of Dijkstra's algorithm[2] as a simulation of sending out runners over the graph.

Ideally, the simulation works as follows, though we'll see that Dijkstra's algorithm works slightly differently. It starts by sending out runners from the source vertex to all adjacent vertices. The first time a runner arrives at any vertex, runners immediately leave that vertex, headed to all of its adjacent vertices. Look at part (a) of this figure:

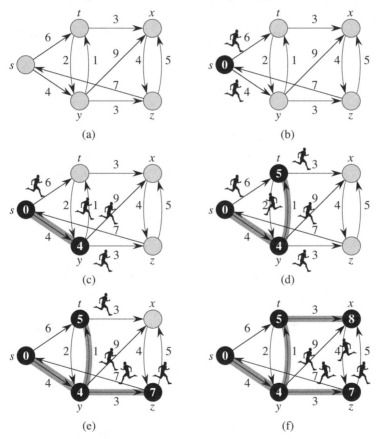

It shows a directed graph with source vertex *s* and weights next to the edges. Think of the weight of an edge as the number of minutes it would take a runner to traverse the edge.

---

[2]Named after Edsger Dijkstra, who proposed the algorithm in 1959.

Part (b) illustrates the start of the simulation, at time 0. At that time, shown inside vertex s, runners leave s and head toward its two adjacent vertices, t and y. The blackened vertex s indicates that we know that $shortest[s] = 0$.

Four minutes later, at time 4, the runner to vertex y arrives, shown in part (c). Because this runner is the first to arrive at y, we know that $shortest[y] = 4$, and so y is blackened in the figure. The shaded edge (s, y) indicates that the first runner to arrive at vertex y came from vertex s, so that $pred[y] = s$. At time 4, the runner from vertex s to vertex t is still in transit, and runners leave vertex y at time 4, headed toward vertices t, x, and z.

The next event, displayed in part (d), occurs one minute later, at time 5, when the runner from vertex y arrives at vertex t. The runner from s to t has yet to arrive. Because the first runner to arrive at vertex t arrived from vertex y at time 5, we set $shortest[t]$ to 5 and $pred[t]$ to y (indicated by the shaded edge (y, t)). Runners leave vertex t, headed toward vertices x and y at this time.

The runner from vertex s finally arrives at vertex t at time 6, but the runner from vertex y had already arrived there a minute earlier, and so the effort of the runner from s to t went for naught.

At time 7, depicted in part (e), two runners arrive at their destinations. The runner from vertex t to vertex y arrives, but the runner from s to y had already arrived at time 4, and so the simulation forgets about the runner from t to y. At the same time, the runner from y arrives at vertex z. We set $shortest[z]$ to 7 and $pred[z]$ to y, and runners leave vertex z, headed toward vertices s and x.

The next event occurs at time 8, as shown in part (f), when the runner from vertex t arrives at vertex x. We set $shortest[x]$ to 8 and $pred[x]$ to t, and a runner leaves vertex x, heading to vertex z.

At this point, every vertex has had a runner arrive, and the simulation can stop. All runners still in transit will arrive at their destination vertices after some other runner had already arrived. Once every vertex has had a runner arrive, the *shortest* value for each vertex equals the weight of the shortest path from vertex s and the *pred* value for each vertex is the predecessor on a shortest path from s.

That was how the simulation proceeds ideally. It relied on the time for a runner to traverse an edge equaling the weight of the edge. Dijkstra's algorithm works slightly differently. It treats all edges the same, so that when it considers the edges leaving a vertex, it processes the adjacent vertices together, and in no particular order. For example, when Dijkstra's algorithm processes the edges leaving vertex s in the figure on page 92, it declares that $shortest[y] = 4$, $shortest[t] = 6$, and $pred[y]$ and $pred[t]$ are both s—*so far*. When Dijkstra's algorithm later considers the edge (y, t), it decreases the weight of the shortest path to vertex t that it has found so far, so that $shortest[t]$ goes from 6 to 5 and $pred[t]$ switches from s to y.

Dijkstra's algorithm works by calling the RELAX procedure from page 86 once per edge. Relaxing an edge (u, v) corresponds to a runner from vertex u arriving at vertex v. The algorithm maintains a set Q of vertices for which the final *shortest* and *pred* values are not yet known; all vertices *not* in Q have their final *shortest* and *pred* values. After initializing *shortest*$[s]$ to 0 for the source vertex s, *shortest*$[v]$ to ∞ for all other vertices, and *pred*$[v]$ to NULL for all vertices, it repeatedly finds the vertex u in set Q with the lowest *shortest* value, removes that vertex from Q, and relaxes all the edges leaving u. Here is the procedure:

Procedure DIJKSTRA(G, s)

Inputs:

- G: a directed graph containing a set V of n vertices and a set E of m directed edges with nonnegative weights.
- s: a source vertex in V.

Result: For each non-source vertex v in V, *shortest*$[v]$ is the weight $sp(s, v)$ of a shortest path from s to v and *pred*$[v]$ is the vertex preceding v on some shortest path. For the source vertex s, *shortest*$[s] = 0$ and *pred*$[s] = $ NULL. If there is no path from s to v, then *shortest*$[v] = \infty$ and *pred*$[v] = $ NULL. (Same as DAG-SHORTEST-PATHS on page 87.)

1. Set *shortest*$[v]$ to ∞ for each vertex v except s, set *shortest*$[s]$ to 0, and set *pred*$[v]$ to NULL for each vertex v.
2. Set Q to contain all vertices.
3. While Q is not empty, do the following:
    A. Find the vertex u in set Q with the lowest *shortest* value and remove it from Q.
    B. For each vertex v adjacent to u:
        i. Call RELAX(u, v).

In the following figure, each part shows the *shortest* value (appearing within each vertex), the *pred* value (indicated by shaded edges), and the set Q (the vertices that are shaded, not blackened) just before each iteration of the loop in step 3.

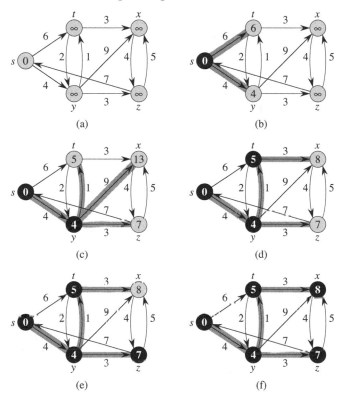

The vertex that is newly blackened in each part of the figure is the vertex chosen as vertex u in step 3A. In the simulation with runners, once a vertex receives *shortest* and *pred* values, they cannot change, but here a vertex could receive *shortest* and *pred* values from relaxing one edge, and a later relaxation of some other edge could change these values. For example, after edge (y, x) is relaxed in part (c) of the figure, the value of *shortest*[x] decreases from ∞ to 13, and *pred*[x] becomes y. The next iteration of the loop in step 3 (part (d)) relaxes edge (t, x), and *shortest*[x] decreases further, to 8, and *pred*[x] becomes t. In the next iteration (part (e)), edge (z, x) is relaxed, but this time *shortest*[x] does not change, because its value, 8, is less than *shortest*[z] + *weight*(z, x), which equals 12.

Dijkstra's algorithm maintains the following loop invariant:

At the start of each iteration of the loop in step 3, *shortest*[*v*] = *sp*(*s*, *v*) for each vertex *v* not in the set *Q*. That is, for each vertex *v* not in *Q*, the value of *shortest*[*v*] is the weight of a shortest path from *s* to *v*.

Here's a simplified version of the reasoning behind this loop invariant. (A formal proof is a bit more involved.) Initially, all vertices are in set *Q*, and so the loop invariant applies to no vertices upon entering the first iteration of the loop in step 3. Assume that as we enter an iteration of this loop, all vertices not in the set *Q* have their correct shortest-path weights in their *shortest* values. Then every edge leaving these vertices has been relaxed in some execution of step 3Bi. Consider the vertex *u* in *Q* with the lowest *shortest* value. Its *shortest* value can never again decrease. Why not? Because the only edges remaining to be relaxed are edges leaving vertices in *Q*, and every vertex in *Q* has a *shortest* value at least as large as *shortest*[*u*]. Since all edge weights are nonnegative, we must have *shortest*[*u*] ≤ *shortest*[*v*] + *weight*(*v*, *u*) for every vertex *v* in *Q*, and so no future relaxation step will decrease *shortest*[*u*]. Therefore, *shortest*[*u*] is as low as it can go, and we can remove vertex *u* from set *Q* and relax all edges leaving *u*. When the loop of step 3 terminates, the set *Q* is empty, and so all vertices have their correct shortest-path weights in their *shortest* values.

We can begin to analyze the running time of the DIJKSTRA procedure, but to analyze it in full, we are going to have to first decide upon some implementation details. Recall from Chapter 5 that we denote the number of vertices by *n* and the number of edges by *m*, and *m* ≤ *n*². We know that step 1 takes $\Theta(n)$ time. We also know that the loop of step 3 iterates exactly *n* times, because the set *Q* initially contains all *n* vertices, each iteration of the loop removes one vertex from *Q*, and vertices are never added back into *Q*. The loop of step 3A processes each vertex and each edge exactly once over the course of the algorithm (we saw the same idea in the TOPOLOGICAL-SORT and DAG-SHORTEST-PATHS procedures in Chapter 5).

What's left to analyze? We need to understand how long it takes to put all *n* vertices into the set *Q* (step 2), how long it takes to determine which vertex in *Q* has the lowest *shortest* value and remove this vertex from *Q* (step 3A), and what bookkeeping adjustments we need to make, if any, when a vertex's *shortest* and *pred* values change due to calling RELAX. Let's name these operations:

- INSERT(Q, v) inserts vertex v into set Q. (Dijkstra's algorithm calls INSERT n times.)

- EXTRACT-MIN(Q) removes the vertex in Q with the minimum *shortest* value and returns this vertex to its caller. (Dijkstra's algorithm calls EXTRACT-MIN n times.)

- DECREASE-KEY(Q, v) performs whatever bookkeeping is necessary in Q to record that *shortest*[v] was decreased by a call of RELAX. (Dijkstra's algorithm calls DECREASE-KEY up to m times.)

These three operations, taken together, define a ***priority queue***.

The descriptions of the priority queue operations say just *what* the operations do, and not *how* they do it. In software design, separating *what* operations do from *how* they do it is known as ***abstraction***. We call the set of operations, specified by *what* they do but not *how* they do it, an ***abstract data type***, or ***ADT***, so that a priority queue is an ADT.

We can implement the priority queue operations—the *how*—by any one of several data structures. A ***data structure*** is a specific way to store and access data in a computer—for example, an array. In the case of priority queues, we'll see three different data structures that can implement the operations. Software designers should be able to plug in any data structure that implements the operations of an ADT. But it's not quite so simple when we think about algorithms. That's because for different data structures, the way they implement operations may take differing amounts of time. Indeed, the three different data structures we'll see for implementing the priority queue ADT yield different running times for Dijkstra's algorithm.

A rewritten version of the DIJKSTRA procedure, explicitly calling the priority queue operations, appears on the following page. Let's examine the three data structures to implement the priority queue operations and see how they affect the running time of Dijkstra's algorithm.

Simple array implementation

The simplest way to implement the priority queue operations is to store the vertices in an array with n positions. If the priority queue currently contains k vertices, then they are in the first k positions of the array, in no particular order. Along with the array, we need to maintain a count of how many vertices it currently contains. The INSERT operation is easy: just add the vertex to the next unused position in the array and increment the count. DECREASE-KEY is even easier: do nothing! Both of these operations take constant time. The EXTRACT-MIN operation

Procedure DIJKSTRA(G, s)

Inputs and Result: Same as before.

1. Set *shortest*$[v]$ to ∞ for each vertex v except s, set *shortest*$[s]$ to 0, and set *pred*$[v]$ to NULL for each vertex v.
2. Make Q an empty priority-queue.
3. For each vertex v:
   A. Call INSERT(Q, v).
4. While Q is not empty, do the following:
   A. Call EXTRACT-MIN(Q) and set u to hold the returned vertex.
   B. For each vertex v adjacent to u:
      i. Call RELAX(u, v).
      ii. If the call to RELAX(u, v) decreased the value of *shortest*$[v]$, then call DECREASE-KEY(Q, v).

takes $O(n)$ time, however, since we have to look at all the vertices currently in the array to find the one with the lowest *shortest* value. Once we identify this vertex, deleting it is easy: just move the vertex in the last position into the position of the deleted vertex and then decrement the count. The n EXTRACT-MIN calls take $O(n^2)$ time. Although the calls to RELAX take $O(m)$ time, recall that $m \leq n^2$. With this implementation of the priority queue therefore, Dijkstra's algorithm takes $O(n^2)$ time, with the time dominated by the time spent in EXTRACT-MIN.

Binary heap implementation

A binary heap organizes data as a binary tree stored in an array. A *binary tree* is a type of graph, but we refer to its vertices as *nodes*, the edges are undirected, and each node has 0, 1, or 2 nodes below it, which are its *children*. On the left side of the figure on the next page is an example of a binary tree, with the nodes numbered. Nodes with no children, such as nodes 6 through 10, are *leaves*.[3]

---

[3]Computer scientists find it easier to draw trees with the root at the top and branches heading downward than to draw them like real trees, with the root at the bottom and branches heading upward.

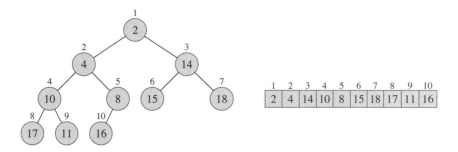

A ***binary heap*** is a binary tree with three additional properties. First, the tree is completely filled on all levels, except possibly the lowest, which is filled from the left up to a point. Second, each node contains a key, shown inside each node in the figure. Third, the keys obey the ***heap property***: the key of each node is less than or equal to the keys of its children. The binary tree in the figure is also a binary heap.

We can store a binary heap in an array, as shown on the right in the figure. Because of the heap property, the node with the minimum key must always be at position 1. The children of the node at position i are at positions $2i$ and $2i + 1$, and the node above the node at position i — its ***parent*** — is at position $\lfloor i/2 \rfloor$. It is easy to navigate up and down within a binary heap when we store it in an array.

A binary heap has one other important characteristic: if it consists of n nodes, then its ***height*** — the number of edges from the root down to the farthest leaf — is only $\lfloor \lg n \rfloor$. Therefore, we can traverse a path from the root down to a leaf, or from a leaf up to the root, in only $O(\lg n)$ time.

Because binary heaps have height $\lfloor \lg n \rfloor$, we can perform the three priority queue operations in $O(\lg n)$ time each. For INSERT, add a new leaf at the first available position. Then, as long as the key in the node is less than the key in its parent, exchange the contents[4] of the node with the contents of its parent, and move up one level toward the root. In other words, "bubble up" the contents toward the root until the heap property holds. Since the path to the root has at most $\lfloor \lg n \rfloor$ edges, at most $\lfloor \lg n \rfloor - 1$ exchanges occur, and so INSERT takes $O(\lg n)$ time. To perform DECREASE-KEY, use the same idea: decrease the key and then

---

[4]The contents of a node includes the key and any other information associated with the key, such as which vertex is associated with this node.

bubble up the contents toward the root until the heap property holds, again taking $O(\lg n)$ time. To perform EXTRACT-MIN, save the contents of the root to return to the caller. Next, take the last leaf (the highest-numbered node) and put its contents into the root position. Then "bubble down" the contents of the root, exchanging the contents of the node and the child whose key is smaller, until the heap property holds. Finally, return the saved contents of the root. Again, because the path from the root down to a leaf has at most $\lfloor \lg n \rfloor$ edges, at most $\lfloor \lg n \rfloor - 1$ exchanges occur, and so EXTRACT-MIN takes $O(\lg n)$ time.

When Dijkstra's algorithm uses the binary-heap implementation of a priority queue, it spends $O(n \lg n)$ time inserting vertices, $O(n \lg n)$ time in EXTRACT-MIN operations, and $O(m \lg n)$ time in DECREASE-KEY operations. (Actually, inserting the n vertices takes just $\Theta(n)$ time, since initially just the source vertex s has a *shortest* value of 0 and all other vertices have *shortest* values of ∞.) When the graph is *sparse*—the number m of edges is much less than n^2—implementing the priority queue with a binary heap is more efficient than using a simple array. Graphs that model road networks are sparse, since the average intersection has about four roads leaving it, and so m would be about $4n$. On the other hand, when the graph is *dense*—m is close to n^2, so that the graph contains many edges—the $O(m \lg n)$ time that Dijkstra's algorithm spends in DECREASE-KEY calls can make it slower than using a simple array for the priority queue.

One other thing about binary heaps: we can use them to sort in $O(n \lg n)$ time:

Procedure HEAPSORT(A, n)

Inputs:
- A: an array.
- n: the number of elements in A to sort.

Output: An array B containing the elements of A, sorted.

1. Build a binary heap Q from the elements of A.
2. Let $B[1 .. n]$ be a new array.
3. For $i = 1$ to n:

    A. Call EXTRACT-MIN(Q) and set $B[i]$ to the value returned.
4. Return the B array.

Step 1 converts the input array into a binary heap, which we can do in one of two ways. One way is to start with an empty binary heap and then insert each element of the array, taking $O(n \lg n)$ time. The other way builds the binary heap directly within the array, working from the bottom up, taking only $O(n)$ time. It's also possible to sort using a heap in place, so that we don't need the extra B array.

Fibonacci heap implementation

We can also implement a priority queue by a complicated data structure called a "Fibonacci heap," or "F-heap." With an F-heap, the n INSERT and EXTRACT-MIN calls take a total of $O(n \lg n)$ time, and the m DECREASE-KEY calls take a total of $\Theta(m)$ time, and so Dijkstra's algorithm takes only $O(n \lg n + m)$ time. In practice, people do not often use F-heaps, for a couple of reasons. One is that an individual operation might take much longer than the average, although in total the operations take the times given above. The second reason is that F-heaps are a bit complicated, and so the constant factors hidden in the asymptotic notation are not as good as for binary heaps.

The Bellman-Ford algorithm

If some edge weights are negative, then Dijkstra's algorithm could return incorrect results. The Bellman-Ford algorithm[5] can handle negative edge weights, and we can use its output to detect and help identify a negative-weight cycle.

The Bellman-Ford algorithm is remarkably simple. After initializing the *shortest* and *pred* values, it just relaxes all m edges $n - 1$ times. The procedure appears on the next page, and the figure below it demonstrates how the algorithm operates on a small graph. The source vertex is s, the *shortest* values appear within the vertices, and the shaded edges indicate *pred* values: if edge (u, v) is shaded, then $pred[v] = u$. In this example, we assume that each pass over all the edges relaxes them in the fixed order $(t, x), (t, y), (t, z), (x, t), (y, x), (y, z), (z, x), (z, s),$ $(s, t), (s, y)$. Part (a) shows the situation just before the first pass, and parts (b) through (e) show the situation after each successive pass. The *shortest* and *pred* values in part (e) are the final values.

---

[5] Based on separate algorithms by Richard Bellman from 1958 and Lester Ford from 1962.

Procedure BELLMAN-FORD(G, s)

Inputs:
- G: a directed graph containing a set V of n vertices and a set E of m directed edges with arbitrary weights.
- s: a source vertex in V.

Result: Same as DIJKSTRA (page 94).

1. Set *shortest*[v] to ∞ for each vertex v except s, set *shortest*[s] to 0, and set *pred*[v] to NULL for each vertex v.
2. For $i = 1$ to $n - 1$:
   A. For each edge (u, v) in E:
      i. Call RELAX(u, v).

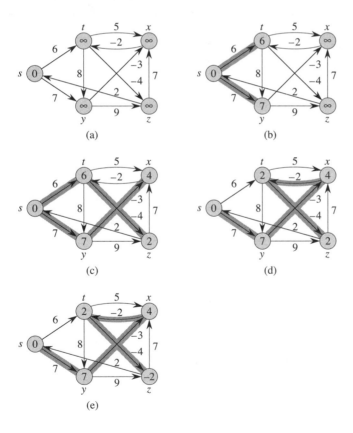

How can an algorithm this simple possibly produce the right answer? Consider a shortest path from the source s to any vertex v. Recall from page 86 that if we relax the edges, in order, along a shortest path from s to v, then *shortest*[v] and *pred*[v] are correct. Now, if negative-weight cycles are disallowed, then there is always a shortest path from s to v that does not contain a cycle. Why? Suppose that a shortest path from s to v contains a cycle. Because the cycle must have nonnegative weight, we could excise the cycle and end up with a path from s to v whose weight is no higher than the path containing the cycle. Every acyclic path must contain at most $n - 1$ edges, for if a path contains n edges then it must visit some vertex twice, which would make a cycle. Thus, if there is a shortest path from s to v, then there is one that contains at most $n - 1$ edges. The first time that step 2A relaxes all edges, it must relax the first edge on this shortest path. The second time that step 2A relaxes all edges, it must relax the second edge on the shortest path, and so on. After the $(n - 1)$st time, all edges on the shortest path have been relaxed, in order, and therefore *shortest*[v] and *pred*[v] are correct. Pretty slick!

Now suppose that the graph contains a negative-weight cycle and we've already run the BELLMAN-FORD procedure on it. You can go around and around a negative-weight cycle, getting a lower-weight path each time around. That means that there is at least one edge (u, v) on the cycle for which *shortest*[v] will decrease if you relax it again—even though this edge has already been relaxed $n - 1$ times.

So here's how to find a negative-weight cycle, if one exists, after running BELLMAN-FORD. Go through the edges once again. If we find an edge (u, v) for which *shortest*[u] + *weight*(u, v) < *shortest*[v], then we know that vertex v is either on a negative-weight cycle or is reachable from one. We can find a vertex on the negative-weight cycle by tracing back the *pred* values from v, keeping track of which vertices we've visited until we reach a vertex x that we've visited before. Then we can trace back *pred* values from x until we get back to x, and all vertices in between, along with x, will constitute a negative-weight cycle. The procedure FIND-NEGATIVE-WEIGHT-CYCLE on the next page shows how to determine whether a graph has a negative-weight cycle, and how to construct one if it does.

It's easy to analyze the running time of the Bellman-Ford algorithm. The loop of step 2 iterates $n - 1$ times, and each time it runs, the loop of step 2A iterates m times, once per edge. The total running time,

Procedure FIND-NEGATIVE-WEIGHT-CYCLE(G)

Input: G: a directed graph containing a set V of n vertices and a set E of m directed edges with arbitrary weights on which the BELLMAN-FORD procedure has already been run.

Output: Either a list of vertices in a negative-weight cycle, in order, or an empty list if the graph has no negative-weight cycles.

1. Go through all edges to find any edge (u, v) such that $shortest[u] + weight(u, v) < shortest[v]$.
2. If no such edge exists, then return an empty list.
3. Otherwise (there is some edge (u, v) for which $shortest[u] + weight(u, v) < shortest[v]$), do the following:
   A. Let *visited* be a new array with one element for each vertex. Set all elements of *visited* to FALSE.
   B. Set x to v.
   C. While *visited*$[x]$ is FALSE, do the following:
      i. Set *visited*$[x]$ to TRUE.
      ii. Set x to *pred*$[x]$
   D. At this point, we know that x is a vertex on a negative-weight cycle. Set v to *pred*$[x]$.
   E. Create a list *cycle* of vertices initially containing just x.
   F. While v is not x, do the following:
      i. Insert vertex v at the beginning of *cycle*.
      ii. Set v to *pred*$[v]$.
   G. Return *cycle*.

therefore, is $\Theta(nm)$. To find whether a negative-weight cycle exists, relax each edge once more until either relaxing changes a *shortest* value or all edges have been relaxed, taking $O(m)$ time. If there is a negative-weight cycle, it can contain at most n edges, and so the time to trace it out is $O(n)$.

At the beginning of this chapter, I promised to show how negative-weight cycles relate to arbitrage opportunities in currency trading. Exchange rates for currencies fluctuate rapidly. Imagine that at some moment in time, the following exchange rates are in effect:

> 1 U.S. dollar buys 0.7292 euros
> 1 euro buys 105.374 Japanese yen
> 1 Japanese yen buys 0.3931 Russian rubles
> 1 Russian ruble buys 0.0341 U.S. dollars

Then you could take 1 U.S. dollar, buy 0.7292 euros with it, take the 0.7292 euros and buy 76.8387 yen (because $0.7292 \cdot 105.374 = 76.8387$, to four decimal places), take the 76.8387 yen and buy 30.2053 rubles (because $76.8387 \cdot 0.3931 = 30.2053$, to four decimal places), and finally take the 30.2053 rubles and buy 1.03 dollars (because $30.2053 \cdot 0.0341 = 1.0300$, to four decimal places). If you could perform all four transactions before the exchange rates change, you could make a 3% return on your 1-dollar investment. Start with one million dollars, and you make a 30-thousand-dollar profit for doing nothing!

Such a scenario is an ***arbitrage opportunity***. Here's how to find an arbitrage opportunity by finding a negative-weight cycle. Suppose that you're looking at n currencies $c_1, c_2, c_3, \ldots, c_n$, and you have all the exchange rates between pairs of currencies. Suppose that with 1 unit of currency c_i you can buy r_{ij} units of currency c_j, so that r_{ij} is the exchange rate between currencies c_i and c_j. Here, both i and j range from 1 to n. (Presumably, $r_{ii} = 1$ for each currency c_i.)

An arbitrage opportunity would correspond to a sequence of k currencies $\langle c_{j_1}, c_{j_2}, c_{j_3}, \ldots, c_{j_k} \rangle$ such that when you multiply out the exchange rates, you get a product strictly greater than 1:

$$r_{j_1, j_2} \cdot r_{j_2, j_3} \cdots r_{j_{k-1}, j_k} \cdot r_{j_k, j_1} > 1 .$$

Now take logarithms of both sides. It doesn't matter what base we use, so let's make like computer scientists and use base 2. Because the logarithm of a product is the sum of the individual logarithms—that is, $\lg(x \cdot y) = \lg x + \lg y$—we're looking for a situation in which

$$\lg r_{j_1, j_2} + \lg r_{j_2, j_3} + \cdots + \lg r_{j_{k-1}, j_k} + \lg r_{j_k, j_1} > 0 .$$

Negating both sides of this inequality gives

$$(-\lg r_{j_1, j_2}) + (-\lg r_{j_2, j_3}) + \cdots + (-\lg r_{j_{k-1}, j_k}) + (-\lg r_{j_k, j_1}) < 0 ,$$

which corresponds to a cycle with edge weights that are the negatives of the logarithms of the exchange rates.

To find an arbitrage opportunity, if one exists, construct a directed graph with one vertex v_i for each currency c_i. For each pair of currencies c_i and c_j, create directed edges (v_i, v_j) and (v_j, v_i) with weights

$-\lg r_{ij}$ and $-\lg r_{ji}$, respectively. Add a new vertex s with a 0-weight edge (s, v_i) to each of the vertices v_1 through v_n. Run the Bellman-Ford algorithm on this graph with s as the source vertex, and use the result to determine whether it contains a negative-weight cycle. If it does, then the vertices on that cycle correspond to the currencies in an arbitrage opportunity. The total number of edges m is $n + n(n-1) = n^2$, and so the Bellman-Ford algorithm takes $O(n^3)$ time, plus another $O(n^2)$ to find whether there is a negative-weight cycle, and another $O(n)$ to trace it out, if one exists. Although $O(n^3)$ time seems slow, in practice it's not so bad because the constant factors in the running times of the loops are low. I coded up the arbitrage program on my 2.4-GHz MacBook Pro and ran it with 182 currencies, which is how many the entire world has. Once I had loaded in the exchange rates (I chose random values for the exchange rates), the program took approximately 0.02 seconds to run.

The Floyd-Warshall algorithm

Now suppose that you want to find a shortest path from every vertex to every vertex. That's the *all-pairs shortest-paths* problem.

The classic example of all-pairs shortest paths—which I have seen several authors refer to—is the table that you see in a road atlas giving distances between several cities. You find the row for one city, you find the column for the other city, and the distance between them lies at the intersection of the row and column.

There is one problem with this example: *it's not all-pairs*. If it were all pairs, the table would have one row and one column for every intersection, not for just every city. The number of rows and columns for just the U.S. would be in the millions. No, the way to make the table you see in an atlas is to find single-source shortest paths from each city and then put a subset of the results—shortest paths to just the other cities, not to all intersections—into the table.

What would be a legitimate application of all-pairs shortest paths? Finding the *diameter* of a network: the longest of all shortest paths. For example, suppose that a directed graph represents a communication network, and the weight of an edge gives the time it takes for a message to traverse a communication link. Then the diameter gives you the longest possible transit time for a message in the network.

Of course, we can compute all-pairs shortest paths by computing single-source shortest paths from each vertex in turn. If all edge weights are nonnegative, we can run Dijkstra's algorithm from each of the n

vertices, each call taking $O(m \lg n)$ time if we use a binary heap or $O(n \lg n + m)$ time if we use a Fibonacci heap, for a total running time of either $O(nm \lg n)$ or $O(n^2 \lg n + nm)$. If the graph is sparse, that approach works well. But if the graph is dense, so that m is near n^2, then $O(nm \lg n)$ is $O(n^3 \lg n)$. Even with a dense graph and a Fibonacci heap, $O(n^2 \lg n + mn)$ is $O(n^3)$, and the constant factor induced by the Fibonacci heap can be significant. Of course, if the graph may contain negative-weight edges, then we cannot use Dijkstra's algorithm, and running the Bellman-Ford algorithm from each of n vertices on a dense graph gives a running time of $\Theta(n^2 m)$, which is $\Theta(n^4)$.

Instead, by using the Floyd-Warshall algorithm,[6] we can solve the all-pairs problem in $\Theta(n^3)$ time—regardless of whether the graph is sparse, dense, or in between, and even allowing the graph to have negative-weight edges but no negative-weight cycles—and the constant factor hidden in the Θ-notation is small. Moreover, the Floyd-Warshall algorithm illustrates a clever algorithmic technique called "dynamic programming."

The Floyd-Warshall algorithm relies on an obvious property of shortest paths. Suppose that you're driving from New York City to Seattle along a shortest route, and that this shortest route from New York to Seattle passes through Chicago and then through Spokane before arriving at Seattle. Then the portion of the shortest route from New York to Seattle that goes from Chicago to Spokane must itself be a shortest route from Chicago to Spokane. Why is that? Because if there were a shorter route from Chicago to Spokane, we would have used it in the shortest route from New York to Seattle! Like I said, obvious. To apply this principle to directed graphs:

> If a shortest path, call it p, from vertex u to vertex v goes from vertex u to vertex x to vertex y to vertex v, then the portion of p that is between x and y is itself a shortest path from x to y. That is, *any subpath of a shortest path is itself a shortest path.*

The Floyd-Warshall algorithm keeps track of path weights and vertex predecessors in arrays indexed in not just one dimension, but in three dimensions. You can think of a one-dimensional array as a table, just as we saw on page 11. A two-dimensional array would be like a matrix, such as the adjacency matrix on page 79; you need two indices

---

[6]Named after Robert Floyd and Stephen Warshall.

(row and column) to identify an entry. You can also think of a two-dimensional array as a one-dimensional array in which each entry is itself a one-dimensional array. A three-dimensional array would be like a one-dimensional array of two-dimensional arrays; you need an index in each of the three dimensions to identify an entry. We'll use commas to separate the dimensions when indexing into a multidimensional array.

In the Floyd-Warshall algorithm, we assume that the vertices are numbered from 1 to n. Vertex numbers become important, because the Floyd-Warshall algorithm uses the following definition:

> $shortest[u, v, x]$ is the weight of a shortest path from vertex u to vertex v in which each intermediate vertex—a vertex on the path other than u and v—is numbered from 1 to x.

(So think of u, v, and x as integers in the range 1 to n that represent vertices.) This definition does not require the intermediate vertices to consist of *all* x vertices numbered 1 to x; it just requires each intermediate vertex—however many there are—to be numbered x or lower. Since all vertices are numbered at most n, it must be the case that $shortest[u, v, n]$ equals $sp(u, v)$, the weight of a shortest path from u to v.

Let's consider two vertices u and v, and pick a number x in the range from 1 to n. Consider all paths from u to v in which all intermediate vertices are numbered at most x. Of all these paths, let path p be one with minimum weight. Path p either contains vertex x or it does not, and we know that, other than possibly u or v, it does not contain any vertex numbered higher than x. There are two possibilities:

- First possibility: x is not an intermediate vertex in path p. Then all intermediate vertices of path p are numbered at most $x - 1$. What does this mean? It means that the weight of a shortest path from u to v with all intermediate vertices numbered at most x is the same as the weight of a shortest path from u to v with all intermediate vertices numbered at most $x - 1$. In other words, $shortest[u, v, x]$ equals $shortest[u, v, x - 1]$.

- Second possibility: x appears as an intermediate vertex in path p. Because any subpath of a shortest path is itself a shortest path, the portion of path p that goes from u to x is a shortest path from u to x. Likewise, the portion of p that goes from x to v is a shortest path from x to v. Because vertex x is an endpoint of each of these subpaths, it is not an intermediate vertex in either of them, and so the intermediate vertices in each of these subpaths are all numbered at most $x - 1$. Therefore, the weight of a shortest path from u to v with all intermediate vertices numbered at most x is the sum of the weights of two shortest paths: one from u to x with all intermediate vertices numbered at most $x - 1$, and one from x to v, also with all intermediate vertices numbered at most $x - 1$. In other words, $shortest[u, v, x]$ equals $shortest[u, x, x - 1] + shortest[x, v, x - 1]$.

Because either x is an intermediate vertex in a shortest path from u to v or it's not, we can conclude that $shortest[u, v, x]$ is the smaller of $shortest[u, x, x - 1] + shortest[x, v, x - 1]$ and $shortest[u, v, x - 1]$.

The best way to represent the graph in the Floyd-Warshall algorithm is by a variant of the adjacency-matrix representation from pages 78–79. Instead of each matrix element being constrained to 0 or 1, the entry for edge (u, v) holds the weight of the edge, with a weight of ∞ indicating that the edge is absent. Since $shortest[u, v, 0]$ denotes the weight of a shortest path from u to v with all intermediate vertices numbered at most 0, such a path has no intermediate vertices. That is, it consists of just a single edge, and so this matrix is exactly what we want for $shortest[u, v, 0]$.

Given the $shortest[u, v, 0]$ values (which are the edge weights), the Floyd-Warshall algorithm computes $shortest[u, v, x]$ values first for all pairs of vertices u and v with x set to 1. Then the algorithm computes $shortest[u, v, x]$ values for all pairs of vertices u and v with x set to 2. Then for x set to 3, and so on, up through n.

How about keeping track of predecessors? Let's define $pred[u, v, x]$ analogously to how we defined $shortest[u, v, x]$, as the predecessor of vertex v on a shortest path from vertex u in which all intermediate vertices are numbered at most x. We can update the $pred[u, v, x]$ values as we compute the $shortest[u, v, x]$ values, as follows. If $shortest[u, v, x]$ is the same as $shortest[u, v, x - 1]$, then the shortest path that we've found from u to v with all intermediate vertices numbered at most x is the same as the one with all intermediate vertices numbered at most $x - 1$. Vertex v's predecessor must be the same in both paths, and so we can set $pred[u, v, x]$ to be the same as $pred[u, v, x - 1]$. What about when $shortest[u, v, x]$ is less than $shortest[u, v, x - 1]$? That happens when we find a path from u to v that has vertex x as an intermediate vertex and has lower weight than the shortest path from u to v with all intermediate vertices numbered at most $x - 1$. Because x must be an intermediate vertex on this newly found shortest path, v's predecessor on the path from u must be the same as v's predecessor on the path from x. In this case, we set $pred[u, v, x]$ to be the same as $pred[x, v, x - 1]$.

We now have all the pieces we need to assemble the Floyd-Warshall algorithm. Here's the procedure:

Procedure FLOYD-WARSHALL(G)

Input: G: a graph represented by a weighted adjacency matrix W with n rows and n columns (one row and one column per vertex). The entry in row u and column v, denoted w_{uv}, is the weight of edge (u, v) if this edge is present in G, and it is ∞ otherwise.

Output: For each pair of vertices u and v, the value of $shortest[u, v, n]$ contains the weight of a shortest path from u to v, and $pred[u, v, n]$ is the predecessor vertex of v on a shortest path from u.

1. Let *shortest* and *pred* be new $n \times n \times (n + 1)$ arrays.
2. For each u and v from 1 to n:
   A. Set $shortest[u, v, 0]$ to w_{uv}.
   B. If (u, v) is an edge in G, then set $pred[u, v, 0]$ to u. Otherwise, set $pred[u, v, 0]$ to NULL.
3. For $x = 1$ to n:
   A. For $u = 1$ to n:
      i. For $v = 1$ to n:
         a. If $shortest[u, v, x] < shortest[u, x, x - 1] + shortest[x, v, x - 1]$, then set $shortest[u, v, x]$ to $shortest[u, x, x - 1] + shortest[x, v, x - 1]$ and set $pred[u, v, x]$ to $pred[x, v, x - 1]$.
         b. Otherwise, set $shortest[u, v, x]$ to $shortest[u, v, x - 1]$ and set $pred[u, v, x]$ to $pred[u, v, x - 1]$.
4. Return the *shortest* and *pred* arrays.

For this graph

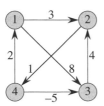

the adjacency matrix W, containing the edge weights, is

$$\begin{pmatrix} 0 & 3 & 8 & \infty \\ \infty & 0 & \infty & 1 \\ \infty & 4 & 0 & \infty \\ 2 & \infty & -5 & 0 \end{pmatrix},$$

which also gives the *shortest*$[u, v, 0]$ values[7] (the weights of paths with at most one edge). For example, *shortest*$[2, 4, 0]$ is 1, because we can get from vertex 2 to vertex 4 directly, with no intermediate vertices, by taking edge $(2, 4)$ with weight 1. Similarly, *shortest*$[4, 3, 0]$ is -5. Here is a matrix giving the *pred*$[u, v, 0]$ values:

$$\begin{pmatrix} \text{NULL} & 1 & 1 & \text{NULL} \\ \text{NULL} & \text{NULL} & \text{NULL} & 2 \\ \text{NULL} & 3 & \text{NULL} & \text{NULL} \\ 4 & \text{NULL} & 4 & \text{NULL} \end{pmatrix}.$$

For example, *pred*$[2, 4, 0]$ is 2 because the predecessor of vertex 4 is vertex 2, using the edge $(2, 4)$, with weight 1, and *pred*$[2, 3, 0]$ is NULL because there is no edge $(2, 3)$.

After running the loop of step 3 for $x = 1$ (to examine paths that may include vertex 1 as an intermediate vertex), the *shortest*$[u, v, 1]$ and *pred*$[u, v, 1]$ values are

$$\begin{pmatrix} 0 & 3 & 8 & \infty \\ \infty & 0 & \infty & 1 \\ \infty & 4 & 0 & \infty \\ 2 & 5 & -5 & 0 \end{pmatrix} \text{ and } \begin{pmatrix} \text{NULL} & 1 & 1 & \text{NULL} \\ \text{NULL} & \text{NULL} & \text{NULL} & 2 \\ \text{NULL} & 3 & \text{NULL} & \text{NULL} \\ 4 & 1 & 4 & \text{NULL} \end{pmatrix}.$$

After the loop runs for $x = 2$, the *shortest*$[u, v, 2]$ and *pred*$[u, v, 2]$ values are

$$\begin{pmatrix} 0 & 3 & 8 & 4 \\ \infty & 0 & \infty & 1 \\ \infty & 4 & 0 & 5 \\ 2 & 5 & -5 & 0 \end{pmatrix} \text{ and } \begin{pmatrix} \text{NULL} & 1 & 1 & 2 \\ \text{NULL} & \text{NULL} & \text{NULL} & 2 \\ \text{NULL} & 3 & \text{NULL} & 2 \\ 4 & 1 & 4 & \text{NULL} \end{pmatrix}.$$

After $x = 3$:

$$\begin{pmatrix} 0 & 3 & 8 & 4 \\ \infty & 0 & \infty & 1 \\ \infty & 4 & 0 & 5 \\ 2 & -1 & -5 & 0 \end{pmatrix} \text{ and } \begin{pmatrix} \text{NULL} & 1 & 1 & 2 \\ \text{NULL} & \text{NULL} & \text{NULL} & 2 \\ \text{NULL} & 3 & \text{NULL} & 2 \\ 4 & 3 & 4 & \text{NULL} \end{pmatrix}.$$

---

[7]Because a three-dimensional array is a one-dimensional array of two-dimensional arrays, for a fixed value of x we can think of *shortest*$[u, v, x]$ as a two-dimensional array.

And our final *shortest*[$u, v, 4$] and *pred*[$u, v, 4$] values, after running the loop for $x = 4$, are

$$
\begin{pmatrix}
0 & 3 & -1 & 4 \\
3 & 0 & -4 & 1 \\
7 & 4 & 0 & 5 \\
2 & -1 & -5 & 0
\end{pmatrix}
\text{ and }
\begin{pmatrix}
\text{NULL} & 1 & 4 & 2 \\
4 & \text{NULL} & 4 & 2 \\
4 & 3 & \text{NULL} & 2 \\
4 & 3 & 4 & \text{NULL}
\end{pmatrix}.
$$

We can see, for example, that the shortest path from vertex 1 to vertex 3 has weight -1. This path goes from vertex 1 to vertex 2 to vertex 4 to vertex 3, which we can see by tracing back: *pred*[$1, 3, 4$] is 4, *pred*[$1, 4, 4$] is 2, and *pred*[$1, 2, 4$] is 1.

I claimed that the Floyd-Warshall algorithm runs in $\Theta(n^3)$ time, and it's easy to see why. We have nested loops three deep, and each one iterates n times. In each iteration of the loop of step 3, the loop of step 3A iterates all n times. Likewise, in each iteration of the loop of step 3A, the loop of step 3Ai iterates all n times. Since the outer loop of step 3 also iterates n times, the innermost loop (step 3Ai) iterates n^3 times in all. Each iteration of the innermost loop takes constant time, and so the algorithm takes $\Theta(n^3)$ time.

It looks as though this algorithm also takes $\Theta(n^3)$ space in memory. After all, it creates two $n \times n \times (n + 1)$ arrays. Since each array entry uses a constant amount of memory, these arrays occupy $\Theta(n^3)$ memory space. It turns out, however, that we can get away with only $\Theta(n^2)$ space in memory. How? Just create *shortest* and *pred* as $n \times n$ arrays, and forget about the third index into *shortest* and *pred* everywhere. Although steps 3Aia and 3Aib keep updating the same *shortest*[u, v] and *pred*[u, v] values, these arrays turn out to have the correct values at the end!

Earlier, I mentioned that the Floyd-Warshall algorithm illustrates a technique called **dynamic programming**. This technique applies only when

1. we are trying to find an optimal solution to a problem,

2. we can break an instance of the problem into instances of one or more subproblems,

3. we use solutions to the subproblem(s) to solve the original problem, and

4. if we use a solution to a subproblem within an optimal solution to the original problem, then the subproblem solution we use must be optimal for the subproblem.

We can summarize these conditions under the umbrella name of ***optimal substructure*** and, put more succinctly, it says that an optimal solution to a problem contains within it optimal solutions to subproblems. In dynamic programming, we have some notion of the "size" of a subproblem, and we often solve the subproblems in increasing order of size, so that we solve the smallest subproblems first, and then once we have optimal solutions to smaller subproblems, we can try to solve larger subproblems optimally using optimal solutions to the smaller subproblems.

This description of dynamic programming sounds rather abstract, so let's see how the Floyd-Warshall algorithm uses it. We state a subproblem as

> Compute $shortest[u, v, x]$, which is the weight of a shortest path from vertex u to vertex v in which each intermediate vertex is numbered from 1 to x.

Here, the "size" of a subproblem is the highest-numbered vertex that we allow to be an intermediate vertex of a shortest path: in other words, the value of x. Optimal substructure comes into play because of the following property:

> Consider a shortest path p from vertex u to vertex v, and let x be the highest-numbered intermediate vertex on this path. Then the portion of p that goes from u to x is a shortest path from u to x with all intermediate vertices numbered from 1 to $x - 1$, and the portion of p that goes from x to v is a shortest path from x to v with all intermediate vertices numbered from 1 to $x - 1$.

We solve the problem of computing $shortest[u, v, x]$ by first computing $shortest[u, v, x - 1]$, $shortest[u, x, x - 1]$, and $shortest[x, v, x - 1]$ and then using the lesser of $shortest[u, v, x - 1]$ and $shortest[u, x, x - 1] + shortest[x, v, x - 1]$. Because we have computed all the *shortest* values where the third index is $x - 1$ before we try to compute any of the *shortest* values where the third index is x, we have all the information we need when we compute $shortest[u, v, x]$.

A common practice in dynamic programming is to store optimal solutions to subproblems ($shortest[u, v, x - 1]$, $shortest[u, x, x - 1]$, and $shortest[x, v, x - 1]$) in a table and then look them up as we compute an optimal solution to the original problem ($shortest[u, v, x]$). We call such an approach "bottom up," since it works from smaller subproblems to larger subproblems. Another approach is to solve subproblems "top down," working from larger subproblems to smaller ones, again storing the result of each subproblem in a table.

Dynamic programming applies to a wide range of optimization problems, only some of which have to do with graphs. We'll see it again in Chapter 7, when we find the longest common subsequence of two strings of characters.

Further reading

Chapter 24 of CLRS [CLRS09] covers Dijkstra's algorithm and the Bellman-Ford algorithm. Chapter 25 of CLRS covers all-pairs shortest-paths algorithms, including Floyd-Warshall; an all-pairs shortest-paths algorithm based on matrix multiplication, running in $\Theta(n^3 \lg n)$ time; and a clever algorithm by Donald Johnson, designed to find all-pairs shortest paths on sparse graphs in $O(n^2 \lg n + nm)$ time.

When edge weights are small nonnegative integers no greater than a known amount C, a more complex implementation of the priority queue in Dijkstra's algorithm yields better asymptotic running times than a Fibonacci heap. For example, Ahuja, Mehlhorn, Orlin, and Tarjan [AMOT90] incorporate a "redistributive heap" into Dijkstra's algorithm, giving a running time of $O(m + n \sqrt{\lg C})$.

7 Algorithms on Strings

A *string* is just a sequence of characters from some underlying character set. For example, this book comprises characters from the set of letters, digits, punctuation symbols, and mathematical symbols, which is a rather large, but finite, character set. Biologists encode strands of DNA as strings over just four characters—A, C, G, T—which represent the base molecules adenine, cytosine, guanine, and thymine.

We can ask all sorts of questions about strings, but in this chapter we'll focus on algorithms for three problems that take strings as inputs:

1. Find a longest common subsequence of two strings.

2. Given a set of operations that can transform one string to another, and the cost of each operation, find a lowest-cost way to transform one string to another.

3. Find all occurrences of a pattern string within a string of text.

The first two of these problems have applications in computational biology. The longer a common subsequence we can find between two strands of DNA, the more similar they are. One way to align strands of DNA is to transform one strand to another; the lower the cost of transforming, the more similar the strands. The last problem, finding occurrences of a pattern within a text, is also known as *string matching*. It comes up in all sorts of programs, such as any time you use a "Find" command. It also comes up in computational biology, because we can look for one strand of DNA within another.

Longest common subsequence

Let's start with what we mean by "sequence" and "subsequence." A *sequence* is a list of items in which the order of items matters. A given item may appear in a sequence multiple times. The particular sequences we'll be working with in this chapter are strings of characters, and we'll use the term "string" instead of "sequence." Likewise, we will assume that the items making up a sequence are characters. For example, the string GACA contains the same character (A) multiple times, and it differs from the string CAAG, which has the same population of characters but in a different order. A **subsequence** Z of a string X is X, possibly with items removed. For example, if X is the string GAC, then it has eight subsequences: GAC (no characters removed), GA (C removed), GC (A removed), AC (G removed), G (A and C removed), A (G and C removed), C (G and A removed), and the empty string (all characters removed). If X and Y are strings, then Z is a **common subsequence** of X and Y if it is a subsequence of both of them. For example, if X is the string CATCGA and Y is the string GTACCGTCA, then CCA is a common subsequence of X and Y consisting of three characters. It is not a **longest common subsequence (LCS)**, however, since the common subsequence CTCA has four characters. Indeed CTCA is a longest common subsequence, but it is not unique, since TCGA is another common subsequence with four characters. The notions of subsequence and substring differ: a **substring** is a subsequence of a string in which the characters must be drawn from contiguous positions in the string. For the string CATCGA, the subsequence ATCG is a substring but the subsequence CTCA is not.

Our goal is, given two strings X and Y, to find a longest common subsequence Z of X and Y. We will use the technique of dynamic programming, which we saw in Chapter 6, to solve this problem.

You can find a longest common subsequence without resorting to dynamic programming, but I don't recommend it. You could try each subsequence of X and check whether it's a subsequence of Y, working from the longest to the smallest subsequences of X, checking each against Y and stopping once you find a subsequence of both X and Y. (You know that you'll eventually find one, since the empty string is a subsequence of all strings.) If X has length m, then it has 2^m subsequences, and so even if we ignore the time to check each subsequence against Y, the time to find an LCS would be at least exponential in the length of X in the worst case.

Recall from Chapter 6 that in order for dynamic programming to apply, we need optimal substructure: an optimal solution to a problem contains optimal solutions to its subproblems. To find an LCS of two strings via dynamic programming, we first need to decide what constitutes a subproblem. Prefixes work. If X is a string $x_1 x_2 x_3 \cdots x_m$, then the **ith prefix** of X is the string $x_1 x_2 x_3 \cdots x_i$, and we denote it by X_i. Here, we require that i be in the range 0 to m, and X_0 is the empty string. For example, if X is CATCGA, then X_4 is CATC.

We can see that an LCS of two strings contains within it an LCS of the prefixes of the two strings. Let's consider two strings $X = x_1 x_2 x_3 \cdots x_m$ and $Y = y_1 y_2 y_3 \cdots y_n$. They have some LCS, say Z, where $Z = z_1 z_2 z_3 \cdots z_k$ for some length k, which could be anywhere from 0 to the smaller of m and n. What can we deduce about Z? Let's look at the last characters in X and Y: x_m and y_n. Either they are equal or they're not.

- If they're equal, then the last character z_k of Z must be the same as that character. What do we know about the rest of Z, which is $Z_{k-1} = z_1 z_2 z_3 \cdots z_{k-1}$? We know that Z_{k-1} must be an LCS of what remains of X and Y, namely $X_{m-1} = x_1 x_2 x_3 \cdots x_{m-1}$ and $Y_{n-1} = y_1 y_2 y_3 \cdots y_{n-1}$. From our example before—where $X = $ CATCGA and $Y = $ GTACCGTCA and an LCS is $Z = $ CTCA—the last character, A, of X and Y is the last character of Z, and we see that $Z_3 = $ CTC must be an LCS of $X_5 = $ CATCG and $Y_8 = $ GTACCGTC.

- If they're not equal, then z_k might be the same as either the last character x_m of X or the last character y_n of Y, but not of both. Or it might not be the same as the last character of either X or Y. If z_k is not the same as x_m, ignore the last character of X: Z must be an LCS of X_{m-1} and Y. Similarly, if z_k is not the same as y_n, ignore the last character of Y: Z must be an LCS of X and Y_{n-1}. Continuing the example from above, let $X = $ CATCG, $Y = $ GTACCGTC, and $Z = $ CTC. Here, z_3 is the same as y_8 (C) but not x_5 (G), and so Z is an LCS of $X_4 = $ CATC and Y.

Therefore, this problem has optimal substructure: an LCS of two strings contains within it an LCS of the prefixes of the two strings.

How to proceed? We need to solve either one or two subproblems, depending on whether the last characters of X and Y are the same. If they are, then we solve just one subproblem—find an LCS of X_{m-1} and Y_{n-1}—and then append that last character to get an LCS of X and Y. If the last characters of X and Y are not the same, then we have to solve two subproblems—find an LCS of X_{m-1} and Y, and find an LCS of X and Y_{n-1}—and use the longer of these two longest common subsequences as an LCS of X and Y. If these two longest common subsequences have the same length, then use either one of them—it doesn't matter which.

We will approach the problem of finding an LCS of X and Y in two steps. First, we'll find the length of an LCS of X and Y, as well as the lengths of the longest common subsequences of all prefixes of X and Y. You might be surprised that we can find the length of an LCS without knowing what the LCS is. After computing the LCS lengths, we will "reverse engineer" how we computed these lengths to find an actual LCS of X and Y.

To make things a little more precise, let's denote the length of an LCS of the prefixes X_i and Y_j by $l[i, j]$. The length of an LCS of X and Y is given by $l[m, n]$. We can start the indices i and j at 0, since if either of the prefixes has length 0, then we know their LCS: it's an empty string. In other words, $l[0, j]$ and $l[i, 0]$ equal 0 for all values of i and j. When both i and j are positive, we determine $l[i, j]$ by looking at smaller values of i and/or j:

- If i and j are positive and x_i is the same as y_j, then $l[i, j]$ equals $l[i - 1, j - 1] + 1$.

- If i and j are positive and x_i differs from y_j, then $l[i, j]$ equals the larger of $l[i, j - 1]$ and $l[i - 1, j]$.

Think of the values of $l[i, j]$ as being stored in a table. We need to compute these values in increasing order of the indices i and j. Here's the $l[i, j]$ table for our example strings (we'll see what the shaded parts mean a little later):

i	x_i	$l[i,j]$	j 0	1	2	3	4	5	6	7	8	9
			y_j	G	T	A	C	C	G	T	C	A
0			0	0	0	0	0	0	0	0	0	0
1	C		0	0	0	0	1	1	1	1	1	1
2	A		0	0	0	1	1	1	1	1	1	2
3	T		0	0	1	1	1	1	1	2	2	2
4	C		0	0	1	1	2	2	2	2	3	3
5	G		0	1	1	1	2	2	3	3	3	3
6	A		0	1	1	2	2	2	3	3	3	4

For example, $l[5, 8]$ is 3, meaning that an LCS of $X_5 = $ CATCG and $Y_8 = $ GTACCGTC has length 3, as we saw on page 117.

In order to compute table values in increasing order of the indices, before we compute a particular entry $l[i, j]$, where both i and j are positive, we need to compute the entries $l[i, j - 1]$ (immediately left of $l[i, j]$), $l[i - 1, j]$ (immediately above $l[i, j]$), and $l[i - 1, j - 1]$

(above and to the left of $l[i, j]$).[1] It's easy to compute the table entries in this way: we can compute them either row by row, from left to right within each row, or column by column, from top to bottom within each column.

The procedure that follows treats the table as a two-dimensional array $l[0 .. m, 0 .. n]$. After filling the leftmost column and top row with 0s, it then fills the remainder of the array row by row.

Procedure COMPUTE-LCS-TABLE(X, Y)

Inputs: X and Y: two strings of length m and n, respectively.

Output: The array $l[0 .. m, 0 .. n]$. The value of $l[m, n]$ is the length of a longest common subsequence of X and Y.

1. Let $l[0 .. m, 0 .. n]$ be a new array.
2. For $i = 0$ to m:

    A. Set $l[i, 0]$ to 0.
3. For $j = 0$ to n:

    A. Set $l[0, j]$ to 0.
4. For $i = 1$ to m:

    A. For $j = 1$ to n:

        i. If x_i is the same as y_j, then set $l[i, j]$ to $l[i - 1, j - 1] + 1$.

        ii. Otherwise (x_i differs from y_j), set $l[i, j]$ to the larger of $l[i, j - 1]$ and $l[i - 1, j]$. If $l[i, j - 1]$ equals $l[i - 1, j]$, it doesn't matter which you choose.
5. Return the array l.

Since it takes constant time to fill in each entry of the table, and the table contains $(m + 1) \cdot (n + 1)$ entries, the running time of COMPUTE-LCS-TABLE is $\Theta(mn)$.

The good news is that, once we compute the $l[i, j]$ table, its lower-right entry, $l[m, n]$, gives us the length of an LCS of X and Y. The bad news is that no single entry in the table tells us the actual characters in an LCS. We can use the table, along with the strings X and Y, to construct an LCS, using $O(m + n)$ additional time. We determine how we got

---

[1]Even mentioning $l[i - 1, j - 1]$ is redundant, since we need to have computed it before computing both of $l[i, j - 1]$ and $l[i - 1, j]$.

the value in $l[i, j]$ by reverse engineering this computation, based on $l[i, j]$ and the values it depends on: x_i, y_j, $l[i - 1, j - 1]$, $l[i, j - 1]$, and $l[i - 1, j]$.

I like to write this procedure recursively, where we assemble an LCS from back to front. The procedure recurses, and when it finds characters in X and Y that are the same, it appends the character to the end of the LCS it constructs. The initial call is ASSEMBLE-LCS(X, Y, l, m, n).

Procedure ASSEMBLE-LCS(X, Y, l, i, j)

Inputs:

- X and Y: two strings.
- l: the array filled in by the COMPUTE-LCS-TABLE procedure.
- i and j: indices into X and Y, respectively, as well as into l.

Output: An LCS of X_i and Y_j.

1. If $l[i, j]$ equals 0, then return the empty string.
2. Otherwise (because $l[i, j]$ is positive, both i and j are positive), if x_i is the same as y_j, then return the string formed by first recursively calling ASSEMBLE-LCS$(X, Y, l, i - 1, j - 1)$ and then appending x_i (or y_j) to the end of the string returned by the recursive call.
3. Otherwise (x_i differs from y_j), if $l[i, j - 1]$ is greater than $l[i - 1, j]$, then return the string returned by recursively calling ASSEMBLE-LCS$(X, Y, l, i, j - 1)$.
4. Otherwise (x_i differs from y_j and $l[i, j - 1]$ is less than or equal to $l[i - 1, j]$), return the string returned by recursively calling ASSEMBLE-LCS$(X, Y, l, i - 1, j)$.

In the table on page 118, the shaded $l[i, j]$ entries are those that the recursion visits with the initial call ASSEMBLE-LCS$(X, Y, l, 6, 9)$, and the shaded x_i characters are those that are appended to the LCS being constructed. To get an idea of how ASSEMBLE-LCS works, start at $i = 6$ and $j = 9$. Here, we find that x_6 and y_9 are both the character A. Therefore, A will be the last character of the LCS of X_6 and Y_9, and we recurse in step 2. The recursive call has $i = 5$ and $j = 8$. This time, we find that x_5 and y_8 are different characters, and we also find that $l[5, 7]$ equals $l[4, 8]$, and so we recurse in step 4. Now the recursive call has $i = 4$ and $j = 8$. And so on. If you read the shaded x_i characters from top to bottom, you get the string CTCA, which is an LCS. If we had broken ties between $l[i, j-1]$ and $l[i-1, j]$ in favor of going left (step 3) rather than going up (step 4), then the LCS produced would have been TCGA.

How is it that the ASSEMBLE-LCS procedure takes $O(m+n)$ time? Observe that in each recursive call, either i decreases, j decreases, or both decrease. After $m+n$ recursive calls, therefore, we are guaranteed that one or the other of these indices hits 0 and the recursion bottoms out in step 1.

Transforming one string to another

Now let's see how to transform one string X to another string Y. We'll start with X, and we'll convert it to Y, character by character. We'll assume that X and Y consist of m and n characters, respectively. As before, we'll denote the ith character of each string by using the lowercase name of the string, subscripted by i, so that the ith character of X is x_i and the jth character of Y is y_j.

To convert X into Y, we'll build a string, which we'll call Z, so that when we're done, Z and Y are the same. We maintain an index i into X and an index j into Z. We are allowed to perform a sequence of specific transformation operations, which may alter Z and these indices. We start with i and j at 1, and we must examine every character in X during the process, which means that we will stop only once i reaches $m+1$.

Here are the operations that we consider:

- *Copy* a character x_i from X to Z by setting z_j to x_i and then incrementing both i and j.

- *Replace* a character x_i from X by another character a by setting z_j to a and then incrementing both i and j.

- *Delete* a character x_i from X by incrementing i but leaving j alone.

- *Insert* a character a into Z by setting z_j to a and then incrementing j but leaving i alone.

Other operations are possible—such as interchanging two adjacent characters, or deleting characters x_i through x_m in a single operation—but we'll consider just the *copy*, *replace*, *delete*, and *insert* operations here.

As an example, here is one sequence of operations that transforms the string ATGATCGGCAT into the string CAATGTGAATC, where the shaded characters are x_i and z_j after each operation:

Operation	X	Z
initial strings	ATGATCGGCAT	
delete A	ATGATCGGCAT	
replace T by C	ATGATCGGCAT	C
replace G by A	ATGATCGGCAT	CA
copy A	ATGATCGGCAT	CAA
copy T	ATGATCGGCAT	CAAT
replace C by G	ATGATCGGCAT	CAATG
replace G by T	ATGATCGGCAT	CAATGT
copy G	ATGATCGGCAT	CAATGTG
replace C by A	ATGATCGGCAT	CAATGTGA
copy A	ATGATCGGCAT	CAATGTGAA
copy T	ATGATCGGCAT	CAATGTGAAT
insert C	ATGATCGGCAT	CAATGTGAATC

Other operation sequences would work, too. For example, we could just delete each character from X in turn and then insert each character from Y into Z.

Each of the transformation operations comes with a cost, which is a constant that depends only on the type of the operation and not on the characters involved. Our goal is to find a sequence of operations that transforms X into Y and has a minimum total cost. Let's denote the cost of the *copy* operation by c_C, the cost of *replace* by c_R, the cost of *delete* by c_D, and the cost of *insert* by c_I. For the sequence of operations in the example above, the total cost would be $5c_C + 5c_R + c_D + c_I$. We should assume that each of c_C and c_R is less than $c_D + c_I$, because otherwise instead of paying c_C to copy a character or paying c_R to replace a character, we would just pay $c_D + c_I$ to delete the character and insert either the same one (instead of copying) or a different one (instead of replacing).

Why would you want to transform one string to another? Computational biology provides one application. Computational biologists often align two DNA sequences in order to measure how similar they are. In one way to align two sequences X and Y, we line up identical characters as much as possible by inserting spaces into the two sequences (including at either end) so that the resulting sequences, let's say X' and Y', have the same length but don't have a space in the same position. That is, we can't have both x_i' and y_i' be a space. After aligning, we assign a score to each position:

- -1 if x_i' and y_i' are the same and not a space.
- $+1$ if x_i' differs from y_i' and neither is a space.
- $+2$ if either x_i' or y_i' is a space.

The score for an alignment is the sum of the scores for the individual positions. The lower the score, the more closely the two strings align. For the strings in the example above, we can align them as follows, where ⊔ indicates a space:

```
X' :  ATGATCG⊔GCAT⊔
Y' :  ⊔CAAT⊔GTGAATC
      *++--*-*-+--*
```

A $-$ under a position indicates a score of -1 for that position, a $+$ indicates a score of $+1$, and a $*$ indicates $+2$. This particular alignment has a total score of $(6 \cdot -1) + (3 \cdot 1) + (4 \cdot 2)$, or 5.

There are many possible ways to insert spaces and align two sequences. To find the way that produces the best match—having the lowest score—we use string transformation with costs $c_C = -1, c_R = +1$, and $c_D = c_I = +2$. The more identical characters get matched up, the better the alignment, and the negative cost of the *copy* operation provides incentive to match up identical characters. A space in Y' corresponds to a deleted character, so that in the above example, the first space in Y' corresponds to deleting the first character (A) of X. A space in X' corresponds to an inserted character, so that in the above example, the first space in X' corresponds to inserting the character T.

So let's see how to transform a string X into a string Y. We'll use dynamic programming, with subproblems of the form "convert the prefix string X_i into the prefix string Y_j," where i runs from 0 to m and j runs from 0 to n. We'll call this subproblem the "$X_i \rightarrow Y_j$ problem," and the problem that we start with is the $X_m \rightarrow Y_n$ problem. Let's denote the cost of an optimal solution to the $X_i \rightarrow Y_j$ problem by $cost[i, j]$. As an example, take $X = \text{ACAAGC}$ and $Y = \text{CCGT}$, so that we want to solve the $X_6 \rightarrow Y_4$ problem, and we'll use the operation costs for aligning DNA sequences: $c_C = -1, c_R = +1$, and $c_D = c_I = +2$. We'll solve subproblems of the form $X_i \rightarrow Y_j$, where i runs from 0 to 6 and j runs from 0 to 4. For example, the $X_3 \rightarrow Y_2$ problem is transforming the prefix string $X_3 = \text{ACA}$ into the prefix string $Y_2 = \text{CC}$.

It's easy to determine $cost[i, j]$ when i or j is 0, because X_0 and Y_0 are empty strings. Convert an empty string into Y_j by j *insert* operations, so that $cost[0, j]$ equals $j \cdot c_I$. Likewise, convert X_i into an empty string by i *delete* operations, so that $cost[i, 0]$ equals $i \cdot c_D$. When both i and j are 0, we are converting the empty string to itself, and so $cost[0, 0]$ is obviously 0.

When i and j are both positive, we need to examine how optimal substructure applies to transforming one string to another. Let's suppose—for the moment—that we know which was the last operation used to convert X_i to Y_j. It was one of the four operations *copy*, *replace*, *delete*, or *insert*.

- If the last operation was a *copy*, then x_i and y_j must have been the same character. The subproblem that remains is converting X_{i-1} to Y_{j-1}, and an optimal solution to the $X_i \rightarrow Y_j$ problem must include an optimal solution to the $X_{i-1} \rightarrow Y_{j-1}$ problem. Why? Because if we had used a solution to the $X_{i-1} \rightarrow Y_{j-1}$ problem that did not have the minimum cost, we could use the minimum-cost solution instead to obtain a better solution to the $X_i \rightarrow Y_j$ problem than the one we got. Therefore, assuming that the last operation was a *copy*, we know that $cost[i, j]$ equals $cost[i - 1, j - 1] + c_C$.

  In our example, let's look at the $X_5 \rightarrow Y_3$ problem. Both x_5 and y_3 are the character G, and so if the last operation was *copy* G, then because $c_C = -1$, we must have $cost[5, 3] = cost[4, 2] - 1$. If $cost[4, 2]$ is 4, then $cost[5, 3]$ must be 3. If we could have found a solution to the $X_4 \rightarrow Y_2$ problem with a cost less than 4, then we could use that solution to find a solution to the $X_5 \rightarrow Y_3$ problem with a cost less than 3.

- If the last operation was a *replace*, and under the reasonable assumption that we can't "replace" a character with itself, then x_i and y_j must differ. Using the same optimal substructure argument as we used for the *copy* operation, we see that, assuming that the last operation was a *replace*, $cost[i, j]$ equals $cost[i - 1, j - 1] + c_R$.

  In our example, consider the $X_5 \rightarrow Y_4$ problem. This time, x_5 and y_4 are different characters (G and T, respectively), and so if the last operation was *replace* G by T, then because $c_R = +1$, we must have $cost[5, 4] = cost[4, 3] + 1$. If $cost[4, 3]$ is 3, then $cost[5, 4]$ must be 4.

- If the last operation was a *delete*, then we have no restrictions on x_i or y_j. Think of the *delete* operation as skipping over the character x_i and leaving the prefix Y_j alone, so that the subproblem we need to solve is the $X_{i-1} \to Y_j$ problem. Assuming that the last operation was a delete, we know that $cost[i, j] = cost[i-1, j] + c_D$.

In our example, consider the $X_6 \to Y_3$ problem. If the last operation was a *delete* (the deleted character must be x_6, which is C), then because $c_D = +2$, we must have $cost[6, 3] = cost[5, 3] + 2$. If $cost[5, 3]$ is 3, then $cost[6, 3]$ must be 5.

- Finally, if the last operation was an *insert*, it leaves X_i alone but adds the character y_j, and the subproblem to solve is $X_i \to Y_{j-1}$. Assuming that the last operation was an *insert*, we know that $cost[i, j] = cost[i, j-1] + c_I$.

In our example, consider the $X_2 \to Y_3$ problem. If the last operation was an *insert* (the inserted character must be y_3, which is G), then because $c_I = +2$, we must have $cost[2, 3] = cost[2, 2] + 2$. If $cost[2, 2]$ is 0, then $cost[2, 3]$ must be 2.

Of course, we don't know in advance which of the four operations was the last one used. We want to use the one that yields the lowest value for $cost[i, j]$. For a given combination of i and j, three of the four operations apply. The *delete* and *insert* operations always apply when both i and j are positive, and exactly one of *copy* and *replace* applies, depending on whether x_i and y_j are the same character. To compute $cost[i, j]$ from other *cost* values, determine which of *copy* and *replace* applies and take the minimum value of $cost[i, j]$ that the three possible operations yield. That is, $cost[i, j]$ is the smallest of the following four values:

- $cost[i-1, j-1] + c_C$, but only if x_i and y_j are the same character,
- $cost[i-1, j-1] + c_R$, but only if x_i and y_j differ,
- $cost[i-1, j] + c_D$,
- $cost[i, j-1] + c_I$.

Just as we did for filling in the l table when computing an LCS, we can fill in the *cost* table row by row. That's because, just like the l table, each entry $cost[i, j]$, where i and j are positive, depends on having already computed the entries immediately to the left, immediately above, and above and to the left.

In addition to the *cost* table, we'll fill in a table *op*, where $op[i, j]$ gives the last operation used to convert X_i to Y_j. We can fill in the entry $op[i, j]$ when we fill in $cost[i, j]$. The procedure COMPUTE-TRANSFORM-TABLES on the following page fills in the $cost$ and op tables, row by row, treating the $cost$ and op tables as two-dimensional arrays.

Page 128 has the $cost$ and op tables computed by COMPUTE-TRANSFORM-TABLES for our example of transforming $X = $ ACAAGC to $Y = $ CCGT with $c_C = -1$, $c_R = +1$, and $c_D = c_I = +2$. Appearing at row i and column j are the values of $cost[i, j]$ and $op[i, j]$, with operation names abbreviated. For example, the last operation used when transforming $X_5 = $ ACAAG to $Y_2 = $ CC replaces G by C, and an optimal sequence of operations to transform ACAAG to CC has a total cost of 6.

The COMPUTE-TRANSFORM-TABLES procedure fills in each entry of the tables in constant time, just as the COMPUTE-LCS-TABLE procedure does. Because each of the tables contains $(m + 1) \cdot (n + 1)$ entries, COMPUTE-TRANSFORM-TABLES runs in $\Theta(mn)$ time.

To construct the sequence of operations that transforms X to Y, we consult the op table, starting at the last entry, $op[m, n]$. We recurse, much as the ASSEMBLE-LCS procedure does, appending each operation encountered from the op table to the end of the sequence of operations. The procedure ASSEMBLE-TRANSFORMATION appears on page 129. The initial call is ASSEMBLE-TRANSFORMATION(op, m, n). The sequence of operations to convert $X = $ ACAAGC into a string Z that is the same as $Y = $ CCGT appears below the $cost$ and op tables on page 128.

Just as in ASSEMBLE-LCS, each recursive call of the ASSEMBLE-TRANSFORMATION procedure decreases either i or j, or both, and so the recursion bottoms out after at most $m + n$ recursive calls. Since each recursive call takes constant time before and after recursing, the ASSEMBLE-TRANSFORMATION procedure runs in $O(m + n)$ time.

One subtlety in the ASSEMBLE-TRANSFORMATION procedure bears closer examination. The recursion bottoms out only once both i and j reach 0. Suppose that one of i and j, but not both, equals 0. Each of the three cases in steps 2A, 2B, and 2C recurses with the value of i or j, or both, decreased by 1. Could there be a recursive call in which i or j has the value -1? Fortunately, the answer is no. Suppose that $j = 0$ and i is positive in a call of ASSEMBLE-TRANSFORMATION. From the way the op table is constructed, $op[i, 0]$ is a *delete* operation, so that step 2B executes. The recursive call in step 2B calls

Procedure COMPUTE-TRANSFORM-TABLES $(X, Y, c_C, c_R, c_D, c_I)$

Inputs:

- X and Y: two strings of length m and n, respectively.
- c_C, c_R, c_D, c_I: the costs of the *copy*, *replace*, *delete*, and *insert* operations, respectively.

Output: Arrays $cost[0..m, 0..n]$ and $op[0..m, 0..n]$. The value in $cost[i, j]$ is the minimum cost of transforming the prefix X_i into the prefix Y_j, so that $cost[m, n]$ is the minimum cost of transforming X into Y. The operation in $op[i, j]$ is the last operation performed when transforming X_i into Y_j.

1. Let $cost[0..m, 0..n]$ and $op[0..m, 0..n]$ be new arrays.
2. Set $cost[0, 0]$ to 0.
3. For $i = 1$ to m:
   A. Set $cost[i, 0]$ to $i \cdot c_D$, and set $op[i, 0]$ to *delete* x_i.
4. For $j = 1$ to n:
   A. Set $cost[0, j]$ to $j \cdot c_I$, and set $op[0, j]$ to *insert* y_j.
5. For $i = 1$ to m:
   A. For $j = 1$ to n:

   (Determine which of *copy* and *replace* applies, and set $cost[i, j]$ and $op[i, j]$ according to which of the three applicable operations minimizes $cost[i, j]$.)

   i. Set $cost[i, j]$ and $op[i, j]$ as follows:
      a. If x_i and y_j are the same, then set $cost[i, j]$ to $cost[i - 1, j - 1] + c_C$ and set $op[i, j]$ to *copy* x_i.
      b. Otherwise (x_i and y_j differ), set $cost[i, j]$ to $cost[i - 1, j - 1] + c_R$ and set $op[i, j]$ to *replace* x_i by y_j.
   ii. If $cost[i - 1, j] + c_D < cost[i, j]$, then set $cost[i, j]$ to $cost[i - 1, j] + c_D$ and set $op[i, j]$ to *delete* x_i.
   iii. If $cost[i, j - 1] + c_I < cost[i, j]$, then set $cost[i, j]$ to $cost[i, j - 1] + c_I$ and set $op[i, j]$ to *insert* y_j.

6. Return the arrays *cost* and *op*.

j	0	1	2	3	4
y_j		C	C	G	T

i	x_i	0	1	2	3	4
0		0	2 *ins* C	4 *ins* C	6 *ins* G	8 *ins* T
1	A	2 *del* A	1 *rep* A *by* C	3 *rep* A *by* C	5 *rep* A *by* G	7 *rep* A *by* T
2	C	4 *del* C	1 *copy* C	0 *copy* C	2 *ins* G	4 *ins* T
3	A	6 *del* A	3 *del* A	2 *rep* A *by* C	1 *rep* A *by* G	3 *rep* A *by* T
4	A	8 *del* A	5 *del* A	4 *rep* A *by* C	3 *rep* A *by* G	2 *rep* A *by* T
5	G	10 *del* G	7 *del* G	6 *rep* G *by* C	3 *copy* G	4 *rep* G *by* T
6	C	12 *del* C	9 *copy* C	6 *copy* C	5 *del* C	4 *rep* C *by* T

Operation	X	Z
initial strings	ACAAGC	
delete A	ACAAGC	
copy C	ACAAGC	C
delete A	ACAAGC	C
replace A *by* C	ACAAGC	CC
copy G	ACAAGC	CCG
replace C *by* T	ACAAGC	CCGT

ASSEMBLE-TRANSFORMATION$(op, i - 1, j)$, so that the value of j in the recursive call stays at 0. Likewise, if $i = 0$ and j is positive, then $op[0, j]$ is an *insert* operation, so that step 2C executes, and in the recursive call to ASSEMBLE-TRANSFORMATION$(op, i, j - 1)$, the value of i stays at 0.

Procedure ASSEMBLE-TRANSFORMATION(op, i, j)

Inputs:
- op: the operation table filled in by
  COMPUTE-TRANSFORM-TABLES.
- i and j: indices into the op table.

Output: A sequence of operations that transforms the string X into the string Y, where X and Y are the strings input to COMPUTE-TRANSFORM-TABLES.

1. If both i and j equal 0, then return an empty sequence.
2. Otherwise (at least one of i and j is positive), do the following:
   A. If $op[i, j]$ is a *copy* or *replace* operation, then return the sequence formed by first recursively calling ASSEMBLE-TRANSFORMATION($op, i - 1, j - 1$) and then appending $op[i, j]$ onto the sequence returned by the recursive call.
   B. Otherwise ($op[i, j]$ is neither a *copy* nor a *replace* operation), then if $op[i, j]$ is a *delete* operation, then return the sequence formed by first recursively calling ASSEMBLE-TRANSFORMATION($op, i - 1, j$) and then appending $op[i, j]$ onto the sequence returned by the recursive call.
   C. Otherwise ($op[i, j]$ is not a *copy*, *replace*, or *delete* operation, and so it must be an *insert* operation), return the sequence formed by first recursively calling ASSEMBLE-TRANSFORMATION($op, i, j - 1$) and then appending $op[i, j]$ onto the sequence returned by the recursive call.

String matching

In the string-matching problem, we have two strings: a ***text string*** T and a ***pattern string*** P. We want to find *all* occurrences of P in T. We'll shorten the names to "text" and "pattern," and we'll assume that the text and pattern consist of n and m characters, respectively, where $m \leq n$ (since it makes no sense to look for a pattern that's longer than the text). We'll denote the characters in P and T by $p_1 p_2 p_3 \cdots p_m$ and $t_1 t_2 t_3 \cdots t_n$, respectively.

Because we want to find all occurrences of the pattern P in the text T, a solution will be all the amounts that we can shift P by to find it in T. Put another way, we say that pattern P **occurs with shift s** in text T if the substring of T that starts at t_{s+1} is the same as the pattern P: $t_{s+1} = p_1, t_{s+2} = p_2$, and so on, up through $t_{s+m} = p_m$. The minimum possible shift would be 0, and because the pattern should not run off the end of the text, the maximum possible shift would be $n - m$. We want to know all the shifts with which P occurs in T. For example, if the text T is GTAACAGTAAACG and the pattern P is AAC, then P occurs in T with shifts 2 and 9.

If we're checking to see whether pattern P occurs in text T with a given shift amount s, then we would have to check all m characters in P against characters of T. Assuming that it takes constant time to check a single character in P against a single character in T, it would take $\Theta(m)$ time to check all m characters in the worst case. Of course, once we find a mismatch between characters of P and T, we don't have to check the rest of the characters. The worst case occurs at each shift amount for which P does occur in T.

It would be easy enough to just check the pattern against the text for every possible shift, running from 0 to $n - m$. Here is how it would work for checking the pattern AAC against the text GTAACAGTAAACG for each possible shift, with character matches shaded:

Shift amount	Text and pattern	Shift amount	Text and pattern
0	GTAACAGTAAACG AAC	6	GTAACAGTAAACG AAC
1	GTAACAGTAAACG AAC	7	GTAACAGTAAACG AAC

2	GTAACAGTAAACG
	  AAC
		8	GTAACAGTAAACG
			        AAC

3	GTAACAGTAAACG
	   AAC
		9	GTAACAGTAAACG
			         AAC

4	GTAACAGTAAACG
	    AAC
		10	GTAACAGTAAACG
			          AAC

5	GTAACAGTAAACG AAC		

This simple approach is rather inefficient, however: with $n - m + 1$ possible shifts, each taking $O(m)$ time to check, the running time would be $O((n - m)m)$. We'd examine almost every character in the text m times.

We can do better, because the simple method of checking the pattern against the text for every possible shift throws away valuable information. In the above example, when we look at shift amount $s = 2$, we have seen all the characters in the substring $t_3 t_4 t_5 = $ AAC. But at the next shift, $s = 3$, we look at t_4 and t_5 again. It would be more efficient to avoid looking at these characters again if at all possible. Let's examine a clever approach to string matching that avoids the wasted time caused by scanning the text repeatedly. Instead of examining text characters m times, it examines each character of the text exactly once.

This more efficient approach relies on a *finite automaton*. Although the name sounds imposing, the concept is quite simple. Applications of finite automata abound, but we'll focus here on using finite automata for string matching. A finite automaton, or *FA* for short, is just a set of *states* and a way to go from state to state based on a sequence of input characters. The FA starts in a particular state and consumes characters from its input, one character at a time. Based on the state it's in and the character it has just consumed, it moves to a new state.

In our string-matching application, the input sequence will be the characters of the text T, and the FA will have $m + 1$ states, one more than the number of characters in the pattern P, numbered from 0 to m. (The "finite" part of the name "finite automaton" stems from the number of states being finite.) The FA starts in state 0. When it's in state k, the k most recent text characters it has consumed match the first k characters of the pattern. Whenever the FA gets to state m, therefore, it has just seen the entire pattern in the text.

Let's look at an example using just the characters A, C, G, and T. Suppose that the pattern is ACACAGA, with $m = 7$ characters. Here is the corresponding FA, with states 0 through 7:

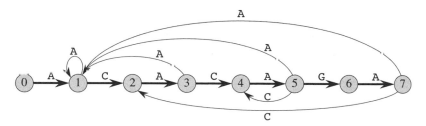

Circles represent states, and arrows, labeled by characters, show how the FA transitions from state to state on input characters. For example, the arrows from state 5 are labeled A, C, and G. The arrow to state 1, labeled A, indicates that when the FA is in state 5 and it consumes the text character A, it moves to state 1. Likewise, the arrow to state 4, labeled C, tells us that when the FA is in state 5 and consumes the text character C, it moves to state 4. Notice that I drew the horizontal "spine" of the FA with extra-heavy arrows and that the labels on the arrows of the spine, read from left to right, give the pattern ACACAGA. Whenever the pattern occurs in the text, the FA moves right by one state for each character, until it reaches the last state, where it declares that it has found an occurrence of the pattern in the text. Notice also that some arrows are missing, such as any arrow labeled T. If an arrow is missing, then the corresponding transition goes to state 0.

The FA internally stores a table *next-state*, which is indexed by all the states and all possible input characters. The value in *next-state*[s, a] is the number of the state to move to if the FA is currently in state s and it has just consumed character a from the text. Here is the entire *next-state* table for the pattern ACACAGA:

	character			
state	A	C	G	T
0	1	0	0	0
1	1	2	0	0
2	3	0	0	0
3	1	4	0	0
4	5	0	0	0
5	1	4	6	0
6	7	0	0	0
7	1	2	0	0

The FA moves one state to the right for each character that matches the pattern, and for each character that fails to match the pattern it moves left, or stays in the same state (*next-state*[1, A] is 1). We'll see how to construct the *next-state* table later on, but first let's trace out what the FA for the pattern AAC does on the input text GTAACAGTAAACG. Here's the FA:

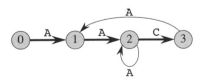

From this drawing, you can tell that the *next-state* table is the following:

state	character			
	A	C	G	T
0	1	0	0	0
1	2	0	0	0
2	2	3	0	0
3	1	0	0	0

Here are the states that the FA moves to and the text characters it consumes to get there:

state	0	0	0	1	2	3	1	0	0	1	2	2	3	0
character	G	T	A	A	C	A	G	T	A	A	A	C	G	

I've shaded the two times that the FA reaches state 3, since whenever it reaches state 3, it has found an occurrence of the pattern AAC.

Here is the procedure FA-STRING-MATCHER for string matching. It assumes that the *next-state* table has already been built.

Procedure FA-STRING-MATCHER $(T, next\text{-}state, m, n)$

Inputs:
- T, n: a text string and its length.
- *next-state*: the table of state transitions, formed according to the pattern being matched.
- m: the length of the pattern. The *next-state* table has rows indexed by 0 to m and columns indexed by the characters that may occur in the text.

Output: Prints out all the shift amounts for which the pattern occurs in the text.

1. Set *state* to 0.
2. For $i = 1$ to n:
   A. Set *state* to the value of *next-state*$[state, t_i]$.
   B. If *state* equals m, then print "The pattern occurs with shift" $i - m$.

If we run FA-STRING-MATCHER on the above example, in which m equals 3, the FA reaches state 3 after consuming the characters t_5 and t_{12}. Therefore, the procedure would print out "Pattern occurs with shift 2" $(2 = 5 - 3)$ and "Pattern occurs with shift 9" $(9 = 12 - 3)$.

Since each iteration of the loop of step 2 takes constant time and this loop runs exactly n iterations, it's plain to see that the running time of FA-STRING-MATCHER is $\Theta(n)$.

That's the easy part. The hard part is constructing the finite automaton's *next-state* table for a given pattern. Recall the idea:

> When the finite automaton is in state k, the k most recent characters it has consumed are the first k characters of the pattern.

To make this idea concrete, let's go back to the FA on page 131 for the pattern ACACAGA and think about why *next-state*[5, C] is 4. If the FA has gotten to state 5, then the five most recent characters it has consumed from the text are ACACA, which you can see by looking at the spine of the FA. If the next character consumed is C, then it does not match the pattern, and the FA cannot continue on to state 6. But the FA doesn't have to go all the way back to state 0, either. Why not? Because now the four most recently consumed characters are ACAC, which are the first four characters of the pattern ACACAGA. That's why when the FA is in state 5 and it consumes a C, it moves to state 4: it has most recently seen the first four characters of the pattern.

We are almost ready to give the rule for constructing the *next-state* table, but we need a couple of definitions first. Recall that, for i in the range 0 to m, the prefix P_i of the pattern P is the substring consisting of the first i characters of P. (When i is 0, the prefix is the empty string.) Define a **suffix** of the pattern accordingly as a substring of characters from the end of P. For example, AGA is a suffix of the pattern ACACAGA. And define the **concatenation** of a string X and a character a to be a new string formed by appending a to the end of X, and we denote it by Xa. For example, the concatenation of the string CA with the character T is the string CAT.

We're finally ready to construct *next-state*[k, a], where k is a state number running from 0 to m and a is any character that might appear in the text. In state k, we have just seen the prefix P_k in the text. That is, the k most recently seen text characters are the same as the first k characters of the pattern. When we see the next character, say a, we have seen $P_k a$ (the concatenation of P_k with a) in the text. At that point, how long a prefix of P have we just seen? Another way to ask this question is how long a prefix of P appears at the end of $P_k a$? That length will be the number of the next state.

More succinctly:

Take the prefix P_k (the first k characters of P) and concatenate it with the character a. Denote the resulting string by $P_k a$. Find the longest prefix of P that is also a suffix of $P_k a$. Then *next-state*$[k, a]$ is the length of this longest prefix.

Yes, there are a few prefixes and suffixes going on, so let's see how we determine that *next-state*$[5, C]$ is 4 for the pattern $P = $ ACACAGA. Since k is 5 in this example, we take the prefix P_5, which is ACACA, and concatenate the character C, giving ACACAC. We want to find the longest prefix of ACACAGA that is also a suffix of ACACAC. Since the string ACACAC has length 6, and a suffix can't be longer than the string that it's a suffix of, we can start by looking at P_6 and then working our way down to shorter and shorter prefixes. Here, P_6 is ACACAG, and it is not a suffix of ACACAC. So now we consider P_5, which is ACACA and is also not a suffix of ACACAC. Next we consider P_4, which is ACAC. But now this prefix *is* a suffix of ACACAC, and so we stop and determine that *next-state*$[5, C]$ should equal 4.

You might wonder whether we can always find a prefix of P that is also a suffix of $P_k a$. The answer is yes, because the empty string is a prefix and a suffix of every string. When the longest prefix of P that is also a suffix of $P_k a$ turns out to be the empty string, we set *next-state*$[k, a]$ to 0. Still using the pattern $P = $ ACACAGA, let's see how to determine *next-state*$[3, G]$. Concatenating P_3 with G gives the string ACAG. We work through the prefixes of P, starting with P_4 (since the length of ACAG is 4) and work our way down. None of the prefixes ACAC, ACA, AC, or A is a suffix of ACAG, and so we settle for the empty string as the longest prefix that works. Since the empty string has length 0, we set *next-state*$[3, G]$ to 0.

How long does it take to fill in the entire *next-state* table? We know that it has one row for each state in the FA, and so it has $m + 1$ rows, numbered 0 to m. The number of columns depends on the number of characters that may occur in the text; let's call this number q, so that the *next-state* table has $q(m + 1)$ entries. To fill in an entry *next-state*$[k, a]$, we do the following:

1. Form the string $P_k a$.
2. Set i to the smaller of $k + 1$ (the length of $P_k a$) and m (the length of P).
3. While P_i is not a suffix of $P_k a$, do the following:
   A. Set i to $i - 1$.

We don't know in advance how many times the loop of step 3 will run, but we know that it makes at most $m + 1$ iterations. We also don't know in advance how many characters of P_i and $P_k a$ must be checked in the test in step 3, but we know that it's always at most i, which is at most m. Since the loop iterates at most $m + 1$ times and each iteration checks at most m characters, it takes $O(m^2)$ time to fill in *next-state*$[k, a]$. Because the *next-state* table contains $q(m + 1)$ entries, the total time to fill it in is $O(m^3 q)$.

In practice, the time to fill in the *next-state* table isn't too bad. I coded up the string-matching algorithm in C++ on my 2.4-GHz Mac-Book Pro and compiled it with optimization level -O3. I gave it the pattern a man, a plan, a canal, panama with the 128-character ASCII character set as the alphabet. The program constructed a *next-state* table with 31 rows and 127 columns (I omitted the column for the null character) in approximately 1.35 milliseconds. With a shorter pattern, the program of course is faster: it took approximately 0.07 milliseconds to construct the table when the pattern was just panama.

Nevertheless, some applications perform string matching frequently, and in these applications the $O(m^3 q)$ time to build the *next-state* table could pose a problem. I won't go into the details, but there is a way to cut the time down to $\Theta(mq)$. In fact, we can do even better. The "KMP" algorithm (developed by Knuth, Morris, and Pratt) uses a finite automaton but avoids creating and filling in the *next-state* table altogether. Instead, it uses an array *move-to* of just m state numbers that allows the FA to emulate having a *next-state* table, and it takes just $\Theta(m)$ time to fill in the *move-to* array. Again, it's a bit too complicated to go into, but I ran the KMP algorithm on my MacBook Pro, and for the pattern a man, a plan, a canal, panama it took about one microsecond to construct the *move-to* array. For the shorter pattern panama, it took about 600 nanoseconds (0.0000006 seconds). Not bad! Like the FA-STRING-MATCHER procedure, the KMP algorithm takes $\Theta(n)$ time to match the pattern against the text, once it has constructed the *move-to* array.

Further reading

Chapter 15 of CLRS [CLRS09] covers dynamic programming in detail, including how to find a longest common subsequence. The algorithm in this chapter for transforming one string to another gives part of the solution to a problem in Chapter 15 of CLRS. (The problem in CLRS includes the two operations, interchanging adjacent characters and deleting a suffix of X, that I did not consider in this chapter. You didn't think I was going to upset my coauthors by giving away the entire solution, did you?)

String matching algorithms appear in Chapter 32 of CLRS. That chapter gives the algorithm based on finite automata and also a full treatment of the KMP algorithm. The first edition of *Introduction to Algorithms* [CLR90] included the Boyer-Moore algorithm, which is particularly efficient when the pattern is long and the number of characters in the alphabet is large.

8 Foundations of Cryptography

When you buy something over the Internet, you probably have to supply your credit-card number to a server on the seller's website or to a server on a third-party payment service's website. To get your credit-card number to a server, you send it over the Internet. The Internet is a public network, and anyone can discern the bits that go over it. Therefore, if your credit-card number were to go out over the Internet without being disguised somehow, then anyone could figure it out and start purchasing goods and services on your account.

Now, it's unlikely that someone is sitting there, just waiting for *you* to send something that looks like a credit-card number over the Internet. It's more likely that someone is waiting for *anyone* to do so, and maybe *you* will be the unfortunate victim. It would be much safer for you to disguise your credit-card number whenever you send it over the Internet. Indeed, you probably do. If you use a secure website—one whose URL begins with "https:" rather than the usual "http:"—then your browser disguises the information it sends by a process called *encryption*. (The https protocol also provides "authentication," so that you know you're connecting to the site you think you're connecting to.) In this chapter, we'll look at encryption, as well as the opposite process, *decryption*, where encrypted information is turned back into its original form. Together, the processes of encryption and decryption form the foundation of the field of cryptography.

Although I consider my credit-card number to be important information to safeguard, I also recognize that it's not all that important in the grand scheme of things. If someone steals my credit-card number, national security is not at risk. But if someone can eavesdrop on instructions from the State Department to a diplomat, or if someone can snoop on military information, national security could indeed be at risk. Therefore, not only do we need ways to encrypt and decrypt information, but these ways need to be highly difficult to defeat.

In this chapter, we'll examine some of the basic ideas underlying encryption and decryption. Modern cryptography goes far, far beyond what I'm presenting here. Don't try to develop a secure system based solely on the material in this chapter; you would need to understand modern cryptography in much greater detail to create a system that is secure in both theory and practice. For example, you would need to follow established standards, such as those published by the National Institute of Standards and Technology. As Ron Rivest (one of the inventors of the RSA cryptosystem, which we'll see later in this chapter) wrote to me, "In general crypto is like a martial arts contest, and to use it in practice you need to understand the latest adversarial approaches." But this chapter will give you a flavor of some algorithms that were motivated by how to encrypt and decrypt information.

In cryptography, we call the original information the ***plaintext*** and the encrypted version the ***ciphertext***. Encryption, therefore, converts plaintext to ciphertext, and decryption converts ciphertext back to its original plaintext. The information needed to convert is known as the cryptographic ***key***.

Simple substitution ciphers

In a ***simple substitution cipher***, you encrypt a text by just substituting one letter for another, and you decrypt an encrypted text by inverting the substitution. Julius Caesar would communicate with his generals by using a ***shift cipher***, in which the sender replaced each letter in a message by the letter that appears three places later in the alphabet, wrapping around at the end. In our 26-letter alphabet, for example, A would be replaced by D, and Y would be replaced by B (after Y comes Z, then A and B). In Caesar's shift cipher, if a general needed more troops, he could encrypt the plaintext *Send me a hundred more soldiers* as the ciphertext *Vhqg ph d kxqguhg pruh vroglhuv*. Upon receiving this ciphertext, Caesar would replace each letter by the letter occurring three places earlier in the alphabet, wrapping around at the front of the alphabet, to recover the original plaintext *Send me a hundred more soldiers*. (In Caesar's time, of course, the message would have been in Latin, using the Latin alphabet of the time.)

If you intercept a message and you know that it was encrypted by a shift cipher, it's ridiculously easy to decrypt, even if you don't know the shift amount (the key) in advance: just try all possible shifts until the decrypted ciphertext makes sense as plaintext. For a 26-character alphabet, you need to try only 25 shifts.

You can make the cipher a little more secure by converting each character to some other, unique, character, but not necessarily the one that appears a fixed number of places later in the alphabet. That is, you create a permutation of the characters and use that as your key. It's still a simple substitution cipher, but it's better than a shift cipher. If you have *n* characters in your character set, then an eavesdropper who intercepts a message would have to discern which of the *n*! (*n*-factorial) permutations you had used. The factorial function grows very quickly in *n*; in fact, it grows faster than an exponential function.

So why not just uniquely convert each character to some other character? If you've ever tried to solve the "cryptoquote" puzzle that appears in many newspapers, you know that you can use letter frequencies and letter combinations to narrow down the choices. Suppose that the plaintext *Send me a hundred more soldiers* converted to the ciphertext *Krcz sr h byczxrz sfxr kfjzgrxk*. In the ciphertext, the letter *r* appears the most often, and you could guess—correctly—that its corresponding plaintext character is *e*, the most commonly occurring letter in English text. Then you could see the two-letter word *sr* in the ciphertext and guess that the plaintext character corresponding to the ciphertext *s* must be one of *b*, *h*, *m*, or *w*, since the only two-letter words in English ending in *e* are *be*, *he*, *me*, and *we*. You could also determine that the plaintext *a* corresponds to the ciphertext *h*, because the only single-letter lowercase word in English is *a*.

Of course, if you're encrypting credit-card numbers, then you don't have to worry too much about letter frequencies or letter combinations. But the ten digits yield only 10! unique ways to convert one digit to another, or 3,628,800. To a computer, that's not very many, especially when compared with the 10^{16} possible credit-card numbers (16 decimal digits), and an eavesdropper could automate attempts to put through purchases on each of the 10! ways—possibly succeeding with credit-card numbers other than yours.

You might have noticed one other problem with using a simple substitution cipher: both the sender and receiver have to agree on the key. Moreover, if you're sending different messages to different parties, and you don't want each party to be able to decrypt messages intended for someone else, then you need to establish a separate key for each party.

Symmetric-key cryptography

When the sender and receiver use the same key, they are practicing *symmetric-key cryptography*. They must somehow agree in advance upon just what key they're using.

One-time pads

Assuming for now that you're fine with using symmetric-key cryptography, but that a simple substitution cipher is not sufficiently secure, another option is the one-time pad. One-time pads work on bits. As you might know, ***bit*** is an abbreviation for "binary digit," and a bit can take on only two values: 0 and 1. Digital computers store information in sequences of bits. Some bit sequences represent numbers, some represent characters (using either the standard ASCII or Unicode character sets), and some even represent instructions that the computer executes.

One-time pads apply the ***exclusive-or***, or ***XOR***, operation to bits. We use $\oplus$ to denote this operation:

$$0 \oplus 0 = 0,$$
$$0 \oplus 1 = 1,$$
$$1 \oplus 0 = 1,$$
$$1 \oplus 1 = 0.$$

The simplest way to think of the XOR operation is that if x is a bit, then $x \oplus 0 = x$ and $x \oplus 1$ gives the opposite of x. Furthermore, if x and y are bits, then $(x \oplus y) \oplus y = x$: XORing x with the same value twice gives x.

Suppose that I want to send you a one-bit message. I could send you either a 0 or a 1 as the ciphertext, and we would have to agree on whether I was sending you the bit value I wanted to send you or the opposite of that bit value. Looked at through the lens of the XOR operation, we would have to agree on whether I was XORing that bit with 0 or with 1. If you were to then XOR the ciphertext bit you received with the bit that I had XORed with—the key—you would recover the original plaintext.

Now suppose that I want to send you a two-bit message. I could leave both bits alone, I could flip both bits, I could flip the first bit but not the second, or I could flip the second bit but not the first. Again, we would have to agree on which bits I was flipping, if any. In terms of the XOR operation on two bits, we would have to agree on which of the two-bit sequences 00, 01, 10, or 11 was the key with which I was XORing the bits of the plaintext to form the ciphertext. And again, you could XOR the two-bit ciphertext with the same two-bit key that I had XORed the plaintext with to recover the original plaintext.

If the plaintext required b bits—perhaps it comprises ASCII or Unicode characters that total b bits—then I could generate a random sequence of b bits as the key, let you know the b bits of the key, and then

XOR, bit by bit, the plaintext with the key to form the ciphertext. Once you received the b-bit ciphertext, you could XOR it, bit by bit, with the key to recover the b-bit plaintext. This system is called a ***one-time pad***,[1] and the key is called the ***pad***.

As long as the bits of the key are randomly chosen—and we'll examine this issue later—it's well nigh impossible for an eavesdropper to decrypt the ciphertext by guessing the key. Even if the eavesdropper knows something about the plaintext—for example, that it's English—for any ciphertext and any *potential* plaintext, there exists a key converting the potential plaintext to the ciphertext,[2] and this key is the bitwise XOR of the potential plaintext and the ciphertext. (That's because if the potential plaintext is t, the ciphertext is c, and the key is k, then not only is $t \oplus k = c$, but also $t \oplus c = k$; the $\oplus$ operation applies bit-by-bit to t, k, and c, so that the ith bit of t XORed with the ith bit of k equals the ith bit of c.) And so encrypting with a one-time pad prevents the eavesdropper from gaining any additional information about the plaintext.

One-time pads give good security, but the keys require as many bits as the plaintext, these bits should be randomly chosen, and the keys need to be shared between the parties in advance. As the name implies, you should use a one-time pad just one time. If you use the same key k for plaintexts t_1 and t_2, then $(t_1 \oplus k) \oplus (t_2 \oplus k) = t_1 \oplus t_2$, which can reveal where the two plaintexts have the same bits.

---

[1] The name comes from the pre-computer realization of the idea, where each party had a pad of paper with a key written on each sheet, and the parties had identical key sequences. A key could be used one time and then its sheet torn off from the pad, exposing the next key. This paper-based system used a shift cipher, but on a letter-by-letter basis, where each corresponding letter of the key gives the shift amount, from 0 for *a* to 25 for *z*. For example, since *z* means to shift by 25, *m* means to shift by 12, and *n* means to shift by 13, the key *zmn* converts the plaintext *dog* to the ciphertext *cat*. Unlike the XOR-based system, however, shifting the letters of the ciphertext in the same direction with the same key does not yield back the plaintext; in this case, it would give *bmg*. Instead, you have to shift the ciphertext letters in the opposite direction.

[2] For the letter-by-letter scheme in the previous footnote, the key *zmn* converts the plaintext *dog* to the ciphertext *cat*, but we can arrive at this ciphertext with a different plaintext, *elk*, and a different key, *ypj*.

Block ciphers and chaining

When the plaintext is long, the pad in a one-time pad has to be equally long, which can be rather unwieldy. Instead, some symmetric-key systems combine two additional techniques: they use a shorter key, and they chop up the plaintext into several blocks, applying the key to each block in turn. That is, they consider the plaintext to be l blocks $t_1, t_2, t_3, \ldots, t_l$, and they encrypt these plaintext blocks into l blocks $c_1, c_2, c_3, \ldots, c_l$ of ciphertext. Such a system is known as a ***block cipher***.

In practice, block ciphers encrypt using a system quite a bit more complicated than the simple XORing of the one-time pad. One frequently used symmetric-key cryptosystem, AES (the Advanced Encryption Standard), incorporates a block cipher. I won't go into details of AES, other than to say that it uses elaborate methods to slice and dice a plaintext block to produce ciphertext. AES uses a key size of 128, 192, or 256 bits and a block size of 128 bits.

There's still a problem with block ciphers, however. If the same block appears twice in the plaintext, then the same encrypted block will appear twice in the ciphertext. One way to solve this problem uses the technique of ***cipher block chaining***. Suppose that you want to send me an encrypted message. You chop up the plaintext t into l blocks $t_1, t_2, t_3, \ldots, t_l$, and you create the l blocks $c_1, c_2, c_3, \ldots, c_l$ of ciphertext as follows. Let's say that you'll encrypt a block by applying some function E to it, and I'll decrypt a block of ciphertext by applying some function D. You create the first block of ciphertext, c_1, as you'd expect: $c_1 = E(t_1)$. But before encrypting the second block, you XOR it, bit by bit, with c_1, so that $c_2 = E(c_1 \oplus t_2)$. For the third block, you first XOR it with c_2: $c_3 = E(c_2 \oplus t_3)$. And so on, so that in general, you compute the ith block of ciphertext based on the $(i-1)$st block of ciphertext and the ith block of plaintext: $c_i = E(c_{i-1} \oplus t_i)$. This formula even works for computing c_1 from t_1 if you start with c_0 being all 0s (because $0 \oplus x$ gives x). To decrypt, I first compute $t_1 = D(c_1)$. From c_1 and c_2, I can compute t_2 by first computing $D(c_2)$, which equals $c_1 \oplus t_2$, and then XORing the result with c_1. In general, I decrypt c_i to determine t_i by computing $t_i = D(c_i) \oplus c_{i-1}$; as with encryption, this scheme works even for computing t_1 if I start with c_0 being all 0s.

We're not quite out of the woods. Even with cipher block chaining, if you send me the same message twice, you'll send the same sequence of ciphertext blocks each time. An eavesdropper would know that you're sending me the same message twice, which could be valuable informa-tion for the eavesdropper to have. One solution is to not start with c_0 being all 0s. Instead, you randomly generate c_0, you use that when en-crypting the first block of plaintext, and I use it when decrypting the first block of ciphertext; we call this randomly generated c_0 an *initialization vector*.

Agreeing on common information

In order for symmetric-key cryptography to work, both the sender and receiver need to agree on the key. In addition, if they're using a block cipher with cipher block chaining, they might also need to agree on the initialization vector. As you can imagine, it's rarely practical to agree on these values in advance. So how do the sender and receiver agree on the key and initialization vector? We will see later in this chapter (page 155) how a hybrid cryptosystem can transmit them securely.

Public-key cryptography

It's obvious that in order for the receiver of an encrypted message to be able to decrypt it, the sender and receiver must both know the key used to encrypt. Right?

Wrong.

In *public-key cryptography*, each party has two keys: a *public key* and a *secret key*. I'll describe public-key cryptography with two parties, you and me, and I'll denote my public key by P and my secret key by S. You have your own public and secret keys. Other parties who participate have their own public and secret keys.

Secret keys are secret, but public keys may be known to everyone. They could even appear in a centralized directory that lets everyone know everyone else's public key. Under the right conditions, you and I can use either of these keys to encrypt and decrypt. By the "right conditions," I mean that there exist functions that use the public and secret keys to either encrypt plaintext to ciphertext or decrypt ciphertext to plaintext. Let's denote the function that I use with my public key by F_P and the function that I use with my secret key by F_S.

The public and secret keys have a special relationship:

$$t = F_S(F_P(t)),$$

so that if you use my public key to encrypt plaintext into ciphertext and then I use my secret key to decrypt the ciphertext, I get back the original plaintext. Some other applications of public-key cryptography require that $t = F_P(F_S(t))$, so that if I encrypt plaintext with my secret key, anyone can decrypt the ciphertext.

Anyone should be able to compute my public-key function F_P efficiently, but only I should be able to compute my secret-key function F_S in any reasonable amount of time. The time required to successfully guess my F_S without knowing my secret key should be prohibitively large for anyone else. (Yes, I'm being vague here, but we'll soon see an actual implementation of public-key cryptography.) The same holds for everyone else's public and secret keys: the public-key function F_P is efficiently computable, but only the holder of the secret key can reasonably compute the secret-key function F_S.

Here's how you can send me a message using public-key cryptography:

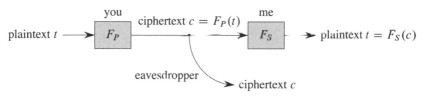

You start with the plaintext t. You find my public key P; maybe you get it directly from me, or maybe you find it in a directory. Once you have P, you encrypt the plaintext to produce the ciphertext $c = F_P(t)$, which you can do efficiently. You send me the ciphertext, so that any eavesdropper who intercepts what you send me sees only the ciphertext. I take the ciphertext c and decrypt it using my secret key, reproducing the plaintext $t = F_S(c)$. You, or anyone else, can encrypt to produce the ciphertext reasonably quickly, but only I can decrypt the ciphertext to reproduce the plaintext in any reasonable amount of time.

In practice, we need to make sure that the functions F_P and F_S work together correctly. We want F_P to produce a different ciphertext for each possible plaintext. Suppose instead that F_P gave the same result for two different plaintexts, t_1 and t_2; that is, $F_P(t_1) = F_P(t_2)$. Then, when I receive a ciphertext $F_P(t_1)$ and try to decrypt it by running it through F_S, I don't know whether I'll get back t_1 or t_2. On the other hand, it's OK — in fact, preferable — for encryption to incorporate an element of randomization, so that the same plaintext is encrypted into different ciphertexts each time it's run through F_P. (The RSA cryptosystem, which we're about to see, is much more secure when the plaintext is only a small portion of what is encrypted, the bulk of the encrypted information being random "padding.") Of course, the decryption function F_S would need to be designed to compensate, so that it could convert multiple ciphertexts into the same plaintext.[3]

A problem arises, however. The plaintext t could take on an arbitrary number of possible values—in fact, it could be arbitrarily long—and the number of ciphertext values that F_P could convert t to has to be at least as many as the number of values that t could take on. How can we construct the functions F_P and F_S under the additional constraints that F_P has to be easy to compute for everyone and F_S has to be easy only for me? It's hard, but it's doable if we can limit the number of possible plaintexts—that is, we use a block cipher.

The RSA cryptosystem

Public-key cryptography is a lovely concept, but it relies on being able to find functions F_P and F_S that work correctly together, F_P is easy for anyone to compute, and F_S is easy for only the holder of the secret key to compute. We call a scheme that fulfills these criteria a **public-key cryptosystem**, and the **RSA cryptosystem**, or just **RSA**,[4] is one such scheme.

RSA depends on several facets of number theory, many of which relate to **modular arithmetic**. In modular arithmetic, we pick a positive integer, let's say n, and whenever we get to n, we immediately wrap back around to 0. It's like regular arithmetic with integers, but we always divide by n and take the remainder. For example, if we're working modulo 5, then the only possible values are $0, 1, 2, 3, 4$, and $3 + 4 = 2$ since 7 divided by 5 gives a remainder of 2. Let's define an operator, mod, to compute remainders, so that we can say 7 mod 5 = 2. Mod-

---

[3]Baseball uses a similar system. Managers and coaches tell players what plays to put on using elaborate systems of gestures, called "signs." For example, touching the right shoulder might mean to execute a hit-and-run play and touching the left thigh might mean to bunt. A manager or coach goes through a long series of signs, but only some of the signs are meaningful; the rest are decoys. The giver and receiver of the signs have a system where they agree on which signs are meaningful, sometimes based on the ordering in the sequence of signs and sometimes based on an "indicator" sign. The manager or coach can give an arbitrarily long series of signs to indicate any particular play, where most of the signs in the series are meaningless.

[4]The name comes from its inventors, Ronald Rivest, Adi Shamir, and Leonard Adleman.

ular arithmetic is like clock arithmetic, but substituting 0 for 12 on the clock face. If you go to sleep at 11 and sleep for eight hours, you wake up at 7: $(11 + 8) \bmod 12 = 7$.

What's particularly nice about modular arithmetic is that we can take mod operations in the middle of expressions and not change the result:[5]

$$(a + b) \bmod n \quad = \quad ((a \bmod n) + (b \bmod n)) \bmod n \ ,$$
$$ab \bmod n \quad = \quad ((a \bmod n)(b \bmod n)) \bmod n \ ,$$
$$a^b \bmod n \quad = \quad (a \bmod n)^b \bmod n \ .$$

Furthermore, for any integer x, we have that $xn \bmod n$ is 0.

In addition, in order for RSA to fulfill the criteria for a public-key cryptosystem, two number-theoretic properties related to prime numbers must hold. As you might know, a ***prime number*** is an integer greater than 1 that has only two integer factors: 1 and itself. For example, 7 is prime, but 6 is not, being factorable as $2 \cdot 3$. The first property that RSA relies on is that if you have a number that is the product of two large secret prime numbers, then nobody else can determine these factors in any reasonable amount of time. Recall from back in Chapter 1 that someone could test all possible odd divisors up to the square root of the number, but if the number is large—hundreds or thousands of digits—then its square root has half as many digits, which could still be large. Although someone could *theoretically* find one of the factors, the resources required (time and/or computing power) would make finding a factor impractical.[6]

---

[5]As an example, to see that $ab \bmod n = ((a \bmod n)(b \bmod n)) \bmod n$, suppose that $a \bmod n = x$ and $b \bmod n = y$. Then there exist integers i and j such that $a = ni + x$ and $b = nj + y$, and so

$$ab \bmod n = (ni + x)(nj + y) \bmod n$$
$$= (n^2 ij + xnj + yni + xy) \bmod n$$
$$= ((n^2 ij \bmod n) + (xnj \bmod n) + (yni \bmod n) + (xy \bmod n)) \bmod n$$
$$= xy \bmod n$$
$$= ((a \bmod n)(b \bmod n)) \bmod n \ .$$

[6]For example, if the number has 1000 bits, then its square root has 500 bits and could be about as large as 2^{500}. Even if someone could test a trillion trillion possible divisors per second, the sun would have burned out long, long before reaching 2^{500}.

The second property is that, even though factoring a number that is the product of two large primes is hard, it's not hard to determine whether a large number is prime. You might think that it's impossible to determine that a number is not prime—that is, the number is ***composite***—without finding at least one nontrivial factor (a factor that is not 1 or the number itself). It is, in fact, possible to do so. One way is the AKS primality test,[7] the first algorithm to determine whether an n-bit number is prime in time $O(n^c)$ for some constant c. Although the AKS primality test is considered theoretically efficient, it is not yet practical for large numbers. Instead, we can use the Miller-Rabin primality test. The downside of the Miller-Rabin test is that it can make errors, declaring a number that is actually composite to be prime. (If it declares a number to be composite, however, then the number is definitely composite.) The good news is that the error rate is 1 in 2^s, where we can pick any positive value of s that we want. So, if we're willing to live with one error in, say, every 2^{50} tests, then we can determine with *almost* perfect certainty whether a number is prime. You might recall from Chapter 1 that 2^{50} is about a million billion, or about 1,000,000,000,000,000. And if you're still uncomfortable with 1 error in 2^{50} tests, with a little more effort, you can make it 1 error in 2^{60} tests; 2^{60} is about a thousand times more than 2^{50}. That's because the time to perform the Miller-Rabin test increases just linearly with the parameter s, and so increasing s by 10, from 50 to 60, increases the running time by only 20%, but decreases the error rate by a factor of 2^{10}, which equals 1024.

Here's how I would set myself up to use the RSA cryptosystem. After we see how RSA works, we'll have to address several details.

1. Pick at random two very large prime numbers, p and q, that are not equal to each other. How large is very large? At least 1024 bits each, or at least 309 decimal digits. Even larger is better.

2. Compute $n = pq$. That's a number with at least 2048 bits, or at least 618 decimal digits.

3. Compute $r = (p-1)(q-1)$, which is almost as large as n.

4. Select a small odd integer e that is ***relatively prime*** to r: the only common divisor of e and r should be 1. Any such small integer is fine here.

---

[7]Named after its inventors, Manindra Agrawal, Neeraj Kayal, and Nitin Saxena.

5. Compute d as the **multiplicative inverse** of e, modulo r. That is, $ed \bmod r$ should equal 1.

6. Declare my **RSA public key** to be the pair $P = (e, n)$.

7. Keep the pair $S = (d, n)$ as my **RSA secret key**, revealed to nobody.

8. Define the functions F_P and F_S by

$$F_P(x) = x^e \bmod n \,,$$
$$F_S(x) = x^d \bmod n \,.$$

These functions can operate on either a block of plaintext or a block of ciphertext, whose bits we interpret as representing large integers.

Let's take an example, but using small numbers so that we can understand what's going on.

1. Pick the prime numbers $p = 17$ and $q = 29$.

2. Compute $n = pq = 493$.

3. Compute $r = (p - 1)(q - 1) = 448$.

4. Select $e = 5$, which is relatively prime to 448.

5. Compute $d = 269$. To check: $ed = 5 \cdot 269 = 1345$, and so $ed \bmod r = 1345 \bmod 448 = (3 \cdot 448 + 1) \bmod 448 = 1$.

6. Declare my RSA public key to be $P = (5, 493)$.

7. Keep $S = (269, 493)$ as my RSA secret key.

8. As an example, let's compute $F_P(327)$:

$$
\begin{aligned}
F_P(327) &= 327^5 \bmod 493 \\
&= 3{,}738{,}856{,}210{,}407 \bmod 493 \\
&= 259 \,.
\end{aligned}
$$

If we compute $F_S(259) = 259^{269} \bmod 493$, we should get 327 back. We do, but you really don't want to see all the digits in the expression 259^{269}. You can search the Internet for an arbitrary-precision calculator, and test it out there. (I did.) Then again, because we're working with modular arithmetic, we don't need to compute the actual value of 259^{269}; we can express all intermediate results modulo 493, so if you wanted to, you could start with the product 1, and 269 times do the following: multiply what you have by 259 and take the product modulo 493. You'll get a result of 327. (I did, or rather, a computer program that I wrote did.)

Here are the details I have to address in order to set up and use RSA:

- How do I work with numbers with hundreds of digits?

- Although testing whether a number is prime isn't an obstacle, how do I know that I can find large prime numbers in a reasonable amount of time?

- How do I find e so that e and r are relatively prime?

- How do I compute d so that it's the multiplicative inverse of e, modulo r?

- If d is large, how do I compute x^d mod n in a reasonable amount of time?

- How do I know that the functions F_P and F_S are inverses of each other?

How to perform arithmetic with large numbers

Clearly, numbers as large as RSA requires are not going to fit in the registers found in most computers, which hold at most 64 bits. Fortunately, several software packages, and even some programming languages—Python, for example—allow you to work with integers that have no fixed limit on their size.

Furthermore, all arithmetic in RSA is modular arithmetic, which allows us to limit the sizes of the integers being calculated. For example, as we are calculating x^d mod n, we'll be calculating intermediate results that are x raised to various powers, but all modulo n, which means that all intermediate results calculated will be in the range from 0 to $n-1$. Moreover, if you fix the maximum sizes of p and q, then you have fixed the maximum size of n, which in turn means that it's feasible to implement RSA in specialized hardware.

How to find a large prime number

I can find a large prime number by repeatedly randomly generating a large odd number and using the Miller-Rabin primality test to determine whether it's prime, stopping once I find a prime number. This scheme presupposes that I'll find a large prime number before too long. What if prime numbers are extremely rare as numbers get large? I could spend a huge amount of time searching for a prime needle in a composite haystack.

I need not worry. The ***Prime Number Theorem*** tells us that, as m approaches infinity, the number of prime numbers less than or equal to m approaches $m/\ln m$, where $\ln m$ is the natural logarithm of m. If I just randomly select an integer m, there's about a 1 in $\ln m$ chance that it's prime. Probability theory tells us that, on average, I need to try only about $\ln m$ numbers near m before I find one that is prime. If I'm looking for prime numbers p and q with 1024 bits, then m is 2^{1024}, and $\ln m$ is approximately 710. A computer can quickly run the Miller-Rabin primality test on 710 numbers.

In practice, I could run a simpler primality test than the Miller-Rabin test. ***Fermat's Little Theorem*** states that if m is a prime number, then x^{m-1} mod m equals 1 for any number x in the range from 1 to $m-1$. The converse—if x^{m-1} mod m equals 1 for any number x in the range from 1 to $m-1$, then m is prime—is not necessarily true, but exceptions are very rare for large numbers. In fact, it's almost always sufficient to just try odd integers m and declare m to be prime if 2^{m-1} mod m equals 1. We'll see on page 153 how to compute 2^{m-1} mod m with only $\Theta(\lg m)$ multiplications.

How to find one number that is relatively prime to another

I need to find a small odd integer e that is relatively prime to r. Two numbers are relatively prime if their greatest common divisor is 1. I'll use an algorithm for computing the greatest common divisor of two integers that dates back to the ancient Greek mathematician Euclid. There's a theorem in number theory that says that if a and b are integers, not both zero, then their greatest common divisor g equals $ai + bj$ for some integers i and j. (Moreover, g is the smallest number that can be formed in this way, but this fact won't matter to us.) One of the coefficients i and j may be negative; for example, the greatest common divisor of 30 and 18 is 6, and $6 = 30i + 18j$ when $i = -1$ and $j = 2$.

On the next page appears Euclid's algorithm in a form that gives the greatest common divisor g of a and b, along with the coefficients i and j. These coefficients will come in handy a little later, when I need to find the multiplicative inverse of e, modulo r. If I have a candidate value for e, I call EUCLID(r, e). If the first element of the triple returned by the call is 1, then the candidate value for e is relatively prime to r. If the first element is any other number, then r and the candidate value for e have a divisor greater than 1 in common, and they are not relatively prime.

Procedure EUCLID(a, b)

Inputs: a and b: Two integers.

Output: A triple (g, i, j) such that g is the greatest common divisor of i and j and $g = ai + bj$.

1. If b equals 0, then return the triple $(a, 1, 0)$.
2. Otherwise (b is not 0), do the following:
   A. Recursively call EUCLID$(b, a \bmod b)$, and assign the returned result to the triple (g, i', j'). That is, set g to the first element of the triple returned, set i' to the second element of the triple returned, and set j' to the third element of the triple returned.
   B. Set i to j'.
   C. Set j to $i' - \lfloor a/b \rfloor j'$.
   D. Return the triple (g, i, j).

I won't go into why this procedure works,[8] nor will I analyze its running time, but I will just tell you that if I call EUCLID(r, e), then the number of recursive calls is $O(\lg e)$. Therefore, I can check quickly whether 1 is the greatest common divisor of r and a candidate value for e. (Remember that e is small.) If not, I can try a different candidate value for e, and so on, until I find one that is relatively prime to r. How many candidates do I expect to have to try? Not many. If I restrict my choices for e to odd prime numbers less than r (easily checked with the Miller-Rabin test or the test based on Fermat's Little Theorem), any choice is highly likely to be relatively prime to r. That's because, by the Prime Number Theorem, approximately $r / \ln r$ prime numbers are less than r, but another theorem shows that r cannot have more than $\lg r$ prime factors. Therefore, I am unlikely to hit a prime factor of r.

---

[8]The call EUCLID$(0, 0)$ returns the triple $(0, 1, 0)$, so that it considers 0 to be the greatest common divisor of 0 and 0. That might strike you as peculiar (I was going to say "odd," but this is the wrong context for that meaning of "odd"), but because r is positive, the parameter a in the first call to EUCLID will be positive, and in any recursive call, a must be positive. So it doesn't matter to us what EUCLID$(0, 0)$ returns.

How to compute multiplicative inverses in modular arithmetic

Once I have r and e, I need to compute d as the inverse of e, modulo r, so that ed mod r equals 1. We already know that the call EUCLID(r, e) returned a triple of the form $(1, i, j)$, that 1 is the greatest common divisor of e and r (because they're relatively prime), and that $1 = ri + ej$. I can just set d to j mod r.[9] That's because we're working modulo r, and so we can take both sides modulo r:

$$\begin{aligned}
1 \bmod r &= (ri + ej) \bmod r \\
&= ri \bmod r + ej \bmod r \\
&= 0 + ej \bmod r \\
&= ej \bmod r \\
&= (e \bmod r) \cdot (j \bmod r) \bmod r \\
&= e(j \bmod r) \bmod r \,.
\end{aligned}$$

(The last line follows because $e < r$, which implies that e mod $r = e$.) And so we have that $1 = e(j \bmod r) \bmod r$, which means that I can set d to the value j in the triple returned by the call EUCLID(r, e), taken modulo r. I use j mod r rather than just j in case j is not in the range from 0 to $r - 1$.

How to raise a number to an integer power quickly

Although e is small, d might be large, and I need to compute x^d mod n in order to compute the function F_S. Although I can work modulo n, which means that all values I work with will be in the range 0 to $n - 1$, I don't want to have to multiply numbers d times. Fortunately, I don't have to. I can multiply numbers just $\Theta(\lg d)$ times, using a technique known as **repeated squaring**. I can use this same technique for the primality test based on Fermat's Little Theorem.

Here's the idea. We know that d is nonnegative. Suppose first that d is even. Then x^d equals $(x^{d/2})^2$. Now suppose that d is odd. Then x^d equals $(x^{(d-1)/2})^2 \cdot x$. These observations give us a nice recursive way to compute x^d, where the base case occurs when d is 0: x^0 equals 1. The

---

[9]Recall that j could be negative. One way to think of j mod r when j is negative and r is positive is to start with j and keep adding r until the number you get is nonnegative. That number equals j mod r. For example, to determine -27 mod 10, you get the numbers -27, -17, -7, and 3. Once you get to 3, you stop and say that -27 mod 10 equals 3.

following procedure embodies this approach, performing all arithmetic modulo n:

Procedure MODULAR-EXPONENTIATION(x, d, n)

Inputs: x, d, n: three integers, with x and d nonnegative and n positive.

Output: Returns the value of x^d mod n.

1. If d equals 0, then return 1.
2. Otherwise (d is positive), if d is even, then recursively call MODULAR-EXPONENTIATION$(x, d/2, n)$, set z to the result of this recursive call, and return z^2 mod n.
3. Otherwise (d is positive and odd), recursively call MODULAR-EXPONENTIATION$(x, (d-1)/2, n)$, set z to the result of this recursive call, and return $(z^2 \cdot x)$ mod n.

The parameter d reduces by at least half in each recursive call. After at most $\lfloor \lg d \rfloor + 1$ calls, d goes down to 0 and the recursion ends. Therefore, this procedure multiplies numbers $\Theta(\lg d)$ times.

Showing that the functions F_P and F_S are inverses of each other

Warning: *Lots of number theory and modular arithmetic ahead. If you're content to accept without proof that the functions F_P and F_S are inverses of each other, skip the next five paragraphs and resume reading at "Hybrid cryptosystems."*

In order for RSA to be a public-key cryptosystem, the functions F_P and F_S must be inverses of each other. If we take a block t of plaintext, treat it as an integer less than n, and feed it into F_P, we get t^e mod n, and if we feed that result into F_S, we get $(t^e)^d$ mod n, which equals t^{ed} mod n. If we reverse the order, first F_S and then F_P, we get $(t^d)^e$ mod n, which again equals t^{ed} mod n. We need to show that for any plaintext block t, interpreted as an integer less than n, we have t^{ed} mod n equals t.

Here's an outline of our approach. Recall that $n = pq$. We will show that t^{ed} mod $p = t$ mod p and that t^{ed} mod $q = t$ mod q. Then, using another fact from number theory, we'll conclude that t^{ed} mod $pq = t$ mod pq—in other words, that t^{ed} mod $n = t$ mod n, which is just t, because t is less than n.

We need to use Fermat's Little Theorem again, and it helps explain why we set r to be the product $(p-1)(q-1)$. (Weren't you wondering where that came from?) Since p is prime, if $t \bmod p$ is nonzero, then $(t \bmod p)^{p-1} \bmod p = 1$.

Recall that we defined e and d so that they are multiplicative inverses, modulo r: $ed \bmod r = 1$. In other words, $ed = 1 + h(p-1)(q-1)$ for some integer h. If $t \bmod p$ is not 0, then we have the following:

$$
\begin{aligned}
t^{ed} \bmod p &= (t \bmod p)^{ed} \bmod p \\
&= (t \bmod p)^{1+h(p-1)(q-1)} \bmod p \\
&= \left((t \bmod p) \cdot ((t \bmod p)^{p-1} \bmod p)^{h(q-1)}\right) \bmod p \\
&= (t \bmod p) \cdot (1^{h(q-1)} \bmod p) \\
&= t \bmod p .
\end{aligned}
$$

Of course, if $t \bmod p$ is 0, then $t^{ed} \bmod p$ equals 0.

A similar argument shows that if $t \bmod q$ is not 0, then $t^{ed} \bmod q$ equals $t \bmod q$, and if $t \bmod q$ is 0, then $t^{ed} \bmod q$ equals 0.

We need one more fact from number theory to finish up: because p and q are relatively prime (each being prime), if both $x \bmod p = y \bmod p$ and $x \bmod q = y \bmod q$, then $x \bmod pq = y \bmod pq$. (This fact comes from the "Chinese Remainder Theorem.") Plugging in t^{ed} for x and t for y, and remembering that $n = pq$ and that t is less than n, gives us $t^{ed} \bmod n = t \bmod n = t$, which is exactly what we needed to show. Whew!

Hybrid cryptosystems

Although we can perform arithmetic with large numbers, in practice we do pay a price in speed. Encrypting and decrypting a long message, containing hundreds or thousands of blocks of plaintext, could cause a noticeable delay. RSA is often used in a hybrid system, part public-key and part symmetric-key.

Here is how you could send me an encrypted message in a hybrid system. We agree on which public-key system and symmetric-key system we're using; let's say RSA and AES. You select a key k for AES and encrypt it with my RSA public key, producing $F_P(k)$. Using the key k, you then encrypt the sequence of plaintext blocks with AES to produce a sequence of ciphertext blocks. You send me $F_P(k)$ and the sequence of ciphertext blocks. I decrypt $F_P(k)$ by computing $F_S(F_P(k))$, which gives me the AES key k, and then I use k to decrypt the ciphertext blocks with AES, thereby recovering the plaintext blocks. If we're using cipher block chaining and we need an initialization vector, then you can encrypt it either with RSA or AES.

Computing random numbers

As we've seen, some cryptosystems require us to generate random numbers—random positive integers, to be precise. Because we represent an integer by a sequence of bits, what we really need is a way to generate random bits, which we can then interpret as an integer.

Random bits can come only from random processes. How can a program running on a computer be a random process? In many cases, it cannot, because a computer program that is built from well defined, deterministic instructions will always produce the same result given the same data to start with. To support cryptographic software, some modern processors provide an instruction that generates random bits based on a random process, such as thermal noise within circuits. Designers of these processors face a threefold challenge: generate the bits at a fast enough rate for applications that demand random numbers, ensure that the bits generated meet basic statistical tests for randomness, and consume a reasonable amount of power while generating and testing the random bits.

Cryptographic programs usually obtain bits from a ***pseudorandom number generator***, or ***PRNG***. A PRNG is a deterministic program that produces a sequence of values, based on an initial value, or ***seed***, and a deterministic rule embodied in the program that says how to generate the next value in the sequence from the current value. If you start a PRNG with the same seed each time, you'll get out the same sequence of values each time. This repeatable behavior is good for debugging, but bad for cryptography. Recent standards for random number generators for cryptosystems require specific implementations of PRNGs.

If you're using a PRNG to generate bits that look random, you want to start with a different seed each time, and that seed should be random. In particular, the seed should be based on bits that are unbiased (not favoring either 0 or 1), independent (no matter what you know about the previous bits generated, anyone has only a 50% chance of correctly guessing the next bit), and unpredictable to an adversary who is trying to break your cryptosystem. If your processor has an instruction that generates random bits, that's a good way to create the PRNG's seed.

Further reading

Cryptography is but one component of security in computer systems. The book by Smith and Marchesini [SM08] covers computer security broadly, including cryptography and ways to attack cryptosystems.

To delve deeper into cryptography, I recommend the books by Katz and Lindell [KL08] and by Menezes, van Oorschot, and Vanstone [MvOV96]. Chapter 31 of CLRS [CLRS09] provides a quick background on the number theory leading up to cryptography, as well as descriptions of RSA and the Miller-Rabin primality test. Diffie and Hellman [DH76] proposed public-key cryptography in 1976, and the original paper describing RSA by Rivest, Shamir, and Adleman [RSA78] appeared two years later.

For more details on approved PRNGs, see Annex C to Federal Information Processing Standards Publication 140-2 [FIP11]. You can read about one hardware implementation of a random number generator based on thermal noise in the article by Taylor and Cox [TC11].

9 Data Compression

In the previous chapter, we examined how to transform information to shield it from an adversary. Protecting information is not the only reason to transform it, however. Sometimes you want to enhance it; for example, you might want to modify an image using a software tool such as Adobe Photoshop in order to remove red-eye or change skin tones. Sometimes you want to add redundancy so that if some bits are incorrect, the errors can be detected and corrected.

In this chapter, we investigate another way to transform information: compressing it. Before we get into some of the methods used to compress and decompress information, we should answer three questions:

1. *Why would we want to compress information?*

   We usually compress information for one of two reasons: to save time and/or to save space.

   Time: When transmitting information over a network, the fewer bits transmitted, the quicker the transmission. Therefore, the sender often compresses the data before sending, sends the compressed data, and then the receiver uncompresses the data that it receives.

   Space: When the amount of storage available could limit how much information you can store, you can store more information if it's compressed. For example, the MP3 and JPEG formats compress sound and images in such a way that most people discern little difference, if any, between the original and compressed materials.

2. *What is the quality of the compressed information?*

   Compression methods can be lossless or lossy. With *lossless compression*, when the compressed information is decompressed, it is identical to the original information. With *lossy compression*, the decompressed information differs from the original, but ideally in an insignificant manner. MP3 and JPEG compression are lossy, but the compression method used by the zip program is lossless.

   Generally speaking, when compressing text, we want lossless compression. Even a difference of one bit can be meaningful. The following sentences differ in just one bit in the ASCII codes of their letters:[1]

```
Don't forget the pop.
Don't forget the pot.
```

These sentences can be construed as requests to remember, respectively, the soft drinks (in the midwest of the U.S. at least) or the marijuana—one bit makes a big difference!

3. *Why is it possible to compress information?*

   This question is easy to answer for lossy compression: you just tolerate how the precision decreases. What about lossless compression? Digital information often contains redundant or useless bits. In ASCII, for example, each character occupies one eight-bit byte, and all commonly used characters (not including accented letters) have a 0 in the most significant (the leftmost) bit. That is, the character codes in ASCII range from 0 to 255, but all commonly used characters fall in the range 0 to 127. In many cases, therefore, one-eighth of the bits in ASCII text are useless, and so it would be easy to compress most ASCII text by 12.5%.

   For a more dramatic example of how to exploit redundancy in lossless compression, consider transmitting a black-and-white image, as fax machines do. Fax machines transmit an image as a series of *pels*:[2] black or white dots that together form the image. Many fax machines transmit the pels from top to bottom, row by row. When the image comprises mostly text, most of the image is white, and so each row likely contains many consecutive white pels. If a row contains part of a horizontal black line, it might have many consecutive black pels. Rather than indicate individually each pel in a run of like color, fax machines compress the information to indicate the length of each run and the color of the pels in the run. For example, in one fax standard, a run of 140 white pels is compressed into the eleven bits 10010001000.

---

[1] The ASCII codes for p and t, respectively, are 01110000 and 01110100.

[2] Pels are like pixels on a screen. Both "pel" and "pixel" are portmanteaus of "picture element."

Data compression is a well studied area, and so I can touch on only a small part of it here. I'll focus on lossless compression, but you can find a couple of good references that cover lossy compression in the "Further reading" section.

In this chapter, unlike the previous chapters, we won't focus on running times. I'll mention them when appropriate, but we're far more interested in the size of the compressed information than in how long compression and decompression take.

Huffman codes

Let's return to strings that represent DNA for the moment. Recall from Chapter 7 that biologists represent DNA as strings over the four characters A, C, G, and T. Suppose that we had a strand of DNA represented by n characters, where 45% of the characters are A, 5% are C, 5% are G, and 45% are T, but the characters appear in the strand in no particular order. If we used the ASCII character set to represent the strand, with each character occupying eight bits, it would take $8n$ bits to represent the entire strand. Of course, we can do better. Since we represent strands of DNA by drawing on only four characters, we really need only two bits to represent each character $(00, 01, 10, 11)$, and so we can reduce the space to $2n$ bits.

But we can do even better by taking advantage of the relative frequencies of the characters. Let's encode the characters with the following bit sequences: $A = 0$, $C = 100$, $G = 101$, $T = 11$. The more frequent characters get the shorter bit sequences. We would encode the 20-character strand **TAATTAGAAATTCTATTATA** by the 33-bit sequence 110011110101000111110011011110110. (We'll see in a moment why I chose this particular encoding and what properties it has.) Given the frequencies of the four characters, to encode the n-character strand, we need only $0.45 \cdot n \cdot 1 + 0.05 \cdot n \cdot 3 + 0.05 \cdot n \cdot 3 + 0.45 \cdot n \cdot 2 = 1.65n$ bits. (Notice that for the sample strand above, $33 = 1.65 \cdot 20$.) By taking advantage of the relative frequencies of the characters, we can do even better than $2n$ bits!

In the encoding we used, not only do the more frequent characters get the shorter bit sequences, but there's something else interesting about the encodings: no code is a prefix of any other code. The code for A is 0, and no other code starts with 0; the code for T is 11, and no other code starts with 11; and so on. We call such a code a ***prefix-free code***.[3]

The prime advantage of prefix-free codes emerges when we decompress. Because no code is a prefix of any other code, we can unambiguously match the compressed bits with their original characters as we decompress bits in order. In the compressed sequence 11001111010100011111001101111010110, for example, no character has the one-bit code 1 and only the code for T begins with 11, and so we know that the first character of the uncompressed text must be T. Stripping off the 11 leaves 001111010100011111001101111010110. Only the code for A begins with 0, and so the first character of what remains must be A. After stripping off the 0 and then the bits 011110, corresponding to the uncompressed characters ATTA, the remaining bits are 10100011111001101111010110. Because only the code for G begins with 101, the next uncompressed character must be G. And so on.

If we measure the efficiency of compression methods according to the average length of the compressed information, then of the prefix-free codes, Huffman codes[4] are the best. One disadvantage of traditional Huffman coding is that it requires the frequencies of all the characters to be known in advance, and therefore compression often requires two passes over the uncompressed text: one to determine character frequencies, and one to map each character to its code. We'll see a little later how to avoid the first pass, at the expense of extra computation.

Once we know the character frequencies, Huffman's method builds a binary tree. (If you've forgotten about binary trees, see page 98.) This tree tells us how to form the codes, and it's also convenient to have when decompressing. Here's what the tree looks like for our example of DNA encoding:

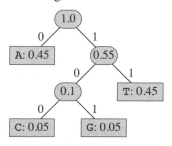

---

[3] In CLRS, we called them "prefix codes." I now prefer the more apt term "prefix-free."

[4] Named after their inventor, David Huffman.

The leaves of the tree, drawn as rectangles, represent the characters, with the frequency of each appearing next to the character. The non-leaves, or **internal nodes**, are drawn with rounded corners, with each internal node containing the sum of the frequencies in the leaves below it. We'll soon see why it pays to store frequencies in the internal nodes.

Next to each edge in the tree appears either a 0 or a 1. To determine the code for a character, follow the path from the root down to the character's leaf, and concatenate the bits along the path. For example, to determine the code for G, start at the root and first take the edge, labeled 1, to its right child; then the edge, labeled 0, to the left child (the internal node with frequency 0.1), and finally the edge, labeled 1, to the right child (the leaf containing G). Concatenating these bits gives the code 101 for G.

Although I always labeled edges to left children by 0 and edges to right children by 1, the labels themselves don't matter much. I could have just as easily labeled the edges this way:

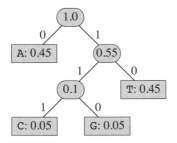

With this tree, the codes would be A = 0, C = 111, G = 110, T = 10. They would still be prefix-free, and the number of bits in each code would be the same as before. That's because the number of bits in the code for a character is the same as the **depth** of the character's leaf: the number of edges in the path from the root down to the leaf. Life is simpler, however, if we always label edges to left children by 0 and edges to right children by 1.

Once we know the frequencies of the characters, we build the binary tree from bottom to top. We start with each of the n leaf nodes, corresponding to the uncompressed characters, as its own individual tree, so that initially, each leaf is also a root. We then repeatedly find the two root nodes with the lowest frequencies, create a new root with these nodes as its children, and give this new root the sum of its children's frequencies. The process continues until all the leaves are under one root. As we progress, we label each edge to a left child by 0 and each edge to a right child by 1, though once we select the two roots with the lowest frequencies, it doesn't matter which we make the left child and which we make the right child of the new root.

For our DNA example, here's how the process unfolds. We start with four nodes, each a leaf representing one character:

The nodes for C and G have the lowest frequencies, so we create a new node, make these two nodes its children, and give it their combined frequencies:

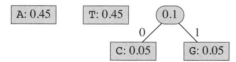

Of the three roots remaining, the one we just created has the lowest frequency, 0.1, and both of the other two have frequencies of 0.45. We can select either of the other two as the second root; we select the one for T, and we make it and the root with frequency 0.1 the children of a new node whose frequency is their sum, 0.55:

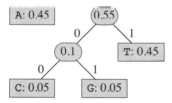

Only two roots remain. We create a new node and make them its children, and its frequency (which we don't need, since we're going to be done) is their sum, 1.0:

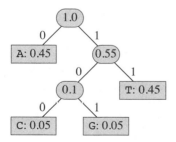

Now that all the leaves are under this new root, we are done building the binary tree.

To be a little more precise, let's define a procedure for building the binary tree. The procedure, BUILD-HUFFMAN-TREE, takes as input two n-element arrays, *char* and *freq*, where *char*[i] contains the ith uncompressed character and *freq*[i] gives the frequency of this character. It also takes the value of n. To find the two roots with the lowest frequencies, the procedure calls the INSERT and EXTRACT-MIN procedures for a priority queue (see pages 96–97).

Procedure BUILD-HUFFMAN-TREE(*char*, *freq*, n)

Inputs:
- *char*: an array of n uncompressed characters.
- *freq*: an array of n character frequencies.
- n: the sizes of the *char* and *freq* arrays.

Output: The root of the binary tree constructed for Huffman codes.

1. Let Q be an empty priority queue.
2. For $i = 1$ to n:

   A. Construct a new node z containing *char*[i] and whose frequency is *freq*[i].
   B. Call INSERT(Q, z).

3. For $i = 1$ to $n - 1$:

   A. Call EXTRACT-MIN(Q), and set x to the node extracted.
   B. Call EXTRACT-MIN(Q), and set y to the node extracted.
   C. Construct a new node z whose frequency is the sum of x's frequency and y's frequency.
   D. Set z's left child to be x and z's right child to be y.
   E. Call INSERT(Q, z).

4. Call EXTRACT-MIN(Q), and return the node extracted.

Once the procedure gets to step 4, only one node remains in the priority queue, and it's the root of the entire binary tree.

You can trace out how this procedure runs with the binary trees on the preceding page. The roots in the priority queue at the start of each iteration of the loop in step 3 appear at the top of each figure.

Let's quickly analyze the running time of BUILD-HUFFMAN-TREE. Assuming that the priority queue is implemented by a binary heap, each INSERT and EXTRACT-MIN operation takes $O(\lg n)$ time. The procedure calls each of these operations $2n - 1$ times, for a total of

$O(n \lg n)$ time. All other work takes a total of $\Theta(n)$ time, and so BUILD-HUFFMAN-TREE runs in $O(n \lg n)$ time.

I mentioned earlier that when decompressing it's convenient to have the binary tree that BUILD-HUFFMAN-TREE constructs. Starting at the root of the binary tree, travel down the tree according to the bits of the compressed information. Strip off each bit, going left if it's a 0 and right if it's a 1. Upon arriving at a leaf, stop, emit a character, and resume searching at the root. Returning to our DNA example, when decompressing the bit sequence 11001111010101000111110011011110110, we strip off the first 1 and go right from the root, then strip off another 1 and go right again, arriving at the leaf for T. We emit T and resume searching at the root. We strip off the next bit, 0, and go left from the root, arriving at the leaf for A, which we emit, and then we go back to the root. Decompression continues in this way until all the bits of the compressed information have been processed.

If we have the binary tree already built before decompressing, then it takes constant time to process each bit. So how does the decompression process gain access to the binary tree? One possibility is to include a representation of the binary tree with the compressed information. Another possibility is to include a decoding table with the processed information. Each entry of the table would include the character, the number of bits in its code, and the code itself. From this table, it's possible to build the binary tree in time linear in the total number of bits in all codes.

The BUILD-HUFFMAN-TREE procedure serves as an example of a **greedy algorithm**, wherein we make the decision that seems best at the moment. Because we want the least-frequently appearing characters far from the root of the binary tree, the greedy approach always selects the two roots with the lowest frequency to place under a new node, which can later become a child of some other node. Dijkstra's algorithm (pages 92–100) is another greedy algorithm, because it always relaxes edges from the vertex with the lowest *shortest* value of those remaining in its priority queue.

I implemented Huffman coding and ran it on an online version of *Moby Dick*. The original text took 1,193,826 bytes, but the compressed version took only 673,579 bytes, or 56.42% the size of the original, not including the encoding itself. Put another way, on average each character required only 4.51 bits to encode. Not too surprisingly, the most frequent character was a space (15.96%), followed by e (9.56%).

The least frequent characters, appearing only twice each, were $, &, [, and].

Adaptive Huffman codes

Practitioners often find that making two passes over the input, one to compute character frequencies and one to encode the characters, is too slow. Instead, the compression and decompression programs work adaptively, updating character frequencies and the binary tree as they compress or decompress in just one pass.

The compression program starts with an empty binary tree. Each character it reads from the input is either new or already in the binary tree. If the character is already in the binary tree, then the compression program emits the character's code according to the current binary tree, increases the character's frequency, and, if necessary, updates the binary tree to reflect the new frequency. If the character is not already in the binary tree, then the compression program emits the character *un*encoded (as is), adds it to the binary tree, and updates the binary tree accordingly.

The decompression program mirrors what the compression program does. It, too, maintains a binary tree as it processes the compressed information. When it sees bits for a character in the binary tree, it goes down the tree to determine which character the bits encode, emits this character, increases the character's frequency, and updates the binary tree. When it sees a character not yet in the tree, the decompression program emits the character, adds it to the binary tree, and updates the binary tree.

Something is amiss here, however. Bits are bits, whether they represent ASCII characters or bits in a Huffman code. How can the decompression program determine whether the bits it's looking at represent an encoded or an unencoded character? Does the bit sequence 101 represent the character currently encoded as 101, or is it the start of an eight-bit unencoded character? The answer is to precede each unencoded character with an *escape code*: a special code indicating that the next set of bits represents an unencoded character. If the original text contains k different characters, then only k escape codes will appear in the compressed information, each one preceding the first occurrence of a character. Escape codes will usually appear infrequently, and so we don't want to assign them short bit sequences at the expense of a more frequently occurring character. A good way to ensure that escape codes are not short is to include an escape code character in the binary tree, but nail down its frequency to be 0 always. As the binary tree is updated, the escape code's bit sequence will change in both the compression and decompression programs, but its leaf will always be the farthest from the root.

Fax machines

Earlier, I mentioned that fax machines compress information to indicate the colors and lengths of runs of identical pels in the rows of the image being transmitted. This scheme is known as ***run-length encoding***. Fax machines combine run-length encoding with Huffman codes. In the standard for fax machines that use regular phone lines, 104 codes indicate runs of different lengths of white pels, and 104 codes indicate runs of different lengths of black pels. The codes for white-pel runs are prefix-free, as are the codes for black-pel runs, though some of the codes for runs of white pels are prefixes of codes for runs of black pels and vice versa.

To determine which codes to use for which runs, a standards committee took a set of eight representative documents and counted how often each run appeared. They then constructed Huffman codes for these runs. The most frequent runs, and hence the shortest codes, were for runs of two, three, and four black pels, with codes 11, 10, and 011, respectively. Other common runs were one black pel (010), five and six black pels (0011 and 0010), two to seven white pels (all with four-bit codes), and other relatively short runs. One fairly frequent run consisted of 1664 white pels, representing an entire row of white pels. Other short codes went to runs of white pels whose lengths are powers of 2 or sums of two powers of 2 (such as 192, which equals $2^7 + 2^6$). Runs can be encoded by concatenating encodings of shorter runs. Earlier, I gave as an example the code for a run of 140 white pels, 10010001000. This code is actually the concatenation of the codes for a run of 128 white pels (10010) and a run of 12 white pels (001000).

In addition to compressing information only within each row of the image, some fax machines compress in both dimensions of the image. Runs of same-color pels can occur vertically as well as horizontally, and so instead of treating each row as if it were encountered in isolation, a row is encoded according to where it differs from the preceding row. For most rows, the difference from the previous row is just a few pels. This scheme entails the risk that errors propagate: an encoding or transmission error causes several consecutive rows to be incorrect. For this reason, fax machines that use this scheme and transmit over phone lines limit the number of consecutive rows that can use it, so that after a certain number of rows, they transmit a full row image using the Huffman coding scheme, rather than transmitting just the differences from the previous row.

LZW compression

Another approach to lossless compression, especially for text, takes advantage of information that recurs in the text, though not necessarily in consecutive locations. Consider, for example, a famous quotation from John F. Kennedy's inaugural address:

> Ask not what your country can do for you—ask what you can do for your country.

Except for the word *not*, each word in the quotation appears twice. Suppose we made a table of the words:

index	word
1	ask
2	not
3	what
4	your
5	country
6	can
7	do
8	for
9	you

Then we could encode the quotation (ignoring capitalization and punctuation) by

1 2 3 4 5 6 7 8 9 1 3 9 6 7 8 4 5

Because this quotation consists of few words, and a byte can hold integers ranging from 0 to 255, we can store each index in a single byte. Thus, we can store this quotation in only 17 bytes, one byte per word, plus whatever space we need to store the table. At one character per byte, the original quotation, without punctuation but with spaces between words, requires 77 bytes.

Of course, the space to store the table matters, for otherwise we could just number every possible word and compress a file by storing only indices of words. For some words, this scheme expands, rather than compresses. Why? Let's be ambitious and assume that there are fewer than 2^{32} words, so that we can store each index in a 32-bit word. We would represent each word by four bytes, and so this scheme loses for words that are three letters or shorter, which require only one byte per letter, uncompressed.

The real obstacle to numbering every possible word, however, is that real text includes "words" that are not words, or rather, not words in the English language. For an extreme example, consider the opening quatrain of Lewis Carroll's "Jabberwocky":

> 'Twas brillig, and the slithy toves
> Did gyre and gimble in the wabe:
> All mimsy were the borogoves,
> And the mome raths outgrabe.

Consider also computer programs, which often use variable names that are not English words. Add in capitalization, punctuation, and *really* long place names,[5] and you can see that if we try to compress text by numbering every possible word, we're going to have to use *a lot* of indices. Certainly more than 2^{32} and, because any combination of char acters *could* appear in text, in reality an unbounded amount.

All is not lost, however, for we can still take advantage of recurring information. We just have to not be so hung up on recurring *words*. Any recurring sequence of characters could help. Several compression schemes rely on recurring character sequences. The one we'll examine is known as *LZW*,[6] and it's the basis for many compression programs used in practice.

LZW makes a single pass over its input for compression and for de compression. In both, it builds a dictionary of character sequences that it has seen, and it uses indices into this dictionary to represent character sequences. Think of the dictionary as an array of character strings. We can index into this array, so that we can speak of its ith entry. Toward the beginning of the input, the sequences tend to be short, and repre senting the sequences by indices could result in expansion, rather than compression. But as LZW progresses through its input, the sequences

---

[5] Such as Llanfairpwllgwyngyllgogerychwyrndrobwllllantysiliogogogoch, a Welsh vil lage.

[6] As you probably guessed, the name honors its inventors. Terry Welch created LZW by modifying the LZ78 compression scheme, which was proposed by Abraham Lempel and Jacob Ziv.

in the dictionary become longer, and representing them by an index can save quite a bit of space. For example, I ran the text of *Moby Dick* through an LZW compressor, and it produced in its output an index representing the 10-character sequence ⊔from⊔the⊔ 20 times. (Each ⊔ indicates one space character.) It also output an index representing the eight-character sequence ⊔of⊔the⊔ 33 times.

Both the compressor and decompressor seed the dictionary with a one-character sequence for each character in the character set. Using the full ASCII character set, the dictionary starts with 256 single-character sequences; the ith entry in the dictionary holds the character whose ASCII code is i.

Before going into a general description of how the compressor works, let's look at a couple of situations it handles. The compressor builds up strings, inserting them into the dictionary and producing as output indices into the dictionary. Let's suppose that the compressor starts building a string with the character T, which it has read from its input. Because the dictionary has every single-character sequence, the compressor finds T in the dictionary. Whenever the compressor finds the string that it's building in the dictionary, it takes the next character from the input and appends that character to the string it's building up. So now let's suppose that the next input character is A. The compressor appends A to the string it's building, getting TA. Let's suppose that TA is also in the dictionary. The compressor then reads the next input character, let's say G. It appends G to the string it's building, resulting in TAG, and this time let's suppose that TAG is *not* in the dictionary. The compressor does three things: (1) it outputs the dictionary index of the string TA; (2) it inserts the string TAG into the dictionary; and (3) it starts building a new string, initially containing just the character (G) that caused the string TAG to not be in the dictionary.

Here is how the compressor works in general. It produces a sequence of indices into the dictionary. Concatenating the strings at these indices gives the original text. The compressor builds up strings in the dictionary one character at a time, so that whenever it inserts a string into the dictionary, that string is the same as some string already in the dictionary but extended by one character. The compressor manages a string s of consecutive characters from the input, maintaining the invariant that the dictionary always contains s in some entry. Even if s is a single character, it appears in the dictionary, because the dictionary is seeded with a single-character sequence for each character in the character set.

Initially, s is just the first character of the input. Upon reading a new character c, the compressor checks to see whether the string $s\,c$, formed by appending c to the end of s, is currently in the dictionary. If it is, then it appends c to the end of s and calls the result s; in other words, it sets s to $s\,c$. The compressor is building a longer string that it will eventually insert into the dictionary. Otherwise, s is in the dictionary but $s\,c$ is not. In this case, the compressor outputs the index of s in the dictionary, inserts $s\,c$ into the next available dictionary entry, and sets s to just the input character c. By inserting $s\,c$ into the dictionary, the compressor has added a string that extends s by one character, and by then setting s to c, it restarts the process of building a string to look up in the dictionary. Because c is a single-character string in the dictionary, the compressor maintains the invariant that s appears somewhere in the dictionary. Once the input is exhausted, the compressor outputs the index of whatever string s remains.

The procedure LZW-COMPRESSOR appears on the next page. Let's run through an example, compressing the text TATAGATCTTAATATA. (The sequence TAG that we saw on the previous page will come up.) The following table shows what happens upon each iteration of the loop in step 3. The values shown for the string s are at the start of the iteration.

Iteration	s	c	Output	New dictionary string
1	T	A	84 (T)	256: TA
2	A	T	65 (A)	257: AT
3	T	A		
4	TA	G	256 (TA)	258: TAG
5	G	A	71 (G)	259: GA
6	A	T		
7	AT	C	257 (AT)	260: ATC
8	C	T	67 (C)	261: CT
9	T	T	84 (T)	262: TT
10	T	A		
11	TA	A	256 (TA)	263: TAA
12	A	T		
13	AT	A	257 (AT)	264: ATA
14	A	T		
15	AT	A		
step 4	ATA		264 (ATA)	

After step 1, the dictionary has one-character strings for each of the 256 ASCII characters in entries 0 through 255. Step 2 sets the string s to hold just the first input character, T. In the first iteration of the main

Procedure LZW-COMPRESSOR (*text*)

Input: text: A sequence of characters in the ASCII character set.

Output: A sequence of indices into a dictionary.

1. For each character *c* in the ASCII character set:

   A. Insert *c* into the dictionary at the index equal to *c*'s numeric code in ASCII.

2. Set *s* to the first character from *text*.
3. While *text* is not exhausted, do the following:

   A. Take the next character from *text*, and assign it to *c*.

   B. If *s c* is in the dictionary, then set *s* to *s c*.

   C. Otherwise (*s c* is not yet in the dictionary), do the following:

       i. Output the index of *s* in the dictionary.

       ii. Insert *s c* into the next available entry in the dictionary.

       iii. Set *s* to the single-character string *c*.

4. Output the index of *s* in the dictionary.

loop of step 3, *c* is the next input character, A. The concatenation *s c* is the string TA, which is not yet in the dictionary, and so step 3C runs. Because the string *s* holds just T, and the ASCII code of T is 84, step 3Ci outputs the index 84. Step 3Cii inserts the string TA into the next available entry in the dictionary, which is at index 256, and step 3Ciii restarts building *s*, setting it to just the character A. In the second iteration of the loop of step 3, *c* is the next input character, T. The string *s c* = AT is not in the dictionary, and so step 3C outputs the index 65 (the ASCII code for A), inserts the string AT into entry 257, and sets *s* to hold T.

We see the benefit of the dictionary upon the next two iterations of the loop of step 3. In the third iteration, *c* becomes the next input character, A. Now the string *s c* = TA is present in the dictionary, and so the procedure doesn't output anything. Instead, step 3B appends the input character onto the end of *s*, setting *s* to TA. In the fourth iteration, *c* becomes G. The string *s c* = TAG is not in the dictionary, and so step 3Ci outputs the dictionary index 256 of *s*. One output number gives not one, but two characters: TA.

Not every dictionary index is output by the time LZW-COMPRESSOR finishes, and some indices may be output more than once. If you concatenate all the characters in parentheses in the output column, you get the original text, `TATAGATCTTAATATA`.

This example is a little too small to show the real benefit of LZW compression. The input occupies 16 bytes, and the output consists of 10 dictionary indices. Each index requires more than one byte. Even if we use two bytes per index in the output, it occupies 20 bytes. If each index occupies four bytes, a common size for integer values, the output takes 40 bytes.

Longer texts tend to yield better results. LZW compression reduces the size of *Moby Dick* from 1,193,826 bytes to 919,012 bytes. Here, the dictionary contains 230,007 entries, and so indices have to be at least four bytes.[7] The output consists of 229,753 indices, or 919,012 bytes. That's not as compressed as the result of Huffman coding (673,579 bytes), but we'll see some ideas a little later to improve the compression.

LZW compression helps only if we can decompress. Fortunately, the dictionary does not have be stored with the compressed information. (If it did, unless the original text contained a huge amount of recurring strings, the output of LZW compression plus the dictionary would constitute an expansion, not a compression.) As mentioned earlier, LZW decompression rebuilds the dictionary directly from the compressed information.

Here is how LZW decompression works. Like the compressor, the decompressor seeds the dictionary with the 256 single-character sequences corresponding to the ASCII character set. It reads a sequence of indices into the dictionary as its input, and it mirrors what the compressor did to build the dictionary. Whenever it produces output, it's from a string that it has added to the dictionary.

Most of the time, the next dictionary index in the input is for an entry already in the dictionary (we'll soon see what happens the rest of the time), and so the LZW decompressor finds the string at that index in the dictionary and outputs it. But how can it build the dictionary? Let's think for a moment about how the compressor operates. When it outputs an index within step 3C, it has found that, although the string *s* is in

---

[7]I'm assuming that we represent integers using the standard computer representations of integers, which occupy one, two, four, or eight bytes. In theory, we could represent indices up to 230,007 using just three bytes, so that the output would take 689,259 bytes.

the dictionary, the string $s\,c$ is not. It outputs the index of s in the dictionary, inserts $s\,c$ into the dictionary, and starts building a new string to store, starting with c. The decompressor has to match this behavior. For each index it takes from its input, it outputs the string s at that index in the dictionary. But it also knows that at the time the compressor output the index for s, the compressor did not have the string $s\,c$ in the dictionary, where c is the character immediately following s. The decompressor knows that the compressor inserted the string $s\,c$ into the dictionary, so that's what the decompressor needs to do—eventually. It cannot insert $s\,c$ yet, because it hasn't seen the character c. That's coming as the first character of the next string that the decompressor will output. But the decompressor doesn't have that next string just yet. Therefore, the decompressor needs to keep track of two consecutive strings that it outputs. If the decompressor outputs strings X and Y, in that order, then it concatenates the first character of Y onto X and then inserts the resulting string into the dictionary.

Let's look at an example, referring to the table on page 171, which shows how the compressor operates on TATAGATCTTAATATA. In iteration 11, the compressor outputs the index 256 for the string TA, and it inserts the string TAA into the dictionary. That's because, at that time, the compressor already had $s =$ TA in the dictionary but not $s\,c =$ TAA. That last A begins the next string output by the compressor, AT (index 257), in iteration 13. Therefore, when the decompressor sees indices 256 and 257, it should output TA, and it also should remember this string so that when it outputs AT, it can concatenate the A from AT with TA and insert the resulting string, TAA, into the dictionary.

On rare occasions, the next dictionary index in the decompressor's input is for an entry not yet in the dictionary. This situation arises so infrequently that when decompressing *Moby Dick*, it occurred for only 15 of the 229,753 indices. It happens when the index output by the compressor is for the string most recently inserted into the dictionary. This situation occurs only when the string at this index starts and ends with the same character. Why? Recall that the compressor outputs the index for a string s only when it finds s in the dictionary but $s\,c$ is not, and then it inserts $s\,c$ into the dictionary, say at index i, and begins a new string s starting with c. If the next index output by the compressor is going to be i, then the string at index i in the dictionary must start with c, but we just saw that this string is $s\,c$. So if the next dictionary index in the decompressor's input is for an entry not yet in the dictionary, the decompressor can output the string it most recently inserted into the dictionary, concatenated with the first character of this string, and insert this new string into the dictionary.

Because these situations are so rare, an example is a bit contrived. The string TATATAT causes it to occur. The compressor does the following: outputs index 84 (T) and inserts TA at index 256; outputs index 65 (A) and inserts AT at index 257; outputs index 256 (TA) and inserts TAT at index 258; and finally outputs index 258 (TAT — the string just inserted). The decompressor, upon reading in index 258, takes the string it had most recently output, TA, concatenates the first character of this string, T, outputs the resulting string TAT, and inserts this string into the dictionary.

Although this rare situation occurs only when the string starts and ends with the same character, this situation does not occur every time the string starts and ends with the same character. For example, when compressing *Moby Dick*, the string whose index was output had the same starting and ending character 11,376 times (a shade under 5% of the time) without being the string most recently inserted into the dictionary.

The procedure LZW-DECOMPRESSOR, on the next page, makes all of these actions precise. The following table shows what happens in each iteration of the loop in step 4 when given as input the indices in the output column in the table on page 171. The strings indexed in the dictionary by *previous* and *current* are output in consecutive iterations, and the values shown for *previous* and *current* in each iteration are after step 4B.

Iteration	*previous*	*current*	Output (*s*)	New dictionary string
Steps 2, 3		84	T	
1	84	65	A	256: TA
2	65	256	TA	257: AT
3	256	71	G	258: TAG
4	71	257	AT	259: GA
5	257	67	C	260: ATC
6	67	84	T	261: CT
7	84	256	TA	262: TT
8	256	257	AT	263: TAA
9	257	264	ATA	264: ATA

Except for the last iteration, the input index is already in the dictionary, so that step 4D runs only in the last iteration. Notice that the dictio-

Procedure LZW-DECOMPRESSOR(*indices*)

Input: indices: a sequence of indices into a dictionary, created by LZW-COMPRESSOR.

Output: The text that LZW-COMPRESSOR took as input.

1. For each character *c* in the ASCII character set:

   A. Insert *c* into the dictionary at the index equal to *c*'s numeric code in ASCII.

2. Set *current* to the first index in *indices*.
3. Output the string in the dictionary at index *current*.
4. While *indices* is not exhausted, do the following:

   A. Set *previous* to *current*.
   B. Take the next number from *indices* and assign it to *current*.
   C. If the dictionary contains an entry indexed by *current*, then do the following:

      i. Set *s* to be the string in the dictionary entry indexed by *current*.
      ii. Output the string *s*.
      iii. Insert, into the next available entry in the dictionary, the string at the dictionary entry indexed by *previous*, concatenated with the first character of *s*.

   D. Otherwise (the dictionary does not yet contain an entry indexed by *current*), do the following:

      i. Set *s* to be the string at the dictionary entry indexed by *previous*, concatenated with the first character of this dictionary entry.
      ii. Output the string *s*.
      iii. Insert, into the next available entry in the dictionary, the string *s*.

nary built by LZW-DECOMPRESSOR matches the one built by LZW-COMPRESSOR.

I haven't addressed how to look up information in the dictionary in the LZW-COMPRESSOR and LZW-DECOMPRESSOR procedures. The latter is easy: just keep track of the last dictionary index used, and if the index in *current* is less than or equal to the last-used index, then the string is in the dictionary. The LZW-COMPRESSOR procedure has a more difficult task: given a string, determine whether it's in the dictionary and, if it is, at what index. Of course, we could just perform a linear search on the dictionary, but if the dictionary contains n items, each linear search takes $O(n)$ time. We can do better by using either one of a couple of data structures. I won't go into the details here, however. One is called a *trie*, and it's like the binary tree we built for Huffman coding, except that each node can have many children, not just two, and each edge is labeled with an ASCII character. The other data structure is a *hash table*, and it provides a simple way to find strings in the directory that is fast on average.

LZW improvements

As I mentioned, I was none too impressed with how well the LZW method compressed the text of *Moby Dick*. Part of the problem stems from the large dictionary. With 230,007 entries, each index requires at least four bytes, and so with an output of 229,753 indices, the compressed version requires four times that, or 919,012 bytes. Then again, we can observe a couple of properties of the indices that the LZW compressor produces. First, many of them are low numbers, meaning that they have many leading zeros in their 32-bit representations. Second, some of the indices are going to occur much more frequently than others.

When both of these properties hold, Huffman coding is likely to yield good results. I modified the Huffman coding program to work with four-byte integers rather than characters, and I ran it with the output of the LZW compressor on *Moby Dick*. The resulting file occupies only 460,971 bytes, or 38.61% of the original size (1,193,826 bytes), which beats Huffman coding alone. Note, however, that I am not including the Huffman encoding's size in this figure. And just as compression entailed two steps—compress the text with LZW and then compress the resulting indices with Huffman coding—decompression would be a two-step process: first decompress with Huffman coding, then decompress with LZW.

Other approaches to LZW compression focus on reducing the number of bits necessary to hold the indices that the compressor outputs. Because many of the indices are small numbers, one approach is to use fewer bits for smaller numbers, but reserve, say, the first two bits to indicate how many bits the number requires. Here's one scheme:

- If the first two bits are 00, then the index is in the range 0 to 63 ($2^6 - 1$), requiring another six bits, and hence one byte in all.

- If the first two bits are 01, then the index is in the range 64 (2^6) to 16,383 ($2^{14} - 1$), requiring another 14 bits, and hence two bytes in all.

- If the first two bits are 10, then the index is in the range 16,384 (2^{14}) to 4,194,303 ($2^{22} - 1$), requiring another 22 bits, and hence three bytes in all.

- Finally, if the first two bits are 11, then the index is in the range 4,194,304 (2^{22}) to 1,073,741,823 ($2^{30} - 1$), requiring another 30 bits, and hence four bytes in all.

In two other approaches, the indices output by the compressor are all the same size, because the compressor limits the size of the dictionary. In one approach, once the dictionary reaches a maximum size, no other entries are ever inserted. In another approach, once the dictionary reaches a maximum size, it is cleared out (except for the first 256 entries), and the process of filling the dictionary restarts from the point in the text where the dictionary filled. In all of these approaches, the decompressor must mirror the compressor's action.

Further reading

Salomon's book [Sal08] is particularly clear and concise, yet it covers a wide range of compression techniques. The book by Storer [Sto88], published 20 years before Salomon's book, is a classic text in the field. Section 16.3 of CLRS [CLRS09] delves into Huffman codes in some detail, though it does not prove that they're the best possible prefix-free codes.

10 Hard? Problems

When I buy material products over the Internet, the seller has to get them delivered to my home. Most of the time, the seller uses a package-delivery company. I won't say which package-delivery company is most often used for the products I purchase, other than to say that brown trucks have been known to stop in front of my driveway every now and then.

Brown trucks

The package-delivery company operates over 91,000 of these brown trucks in the U.S., as well as many others worldwide. At least five days per week, each truck starts and ends at a specific depot and drops off parcels at numerous residential and commercial locations. The package-delivery company has a keen interest in minimizing the cost incurred by each truck as it makes many stops each day. For example, one online source I consulted claimed that once the company mapped out routes for its drivers to reduce the number of left turns, it reduced the total distance traveled by its vehicles by 464,000 miles in an 18-month period, saving over 51,000 gallons of fuel, with the added benefit of decreasing carbon dioxide emissions by 506 metric tons.

How can the company minimize the cost of sending out each truck each day? Suppose that a given truck must deliver parcels to n locations on a particular day. Adding in the depot, there are $n + 1$ locations that the truck must visit. For each of these $n + 1$ locations, the company can calculate the costs of sending the truck from there to each of the other n locations, so that the company has an $(n+1) \times (n+1)$ table of costs from location to location, where the entries on the diagonal are meaningless, since the ith row and the ith column correspond to the same location. The company wants to determine the route that starts and ends at the depot and visits all the other n locations exactly once, such that the total cost of the entire route is as low as possible.

It is possible to write a computer program that will solve this problem. After all, if we consider a particular route and we know the order of stops on the route, then it's just a matter of looking up in the table the costs of going from location to location and adding them up. Then we just have to enumerate all the possible routes and keep track of which one has the lowest total cost. The number of possible routes is finite, and so the program will terminate at some point and give the answer. That program doesn't seem so hard to write, does it?

Indeed, the program isn't hard to write.

It's hard to run.

The hitch is that the number of possible routes that visit n locations is enormous: $n!$ (n-factorial). Why? The truck starts at the depot. From there, any of the other n locations can be the first stop. From the first stop, any of the remaining $n - 1$ locations can be the second stop, and so there are $n \cdot (n - 1)$ possible combinations for the first two stops, in order. Once we settle on the first two stops, any of $n - 2$ locations could be the third stop, giving $n \cdot (n - 1) \cdot (n - 2)$ possible orders for the first three stops. Extending this reasoning to the n delivery locations, the number of possible orders is $n \cdot (n - 1) \cdot (n - 2) \cdots 3 \cdot 2 \cdot 1$, or $n!$.

Recall that $n!$ grows faster than an exponential function; it's super-exponential. In Chapter 8, I pointed out that 10! equals 3,628,800. To a computer, that's not such a big number. But the brown trucks drop off parcels at many more than just 10 locations per day. Suppose that a truck delivers to 20 addresses per day. (In the U.S., the company averages about 170 packages per truck, so even allowing for multiple packages to be delivered to a single location, 20 stops per day doesn't seem like an overestimate.) With 20 stops, a computer program would have to enumerate 20! possible orders, and 20! equals 2,432,902,008,176,640,000. If the company's computers could enumerate and evaluate one trillion orders per second, it would require over 28 days to try them all. And that's for just one day's worth of deliveries for one of over 91,000 trucks.

With this approach, if the company were to acquire and operate the computing power needed to find the lowest-cost routes for all trucks each day, the computing cost would easily wipe out the gains from the more efficient routes. No, this idea of enumerating all possible routes and keeping track of the best, although mathematically sound, is simply not practical. Is there a better way to find the lowest-cost route for each truck?

Nobody knows. (Or if somebody does know, he or she isn't telling.) Nobody has found a better way, yet nobody has proven that a better way cannot exist. How frustrating is that?

It's more frustrating than you might imagine. The problem of finding the lowest-cost routes for brown trucks is better known as the ***traveling-salesman problem***, so called because in its original formulation a traveling salesman[1] has to visit n cities, starting and ending at the same city, and visit all the cities with the shortest possible tour. No algorithm that runs in time $O(n^c)$, for any constant c, has ever been found for the traveling-salesman problem. We don't know of an algorithm that, given the intercity distances among n cities, finds the best possible order to visit the n cities in $O(n^{100})$ time, $O(n^{1000})$ time, or even $O(n^{1,000,000})$ time.

It gets worse. Many problems—*thousands* of them—share this characteristic: for an input of size n, we know of no algorithm that runs in time $O(n^c)$ for any constant c, yet nobody has proven that no such algorithm could exist. These problems come from a wide variety of domains—logic, graphs, arithmetic, and scheduling among them.

To take the frustration to a whole new level, here's the most amazing fact: *if there were an algorithm that ran in $O(n^c)$ time for* any *of these problems, where c is a constant, then there would be an algorithm that ran in $O(n^c)$ time for* all *of these problems*. We call these problems ***NP-complete***. An algorithm that runs in time $O(n^c)$ on an input of size n, where c is a constant, is a ***polynomial-time algorithm***, so called because n^c with some coefficient would be the most significant term in the running time. We know of no polynomial-time algorithm for any NP-complete problem, but nobody has proven that it's impossible to solve some NP-complete problem in polynomial time.

And there's even more frustration: many NP-complete problems are almost the same as problems that we know how to solve in polynomial time. Just a small tweak separates them. For example, recall from Chapter 6 that the Bellman-Ford algorithm finds shortest paths from a single source in a directed graph, even if the graph has negative-weight edges, in $\Theta(nm)$ time, where the graph has n vertices and m edges. If the graph is given as adjacency lists, then the input size is $\Theta(n + m)$. Let's assume that $m \geq n$; then the input size is $\Theta(m)$ and $nm \leq m^2$, and so the running time of the Bellman-Ford algorithm is polynomial in the input size. (You can get the same result if $n > m$.) So finding *shortest*

---

[1] Sorry about the gendered language. The name is historical, and if the problem were first being cast today, I hope that it would be known as the "traveling-salesperson problem."

paths is easy. You might be surprised to learn, however, that finding a
longest acyclic path (that is, a longest path without cycles) between two
vertices is NP-complete. In fact, merely determining whether a graph
contains a path without cycles with at least a given number of edges is
NP-complete.

As another example of related problems, where one is easy and one
is NP-complete, consider Euler tours and hamiltonian cycles. Both of
these problems have to do with finding paths in a connected, undirected
graph. In an ***undirected graph***, edges have no direction, so that (u, v)
and (v, u) are the same edge. We say that edge (u, v) is ***incident*** on
vertices u and v. A ***connected graph*** has a path between every pair of
vertices. An ***Euler tour***[2] starts and ends at the same vertex and visits
each edge exactly once, though it may visit each vertex more than once.
A ***hamiltonian cycle***[3] starts and ends at the same vertex and visits each
vertex exactly once (except, of course, for the vertex at which it starts
and ends). If we ask whether a connected, undirected graph has an
Euler tour, the algorithm is remarkably easy: determine the ***degree*** of
each vertex, that is, how many edges are incident on it. The graph has
an Euler tour if and only if the degree of every vertex is even. But if
we ask whether a connected, undirected graph has a hamiltonian cycle,
that's NP-complete. Notice that the question is not "what is the order of
vertices on a hamiltonian cycle in this graph?" but just the more basic
"yes or no: is it possible to construct a hamiltonian cycle on this graph?"

NP-complete problems come up surprisingly often, which is why
I'm including material on them in this book. If you are trying to find
a polynomial-time algorithm for a problem that turns out to be NP-
complete, you are likely to be in for a big helping of disappointment.
(But see the section on perspective, pages 208–211.) The concept of
NP-complete problems has been around since the early 1970s, and people were trying to solve problems that turned out to be NP-complete
(such as the traveling-salesman problem) well before then. To date, we

---

[2] So named because the mathematician Leonhard Euler proved in 1736 that it was not
possible to tour the city of Königsberg, Prussia, by crossing every one of its seven
bridges exactly once and ending up at the starting point.

[3] The name honors W. R. Hamilton, who in 1856 described a mathematical game on a
graph known as the dodecahedron, in which one player sticks five pins in any five consecutive vertices and the other player must complete the path to form a cycle containing
all the vertices.

don't know whether a polynomial-time algorithm exists for any NP-complete problem, nor do we know that no such algorithm can exist. Many brilliant computer scientists have spent years on this question without resolving it. I'm not saying that *you* cannot find a polynomial-time algorithm for an NP-complete problem, but you would be facing long odds if you were to try.

The classes P and NP and NP-completeness

In the previous chapters, I was concerned about differences in running times such as $O(n^2)$ vs. $O(n \lg n)$. In this chapter, however, we'll be happy if an algorithm runs in polynomial time, so that differences of $O(n^2)$ vs. $O(n \lg n)$ are insignificant. Computer scientists generally regard problems solvable by polynomial-time algorithms as "tractable," meaning "easy to deal with." If a polynomial-time algorithm exists for a problem, then we say that this problem is in the *class* **P**.

At this point, you might be wondering how we could possibly consider a problem that requires $\Theta(n^{100})$ time as tractable. For an input of size $n = 10$, isn't 10^{100} a dauntingly large number? Yes, it is; in fact, the quantity 10^{100} is a googol (the origin of the name "Google"). Fortunately, we don't see algorithms that take $O(n^{100})$ time. The problems in P that we encounter in practice require much less time. I've rarely seen polynomial-time algorithms that take worse than, say, $O(n^5)$ time. Moreover, once someone finds the first polynomial-time algorithm for a problem, others often follow with even more efficient algorithms. So if someone were to devise the first polynomial-time algorithm for a problem but it ran in time $\Theta(n^{100})$, there would be a good chance that others would follow suit with faster algorithms.

Now suppose that you're given a proposed solution to a problem, and you want to verify that the solution is correct. For example, in the hamiltonian-cycle problem, a proposed solution would be a sequence of vertices. In order to verify that this solution is correct, you'd need to check that every vertex appears in the sequence exactly once, except that the first and last vertices should be the same, and if the sequence is $\langle v_1, v_2, v_3, \ldots, v_n, v_1 \rangle$ then the graph must contain edges $(v_1, v_2), (v_2, v_3), (v_3, v_4), \ldots, (v_{n-1}, v_n)$ and back around to (v_n, v_1). You could easily verify that this solution is correct in polynomial time. If it is possible to verify a proposed solution to a problem in time polynomial in the size of the input to the problem, then we say that this problem is in the *class* **NP**.[4] We call the proposed solution a *certificate*, and in order for the problem to be in NP, the time to verify the certificate needs to be polynomial in the size of the input to the problem and the size of the certificate.

If you can solve a problem in polynomial time, then you can certainly verify a certificate for that problem in polynomial time. In other words, every problem in P is automatically in NP. The reverse—is every problem in NP also in P?—is the question that has perplexed computer scientists for all these years. We often call it the "P = NP? problem."

The NP-complete problems are the "hardest" in NP. Informally, a problem is *NP-complete* if it satisfies two conditions: (1) it's in NP and (2) if a polynomial-time algorithm exists for the problem, then there is a way to convert *every* problem in NP into this problem in such a way as to solve them all in polynomial time. If a polynomial-time algorithm exists for *any* NP-complete problem—that is, if any NP-complete problem is in P—then P = NP. Because NP-complete problems are the hardest in NP, if it turns out that any problem in NP is not polynomial-time solvable, then none of the NP-complete problems are. A problem is *NP-hard* if it satisfies the second condition for NP-completeness but may or may not be in NP.

Here's a handy list of the pertinent definitions:

- **P**: problems solvable in polynomial time, i.e., we can solve the problem in time polynomial in the size of the input to the problem.

- *Certificate*: a proposed solution to a problem.

- **NP**: problems verifiable in polynomial time, i.e., given a certificate, we can verify that the certificate is a solution the problem in time polynomial in the size of the input to the problem and the size of the certificate.

- *NP-hard*: a problem such that if there is a polynomial-time algorithm to solve this problem, then we can convert every problem in NP into this problem in such a way to solve every problem in NP in polynomial time.

- *NP-complete*: a problem that is NP-hard and also in NP.

---

[4]You probably surmised that the name P comes from "polynomial time." If you're wondering where the name NP comes from, it's from "nondeterministic polynomial time." It's an equivalent, but not quite as intuitive, way of viewing this class of problems.

Decision problems and reductions

When we talk about the classes P and NP, or about the concept of NP-completeness, we restrict ourselves to *decision problems*: their output is a single bit, indicating "yes" or "no." I couched the Euler-tour and hamiltonian-cycle problems in this way: Does the graph have an Euler tour? Does it have a hamiltonian cycle?

Some problems, however, are optimization problems, where we want to find the best possible solutions, rather than decision problems. Fortunately, we can often bridge part of this gap by recasting an optimization problem as a decision problem. For example, let's consider the shortest-path problem. There, we used the Bellman-Ford algorithm to find shortest paths. How can we pose the shortest-path problem as a yes/no problem? We can ask "Does the graph contain a path between two specific vertices whose path weight is at most a given value k?" We're not asking for the vertices or edges on the path, but just whether such a path exists. Assuming that path weights are integers, we can find the actual weight of the shortest path between the two vertices by asking yes/no questions. How? Pose the question for $k = 1$. If the answer is no, then try with $k = 2$. If the answer is no, try with $k = 4$. Keep doubling the value of k until the answer is yes. If that last value of k was k', then the answer is somewhere between $k'/2$ and k'. Then find the true answer by using binary search with an initial interval of $k'/2$ to k. This approach won't tell us which vertices and edges a shortest path contains, but at least it will tell us the weight of a shortest path.

The second condition for a problem to be NP-complete requires that if a polynomial-time algorithm exists for the problem, then there is a way to convert every problem in NP into this problem in such a way as to solve them all in polynomial time. Focusing on decision problems, let's see the general idea behind converting one decision problem, X, into another decision problem, Y, such that if there's a polynomial-time algorithm for Y then there's a polynomial-time algorithm for X. We call such a conversion a *reduction* because we're "reducing" solving problem X to solving problem Y. Here's the idea:

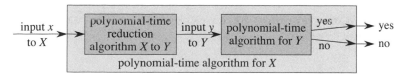

We're given some input x of size n to problem X. We transform this input into an input y to problem Y, and we do so in time polynomial in n, say $O(n^c)$ for some constant c. The way we transform input x into input y has to obey an important property: if algorithm Y decides "yes" on input y, then algorithm X should decide "yes" on input x, and if Y decides "no" on y, then X should decide "no" on x. We call this transformation a ***polynomial-time reduction algorithm***. Let's see how long the entire algorithm for problem X takes. The reduction algorithm takes $O(n^c)$ time, and its output cannot be longer than the time it took, and so the size of the reduction algorithm's output is $O(n^c)$. But this output is the input y to the algorithm for problem Y. Since the algorithm for Y is a polynomial-time algorithm, on an input of size m, it runs in time $O(m^d)$ for some constant d. Here, m is $O(n^c)$, and so the algorithm for Y takes time $O((n^c)^d)$, or $O(n^{cd})$. Because both c and d are constants, so is cd, and we see that the algorithm for Y is a polynomial-time algorithm. The total time for the algorithm for problem X is $O(n^c + n^{cd})$, which makes it, too, a polynomial-time algorithm.

This approach shows that if problem Y is "easy" (solvable in polynomial time), then so is problem X. But we'll use polynomial-time reductions to show not that problems are easy, but that they are hard:

> If problem X is NP-hard and we can reduce it to problem Y in polynomial time, then problem Y is NP-hard as well.

Why should this statement hold? Let's suppose that problem X is NP-hard and that there is a polynomial-time reduction algorithm to convert inputs to X into inputs to Y. Because X is NP-hard, there is a way to convert any problem, say Z, in NP into X such that if X has a polynomial-time algorithm, so does Z. Now you know how that conversion occurs, namely by a polynomial-time reduction:

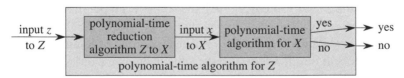

Because we can convert inputs to X into inputs to Y with a polynomial-time reduction, we can expand X as we did earlier:

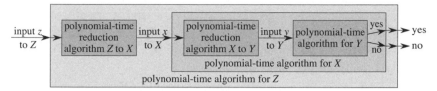

Instead of grouping the polynomial-time reduction for X to Y and the algorithm for Y together, let's group the two polynomial-time reductions together:

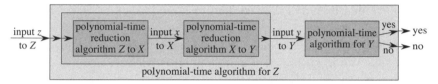

Now we note that if we immediately follow the polynomial-time reduction for Z to X by the polynomial-time reduction from X to Y, we have a polynomial-time reduction from Z to Y:

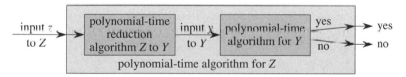

Just to make sure that the two polynomial-time reductions in sequence together constitute a single polynomial-time reduction, we'll use a similar analysis to what we did before. Suppose that the input z to problem Z has size n, that the reduction from Z to X takes time $O(n^c)$, and that the reduction from X to Y on an input of size m takes time $O(m^d)$, where c and d are constants. The output of the reduction from Z to X cannot be longer than the time it took to produce it, and so this output, which is also the input x to the reduction from X to Y, has size $O(n^c)$. Now we know that the size m of the input to the reduction from X to Y has size $m = O(n^c)$, and so the time taken by the reduction from X to Y is $O((n^c)^d)$, which is $O(n^{cd})$. Since c and d are constants, this second reduction takes time polynomial in n.

Furthermore, the time taken in the last stage, the polynomial-time algorithm for Y, is also polynomial in n. Suppose that the algorithm for Y on an input of size p takes time $O(p^b)$, where b is a constant. As before, the output of a reduction cannot exceed the time taken to produce it, and so $p = O(n^{cd})$, which means that the algorithm for Y takes time $O((n^{cd})^b)$, or $O(n^{bcd})$. Since b, c, and d are all constants, the algorithm for Y takes time polynomial in the original input size n. Altogether, the algorithm for Z takes time $O(n^c + n^{cd} + n^{bcd})$, which is polynomial in n.

What have we just seen? We showed that if problem X is NP-hard and there is a polynomial-time reduction algorithm that transforms an input x to X into an input y to problem Y, then Y is NP-hard, too. Because X being NP-hard means that every problem in NP reduces to it in polynomial time, we picked any problem Z in NP that reduces to X in polynomial time and showed that it also reduces to Y in polynomial time.

Our ultimate goal is to show that problems are NP-complete. So now all we have to do to show that a problem Y is NP-complete is

- show that it's in NP, which we can do by showing that there's a way to verify a certificate for Y in polynomial time, and

- take some other problem X that we know to be NP-hard and give a polynomial-time reduction from X to Y.

There is one more little detail that I've ignored so far: the Mother Problem. We need to start with some NP-complete problem M (the **Mother Problem**) that *every* problem in NP reduces to in polynomial time. Then we can reduce M to some other problem in polynomial time to show that the other problem is NP-hard, reduce the other problem to yet some other problem to show that the latter is NP-hard, and so on. Bear in mind, too, that there's no limit on how many other problems we can reduce a single problem to, so that the family tree of NP-complete problems starts with the Mother Problem and then branches out.

A Mother Problem

Different books list different Mother Problems. That's fine, since once you reduce one Mother Problem to some other problem, that other problem could also serve as the Mother Problem. One Mother Problem often seen is boolean formula satisfiability. I'll briefly describe this problem, but I won't prove that every problem in NP reduces to it in polynomial time. The proof is long and—dare I say—tedious.

First off: "boolean" is mathematical lingo for simple logic in which variables may take on only the values 0 and 1 (called boolean values), and operators take one or two boolean values and produce a boolean value. We've already seen exclusive-or (XOR) in Chapter 8. Typical boolean operators are AND, OR, NOT, IMPLIES, and IFF:

- x AND y equals 1 only if both x and y are 1; otherwise (either or both are 0), x AND y equals 0.

- x OR y equals 0 only if both x and y are 0; otherwise (either or both are 1), x OR y equals 1.

- NOT x is the opposite of x: it's 0 if x is 1, and it's 1 if x is 0.

- x IMPLIES y is 0 only if x is 1 and y is 0; otherwise (either x is 0, or x and y are both 1) x IMPLIES y is 1.

- x IFF y means "x if and only if y," and it equals 1 only if x and y are equal (both 0 or both 1); if x and y differ (one of them is 0 and the other is 1), then x IFF y equals 0.

There are 16 possible boolean operators that take two operands, but these are the most common.[5] A ***boolean formula*** consists of boolean-valued variables, boolean operators, and parentheses for grouping.

In the ***boolean formula satisfiability problem***, the input is a boolean formula, and we ask whether there is some way to assign the values 0 and 1 to the variables in the formula so that it evaluates to 1. If there is such a way, we say that the formula is ***satisfiable***. For example, the boolean formula

$$\Big((w \text{ IMPLIES } x) \text{ OR NOT} \Big(((\text{NOT } w) \text{ IFF } y) \text{ OR } z\Big)\Big) \text{ AND (NOT } x)$$

is satisfiable: let $w = 0, x = 0, y = 1$, and $z = 1$. Then the formula evaluates to

$$\Big((0 \text{ IMPLIES } 0) \text{ OR NOT} \Big(((\text{NOT } 0) \text{ IFF } 1) \text{ OR } 1\Big)\Big) \text{ AND (NOT } 0)$$

$$= \Big(1 \text{ OR NOT} \big((1 \text{ IFF } 1) \text{ OR } 1\big)\Big) \text{ AND } 1$$
$$= \big(1 \text{ OR NOT } (1 \text{ OR } 1)\big) \text{ AND } 1$$
$$= (1 \text{ OR } 0) \text{ AND } 1$$
$$= 1 \text{ AND } 1$$
$$= 1.$$

---

[5]Some of these 16 two-operand boolean operators are not terribly interesting, such as the operator that evaluates to 0 regardless of the values of its operands.

On the other hand, here's a simple formula that is not satisfiable:

x AND (NOT x) .

If $x = 0$, then this formula evaluates to 0 AND 1, which is 0; if instead $x = 1$, then this formula evaluates to 1 AND 0, which again is 0.

A sampler of NP-complete problems

With boolean formula satisfiability as our Mother Problem, let's see some of the problems that we can show are NP-complete by using polynomial-time reductions. Here's the family tree of reductions that we'll see:

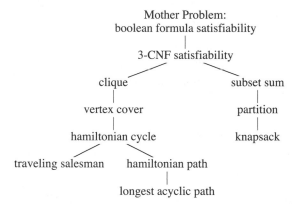

I won't show all the reductions in this family tree, because some of them are rather long and involved. But we'll see a couple that are interesting because they show how to reduce a problem from one domain to a different domain, such as logic (3-CNF satisfiability) to graphs (the clique problem).

3-CNF satisfiability

Because boolean formulas can contain any of the 16 two-operand boolean operators, and because they can be parenthesized in any number of ways, it's difficult to reduce directly from the boolean formula satisfiability problem—the Mother Problem. Instead, we will define a related problem that is also about satisfying boolean formulas, but that has some restrictions on the structure of the formula that is the input to the problem. It will be much easier to reduce from this restricted problem. Let's require that the formula be ANDs of *clauses*, where each clause is an OR of three terms, and each term is a *literal*: either a variable or the negation of a variable (such as NOT x). A boolean formula in this form is in *3-conjunctive normal form*, or *3-CNF*. For example, the boolean formula

$$(w \text{ OR } (\text{NOT } w) \text{ OR } (\text{NOT } x)) \text{ AND } (y \text{ OR } x \text{ OR } z)$$

$$\text{AND } ((\text{NOT } w) \text{ OR } (\text{NOT } y) \text{ OR } (\text{NOT } z))$$

is in 3-CNF. Its first clause is $(w \text{ OR } (\text{NOT } w) \text{ OR } (\text{NOT } x))$.

Deciding whether a boolean formula in 3-CNF has a satisfying assignment to its variables—the *3-CNF satisfiability problem*—is NP-complete. A certificate is a proposed assignment of the values 0 and 1 to the variables. Checking a certificate is easy: just plug in the proposed values for the variables, and verify that the expression evaluates to 1. To show that 3-CNF satisfiability is NP-hard, we reduce from (unrestricted) boolean formula satisfiability. Again, I won't go into the (not so interesting) details. It gets more interesting when we reduce from a problem in one domain to a problem in a different domain, which we're about to do.

Here's a frustrating aspect of 3-CNF satisfiability: although it's NP-complete, there is a polynomial-time algorithm to determine whether a 2-CNF formula is satisfiable. A 2-CNF formula is just like a 3-CNF formula except that it has two literals, not three, in each clause. A small change like that takes a problem from being as hard as the hardest problem in NP to being easy!

Clique

Now we're going to see an interesting reduction, for problems in different domains: from 3-CNF satisfiability to a problem having to do with undirected graphs. A *clique* in an undirected graph G is a subset S of vertices such that the graph has an edge between every pair of vertices in S. The *size of a clique* is the number of vertices it contains.

As you might imagine, cliques play a role in social network theory. Modeling each individual as a vertex and relationships between individuals as undirected edges, a clique represents a group of individuals all of whom have relationships with each other. Cliques also have applications in bioinformatics, engineering, and chemistry.

The *clique problem* takes two inputs, a graph G and a positive integer k, and asks whether G has a *k-clique*: a clique of size k. For example, the graph on the next page has a clique of size 4, shown with heavily shaded vertices, and no other clique of size 4 or greater.

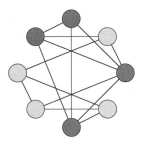

Verifying a certificate is easy. The certificate is the k vertices claimed to form a clique, and we just have to check that each of the k vertices has an edge to the other $k - 1$. This check is easily performed in time polynomial in the size of the graph. Now we know that the clique problem is in NP.

How can a problem in satisfying boolean formulas reduce to a graph problem? We start with a boolean formula in 3-CNF. Suppose that the formula is C_1 AND C_2 AND C_3 AND $\cdots$ AND C_k, where each C_r is one of k clauses. From this formula, we will construct a graph in polynomial time, and this graph will have a k-clique if and only if the 3-CNF formula is satisfiable. We need to see three things: the construction, an argument that the construction runs in time polynomial in the size of the 3-CNF formula, and a proof that the graph has a k-clique if and only if there is some way to assign to the variables of the 3-CNF formula so that it evaluates to 1.

To construct a graph from a 3-CNF formula, let's focus on the rth clause, C_r. It has three literals; let's call them l_1^r, l_2^r, and l_3^r, so that C_r is l_1^r OR l_2^r OR l_3^r. Each literal is either a variable or the negation of a variable. We create one vertex for each literal, so that for clause C_r, we create a triple of vertices, v_1^r, v_2^r, and v_3^r. We add an edge between vertices v_i^r and v_j^s if two conditions hold:

- v_i^r and v_j^s are in different triples; that is, r and s are different clause numbers, and

- their corresponding literals are not negations of each other.

For example, the graph on the next page corresponds to the 3-CNF formula

$$\big(x \text{ OR } (\text{NOT } y) \text{ OR } (\text{NOT } z)\big) \text{ AND } \big((\text{NOT } x) \text{ OR } y \text{ OR } z\big)$$
$$\text{AND } (x \text{ OR } y \text{ OR } z) .$$

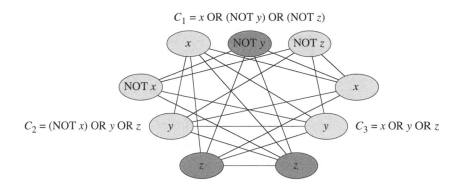

$C_1 = x$ OR (NOT y) OR (NOT z)

$C_2 = $ (NOT x) OR y OR z

$C_3 = x$ OR y OR z

It's easy enough to see that this reduction can be performed in polynomial time. If the 3-CNF formula has k clauses, then it has $3k$ literals, and so the graph has $3k$ vertices. At most, each vertex has an edge to all the other $3k - 1$ vertices, and so the number of edges is at most $3k(3k - 1)$, which equals $9k^2 - 3k$. The size of the graph constructed is polynomial in the size of the 3-CNF input, and it's easy to determine which edges go into the graph.

Finally, we need to show that the constructed graph has a k-clique if and only if the 3-CNF formula is satisfiable. We start by assuming that the formula is satisfiable, and we'll show that the graph has a k-clique. If there exists a satisfying assignment, each clause C_r contains at least one literal l_i^r that evaluates to 1, and each such literal corresponds to a vertex v_i^r in the graph. If we select one such literal from each of the k clauses, we get a corresponding set S of k vertices. I claim that S is a k-clique. Consider any two vertices in S. They correspond to literals in different clauses that evaluate to 1 in the satisfying assignment. These literals cannot be negations of each other, because if they were, then one of them would evaluate to 1 but the other would evaluate to 0. Since these literals are not negations of each other, we created an edge between the two vertices when we constructed the graph. Because we can pick any two vertices in S as this pair, we see that there are edges between all pairs of vertices in S. Hence, S, a set of k vertices, is a k-clique.

Now we have to show the other direction: if the graph has a k-clique S, then the 3-CNF formula is satisfiable. No edges in the graph connect vertices in the same triple, and so S contains exactly one vertex per triple. For each vertex v_i^r in S, assign 1 to its corresponding literal l_i^r in the 3-CNF formula. We don't have to worry about assigning a 1 to both a literal and its negation, since the k-clique cannot contain vertices corresponding to a literal and its negation. Since each clause has a literal that evaluates to 1, each clause is satisfied, and so the entire 3-CNF formula is satisfied. If any variables don't correspond to vertices in the clique, assign values to them arbitrarily; they won't affect whether the formula is satisfied.

In the above example, a satisfying assignment has $y = 0$ and $z = 1$; it doesn't matter what we assign to x. A corresponding 3-clique consists of the heavily shaded vertices, which correspond to NOT y from clause C_i and z from clauses C_2 and C_3.

Thus, we have shown that there exists a polynomial-time reduction from the NP-complete problem of 3-CNF satisfiability to the problem of finding a k-clique. If you were given a boolean formula in 3-CNF with k clauses, and you had to find a satisfying assignment for the formula, you could use the construction we just saw to convert the formula in polynomial time to an undirected graph, and determine whether the graph had a k-clique. If you could determine in polynomial time whether the graph had a k-clique, then you would have determined in polynomial time whether the 3-CNF formula had a satisfying assignment. Since 3-CNF satisfiability is NP-complete, so is determining whether a graph contains a k-clique. As a bonus, if you could determine not only whether the graph had a k-clique, but which vertices constituted the k-clique, then you could use this information to find the values to assign to the variables of the 3-CNF formula in a satisfying assignment.

Vertex cover

A ***vertex cover*** in an undirected graph G is a subset S of the vertices such that every edge in G is incident on at least one vertex in S. We say that each vertex in S "covers" its incident edges. The ***size of a vertex cover*** is the number of vertices it contains. As in the clique problem, the ***vertex-cover problem*** takes as input an undirected graph G and a positive integer m. It asks whether G has a vertex cover of size m. Like the clique problem, the vertex-cover problem has applications in bioinformatics. In another application, you have a building with hallways and cameras that can scan up to 360 degrees located at the intersections of hallways, and you want to know whether m cameras will allow you to see all the hallways. Here, edges model hallways and vertices model intersections. In yet another application, finding vertex covers helps in designing strategies to foil worm attacks on computer networks.

A certificate for the vertex-cover problem is, not surprisingly, a proposed vertex cover. It's easy to verify in time polynomial in the size of the graph that the proposed vertex cover has size m and really does cover all the edges, and so we see that this problem is in NP.

The NP-completeness family tree on page 190 tells you that we reduce the clique problem to the vertex-cover problem. Suppose that the input to the clique problem is an undirected graph G with n vertices and a positive integer k. In polynomial time, we'll produce an input graph $\overline{G}$ to the vertex-cover problem such that G has a clique of size k if and only if $\overline{G}$ has a vertex cover of size $n - k$. This reduction is really easy. The graph $\overline{G}$ has the same vertices as G, and it has exactly the opposite edges as G. In other words, edge (u, v) is in $\overline{G}$ if and only if (u, v) is *not* in G. You might have guessed that the vertex cover of size $n - k$ in $\overline{G}$ consists of the vertices *not* in the clique of k vertices in G — and you would be correct! Here are examples of graphs G and $\overline{G}$, with eight vertices. The five vertices forming a clique in G and the remaining three vertices forming a vertex cover in $\overline{G}$ are heavily shaded:

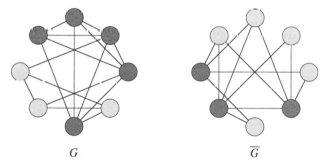

$\qquad\qquad G \qquad\qquad\qquad\qquad\qquad\qquad \overline{G}$

Note that every edge in $\overline{G}$ is incident on at least one heavily shaded vertex.

We need to show that G has a k-clique if and only if $\overline{G}$ has a vertex cover of size $n - k$. Start by supposing that G has a k-clique C. Let S consist of the $n - k$ vertices not in C. I claim that every edge in $\overline{G}$ is incident on at least one vertex in S. Let (u, v) be any edge in $\overline{G}$. It's in $\overline{G}$ because it was not in G. Because (u, v) is not in G, at least one of the vertices u and v is not in the clique C of G, because an edge connects every pair of vertices in C. Since at least one of u and v is not in C, at least one of u and v is in S, which means that edge (u, v) is incident on at least one of the vertices in S. Since we chose (u, v) to be any edge in $\overline{G}$, we see that S is a vertex cover for $\overline{G}$.

Now we go the other way. Suppose that $\overline{G}$ has a vertex cover S containing $n - k$ vertices, and let C consist of the k vertices not in S. Every edge in $\overline{G}$ is incident on some vertex in S. In other words, if (u, v) is an edge in $\overline{G}$, then at least one of u and v is in S. If you recall the definition of contrapositive on page 22, you can see that the contrapositive of this implication is that if neither u nor v is in S, then (u, v) is not in $\overline{G}$—and therefore, (u, v) is in G. In other words, if both u and v are in C, then the edge (u, v) is present in G. Since u and v are any pair of vertices in C, we see that there is an edge in G between all pairs of vertices in C. That is, C is a k-clique.

Thus, we have shown that there exists a polynomial-time reduction from the NP-complete problem of determining whether an undirected graph contains a k-clique to the problem of determining whether an undirected graph contains a vertex cover of size $n - k$. If you were given an undirected graph G and you wanted to know whether it contained a k-clique, you could use the construction we just saw to convert G in polynomial time to $\overline{G}$, and determine whether $\overline{G}$ contained a vertex cover with $n - k$ vertices. If you could determine in polynomial time whether $\overline{G}$ had a vertex cover of size $n - k$, then you would have determined in polynomial time whether G had a k-clique. Since the clique problem is NP-complete, so is the vertex-cover problem. As a bonus, if you could determine not only whether $\overline{G}$ had a vertex cover of $n - k$ vertices, but which vertices constituted the cover, then you could use this information to find the vertices in the k-clique.

Hamiltonian cycle and hamiltonian path

We've already seen the hamiltonian-cycle problem: does a connected, undirected graph contain a hamiltonian cycle (a path that starts and ends at the same vertex and visits all other vertices exactly once)? The applications of this problem are a bit arcane, but from the NP-completeness family tree on page 190, you can see that we use this problem to show that the traveling-salesman problem is NP-complete, and we've seen how the traveling-salesman problem comes up in practice.

A closely related problem is the **hamiltonian-path problem**, which asks whether the graph contains a path that visits each vertex exactly once, but does not require that the path be a closed cycle. This problem, too, is NP-complete, and we will use it on page 199 to show that the longest-acyclic-path problem is NP-complete.

For both of the hamiltonian problems, the certificate is obvious: the order of the vertices in the hamiltonian cycle or path. (For a hamiltonian cycle, don't repeat the first vertex at the end.) Given a certificate, we need only check that each vertex appears exactly once in the list and that the graph contains an edge between each pair of consecutive vertices in the ordering. For the hamiltonian-cycle problem, we also have to check that an edge exists between the first and last vertices.

I won't detail the polynomial-time reduction from the vertex-cover problem to the hamiltonian-cycle problem, which shows that the latter is NP-hard. It's quite complicated and relies on a *widget*, which is a piece of a graph that enforces certain properties. The widget used in the reduction has the property that any hamiltonian cycle in the graph constructed by the reduction can traverse the widget in one of only three ways.

To reduce the hamiltonian-cycle problem to the hamiltonian-path problem, we start with a connected, undirected graph G with n vertices, and from it we will form a new connected, undirected graph G' with $n + 3$ vertices. We pick any vertex u in G, and let its adjacent vertices be $v_1, v_2, \ldots, v_k$. To construct G', we add three new vertices, x, y, and z, and we add edges (u, x) and (y, z), along with edges $(v_1, y), (v_2, y), \ldots, (v_k, y)$ between y and all the vertices adjacent to u. Here's an example:

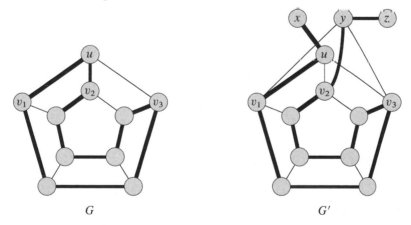

G G'

Heavy edges indicate a hamiltonian cycle in G and a corresponding hamiltonian path in G'. This reduction takes polynomial time, since G' contains just three more vertices than G and at most $n + 1$ additional edges.

As usual, we need to show that the reduction works: that G has a hamiltonian cycle if and only if G' has a hamiltonian path. Suppose that G has a hamiltonian cycle. It must contain an edge (u, v_i) for some vertex v_i adjacent to u and, therefore, adjacent to y in G'. To form a hamiltonian path in G, going from x to z, take all the edges of the hamiltonian cycle except for (u, v_i) and add the edges (u, x), (v_i, y), and (y, z). In the above example, v_i is vertex v_2, and so the hamiltonian path omits edge (v_2, u) and adds edges (u, x), (v_2, y), and (y, z).

Now suppose that G' has a hamiltonian path. Because vertices x and z each have only one incident edge, the hamiltonian path must go from x to z, and it must contain an edge (v_i, y) for some vertex adjacent to y and, therefore, adjacent to u. To find a hamiltonian cycle in G, remove x, y, and z and all their incident edges, and use all the edges in the hamiltonian path in G', along with (v_i, u).

A similar denouement to those of our previous reductions holds here. There exists a polynomial-time reduction from the NP-complete problem of determining whether a connected, undirected graph contains a hamiltonian cycle to the problem of determining whether a connected, undirected graph contains a hamiltonian path. Since the former is NP-complete, so is the latter. Moreover, knowing the edges in the hamiltonian path gives the edges in the hamiltonian cycle.

Traveling salesman

In the decision version of the ***traveling-salesman problem***, we are given a complete undirected graph with a nonnegative integer weight on each edge, and a nonnegative integer k. A ***complete graph*** has an edge between every pair of vertices, so that if a complete graph has n vertices, then it has $n(n - 1)$ edges. We ask whether the graph has a cycle containing all vertices whose total weight is at most k.

It's pretty easy to show that this problem is in NP. A certificate consists of the vertices of the cycle, in order. We can easily check in polynomial time whether the edges on this cycle visit all the vertices and have a total weight of k or less.

To show that the traveling-salesman problem is NP-hard, we reduce from the hamiltonian-cycle problem, another simple reduction. Given a graph G as input to the hamiltonian-cycle problem, we construct a complete graph G' with the same vertices as G. Set the weight of edge (u, v) in G' to 0 if (u, v) is an edge in G, and set it to 1 if there is no edge (u, v) in G. Set k to 0. This reduction takes time polynomial in the size of G, since it adds at most $n(n - 1)$ edges.

To show that the reduction works, we need to show that G has a hamiltonian cycle if and only if G' has a cycle of weight 0 that includes all the vertices. Once again, the argument is easy. Suppose that G has a hamiltonian cycle. Then each edge on the cycle is in G, and so each of these edges gets a weight of 0 in G'. Thus, G' has a cycle containing all the vertices, and the total weight of this cycle is 0. Conversely, now suppose that G' has a cycle containing all the vertices and whose total weight is 0. Then each edge on this cycle must also be in G, and so G has a hamiltonian cycle.

I don't need to repeat the now-familiar denouement, do I?

Longest acyclic path

In the decision version of the ***longest-acyclic-path problem***, we are given an undirected graph G and an integer k, and we ask whether G contains two vertices that have an acyclic path between them with at least k edges.

Once again, a certificate for the longest-acyclic-path problem is easy to verify. It consists of the vertices in the proposed path, in order. We can check in polynomial time that the list contains at least $k+1$ vertices ($k+1$ because a path with k edges contains $k+1$ vertices) with no vertex repeated and that there is an edge between every pair of consecutive vertices in the list.

Yet another simple reduction shows that this problem is NP-hard. We reduce from the hamiltonian-path problem. Given a graph G with n vertices as input to the hamiltonian-path problem, the input to the longest-acyclic-path problem is the graph G, unchanged, and the integer $k = n - 1$. If this isn't a polynomial time reduction, I don't know what is.

We show that the reduction works by showing that G has a hamiltonian path if and only if it has an acyclic path containing at least $n - 1$ edges. But a hamiltonian path *is* an acyclic path containing $n-1$ edges, so we're done!

Subset sum

In the ***subset-sum problem***, the input is a finite set S of positive integers, in no particular order, and a target number t, which is also a positive integer. We ask whether there exists a subset S' of S whose elements sum to exactly t. For example, if S is the set $\{1, 2, 7, 14, 49, 98, 343, 686, 2409, 2793, 16808, 17206, 117705, 117993\}$ and $t = 138457$, then the subset $S' = \{1, 2, 7, 98, 343, 686, 2409, 17206, 117705\}$ is a solution. A certificate is, of course, a subset of S, which we can verify by just adding up the numbers in the subset and checking that their sum equals t.

As you can see from the NP-completeness family tree on page 190, we show that the subset-sum problem is NP-hard by reducing from 3-CNF satisfiability. Here is another reduction that crosses problem domains, transforming a problem in logic into an arithmetic problem. You'll see that the transformation is clever but, ultimately, quite straightforward.

We start with a 3-CNF boolean formula F that has n variables and k clauses. Let's name the variables $v_1, v_2, v_3, \ldots, v_n$ and the clauses $C_1, C_2, C_3, \ldots, C_k$. Each clause contains exactly three literals (remember that each literal is either v_i or NOT v_i) joined together by ORs, and the entire formula F is C_1 AND C_2 AND C_3 AND $\cdots$ AND C_k. Put another way, for a given assignment of 0 or 1 to each variable, each clause is satisfied if any of its literals evaluates to 1, and the full formula F is satisfied only if all of its clauses are satisfied.

Before we construct the set S for the subset-sum problem, let's construct the target number t from the 3-CNF formula F. We'll construct it as a decimal integer with $n + k$ digits. The least significant k digits (the rightmost k digits) of t correspond to the k clauses of F, and each of these digits is a 4. The most significant n digits of t correspond to the n variables of F, and each of these digits is a 1. If the formula F has, say, three variables and four clauses, then t comes out to 1114444. As we'll see, if there is a subset of S that sums to t, then the digits of t that correspond to the variables (the 1s) will ensure that we assign a value to each variable in F, and the digits of t that correspond to the clauses (the 4s) will ensure that each clause of F is satisfied.

The set S will consist of $2n + 2k$ integers. It contains integers x_i and x'_i for each of the n variables v_i in the 3-CNF formula F, and it contains integers q_j and q'_j for each of the k clauses C_j in F. We construct each integer in S digit by digit, in decimal. Let's see an example with $n = 3$ variables and $k = 4$ clauses, so that the 3-CNF formula is $F = C_1$ AND C_2 AND C_3 AND C_4, and let the clauses be

$$C_1 \ = \ v_1 \text{ OR (NOT } v_2) \text{ OR (NOT } v_3) ,$$
$$C_2 \ = \ (\text{NOT } v_1) \text{ OR (NOT } v_2) \text{ OR (NOT } v_3) ,$$
$$C_3 \ = \ (\text{NOT } v_1) \text{ OR (NOT } v_2) \text{ OR } v_3 ,$$
$$C_4 \ = \ v_1 \text{ OR } v_2 \text{ OR } v_3 .$$

Here are the corresponding set S and target t:

		v_1	v_2	v_3	C_1	C_2	C_3	C_4
x_1	=	1	0	0	1	0	0	1
x_1'	=	1	0	0	0	1	1	0
x_2	=	0	1	0	0	0	0	1
x_2'	=	0	1	0	1	1	1	0
x_3	=	0	0	1	0	0	1	1
x_3'	=	0	0	1	1	1	0	0
q_1	=	0	0	0	1	0	0	0
q_1'	=	0	0	0	2	0	0	0
q_2	=	0	0	0	0	1	0	0
q_2'	=	0	0	0	0	2	0	0
q_3	=	0	0	0	0	0	1	0
q_3'	=	0	0	0	0	0	2	0
q_4	=	0	0	0	0	0	0	1
q_4'	=	0	0	0	0	0	0	2
t	=	1	1	1	4	4	4	4

Note that the shaded elements of S — 1000110, 101110, 10011, 1000, 2000, 200, 10, 1, and 2 — sum to 1114444. We'll soon see what these elements correspond to in the 3 CNF formula F.

We construct the integers in S so that, digit by digit, every column in the above diagram sums to either 2 (the leftmost n columns) or 6 (the rightmost k columns). Note that when elements in S are added up, no carries out of any digit position can occur and we can work with the numbers digit by digit.

In the diagram, each row is labeled by an element in S. The first $2n$ rows correspond to the n variables of the 3-CNF formula, and the last $2k$ rows are "slack" whose purpose we'll see a little later. The rows labeled by elements x_i and x_i' correspond respectively to occurrences of the literals v_i and NOT v_i in F. We'll say that these rows "are" the literals, understanding that we mean that they correspond to the literals. The goal is to include in the subset S' exactly n of the first $2n$ rows — indeed, just one of each x_i, x_i' pair — which will correspond to a satisfying assignment for the 3-CNF formula F. Because we require that the rows we choose from the literals add up to 1 in each of the leftmost n columns, we ensure that, for each variable v_i in the 3-CNF formula, we include in S' a row for one of x_i and x_i', but not both. The rightmost k columns ensure that the rows we include in S' are literals that satisfy each clause in the 3-CNF formula.

Let's focus for the moment on the n leftmost columns, which are labeled by the variables $v_1, v_2, \ldots, v_n$. For a given variable v_i, both x_i and x'_i have a 1 in the digit corresponding to v_i, and they have 0 in all other digit positions corresponding to other variables. For example, the leftmost three digits of both x_2 and x'_2 are 010. The digits of the last $2k$ rows in the leftmost n columns are 0. Because the target t has a 1 in each of the variable positions, exactly one of x_i and x'_i must be in the subset S' in order to contribute to the sum. Having x_i in S' corresponds to setting v_i to 1, and having x'_i in S' corresponds to setting v_i to 0.

Now we turn our attention to the rightmost k columns, which correspond to the clauses. These columns ensure that each clause is satisfied, as we will see below. If the literal v_i appears in clause C_j, then x_i has a 1 in the column for C_j; if the literal NOT v_i appears in clause C_j, then x'_i has a 1 in the C_j column. Because each clause in a 3-CNF formula contains exactly three distinct literals, the column for each clause must contain exactly three 1s among all the x_i and x'_i rows. For a given clause C_j, the rows among the first $2n$ that are included in S' correspond to satisfying 0, 1, 2, or 3 of the literals in C_j, and so these rows contribute 0, 1, 2, or 3 to the sum for C_j's column.

But the target digit for each clause is 4, and that's where the "slack" elements q_j and q'_j, for $j = 1, 2, 3, \ldots, k$, come in. They ensure that for each clause, the subset S' includes some literal in the clause (some x_i or x'_i that has a 1 in the column for that clause). The row for q_j has a 1 in the column for clause C_j and 0 everywhere else, and the row for q'_j is the same except that it has a 2. We can add in these rows to achieve the target digit of 4, but only if the subset S' includes at least one literal from C_j. Which of these slack rows need to be added in depends on how many of the literals of clause C_j are included in S'. If S' includes just one literal, then both slack rows are needed, because the sum in the column is 1 from the literal, plus 1 from q_j, plus 2 from q'_j. If S' includes two literals, then just q'_j is needed, because the column sum is 2 from the two literals, plus 2 from q'_j. If S' includes three literals, then just q_j is needed, because the column sum is 3 from the three literals, plus 1 from q_j. But, if no literals from clause C_j are included in S', then $q_j + q'_j = 3$ is not enough to achieve the target digit of 4. Therefore, we can achieve the target digit of 4 for each clause only if some literal in the clause is included in the subset S'.

Now that we've seen the reduction, we can see that it takes polynomial time. We're creating $2n + 2k + 1$ integers (including the target t), each with $n + k$ digits. You can see from the diagram that of the integers constructed, no two are equal, and so S really is a set. (The definition of a set does not allow repeated elements.)

To show that the reduction works, we need to show that the 3-CNF formula F has a satisfying assignment if and only if there exists a subset S' of S that sums to exactly t. At this point, you've seen the idea, but let's recap. First, suppose that F has a satisfying assignment. If this assignment sets v_i to 1, then include x_i in S'; otherwise, include x_i'. Because exactly one of x_i and x_i' is in S, the column for v_i must sum to 1, matching the appropriate digit of t. Because the assignment satisfies each clause C_j, the x_i and x_i' rows must contribute 1, 2, or 3 (the number of literals in C_j that are 1) to the sum in C_j's column. Including the necessary slack rows q_j and/or q_j' in S' achieves the target digit 4.

Conversely, suppose that S has a subset S' that sums to exactly t. In order for t to have a 1 in the leftmost n positions, S' must include exactly one of x_i and x_i' for each variable v_i. If it includes x_i, then set v_i to 1; if it includes x_i', then set v_i to 0. Because the slack rows q_j and q_j' summed together cannot achieve the target digit 4 in the column for clause C_j, the subset S' must also include at least one row x_i or x_i' with a 1 in C_j's column. If it includes x_i, then the literal v_i appears in clause C_j, and the clause is satisfied. If S' includes x_i', then the literal NOT v_i appears in clause C_j, and the clause is satisfied. Thus, each clause is satisfied, and there exists a satisfying assignment for the 3-CNF formula F.

And so we see that if we could solve the subset-sum problem in polynomial time, we could also determine whether a 3-CNF formula is satisfiable in polynomial time. Since 3-CNF satisfiability is NP-complete, so is the subset-sum problem. Moreover, if we know which integers in the constructed set S sum to the target t, we can determine how to set the variables in the 3-CNF formula so that it evaluates to 1.

One other note about the reduction I used: the digits don't have to be decimal digits. What matters is that no carries from one place to another can occur when adding up the integers. Since no column's sum can exceed 6, interpreting the numbers in any base 7 or greater would be fine. Indeed, the example I gave on page 199 comes from the numbers in the diagram, but interpreted in base 7.

Partition

The *partition problem* is closely related to the subset-sum problem. In fact, it's a special case of the subset-sum problem: if z equals the sum of all the integers in the set S, then the target t is exactly $z/2$. In other words, the goal is to determine whether there exists a partition of the set S into two disjoint sets S' and S'' such that each integer in S is in either S' or S'' but not both (that's what it means for S' and S'' to partition S) and the sum of the integers in S' equals the sum of the integers in S''. As in the subset-sum problem, a certificate is a subset of S.

To show that the partition problem is NP-hard, we reduce from the subset-sum problem. (No big surprise there.) Given a set R of positive integers and a positive integer target t as input to the subset-sum problem, in polynomial time we construct a set S as input to the partition problem. First, compute z as the sum of all the integers in R. We assume that z is not equal to $2t$, because if it is, then the problem is already a partition problem. (If $z = 2t$, then $t = z/2$, and we're trying to find a subset of R that sums to the same total as the integers not in the subset.) Then choose any integer y that is greater than both $t + z$ and $2z$. Define the set S to contain all the integers in R and two additional integers: $y - t$ and $y - z + t$. Because y is greater than both $t + z$ and $2z$, we know that both $y - t$ and $y - z + t$ are greater than z (the sum of the integers in R), and so these two integers cannot be in R. (Remember that because S is a set, all of its elements must be unique. We also know that, because z is not equal to $2t$, we must have $y - t \neq y - z + t$, and so the two new integers are unique.) Note that the sum of all the integers in S equals $z + (y - t) + (y - z + t)$, which is just $2y$. Therefore, if S is partitioned into two disjoint subsets with equal sums, each subset must sum to y.

To show that the reduction works, we need to show that there exists a subset R' of R whose integers sum to t if and only if there exists a partition of S into S' and S'' such that the integers in S' and the integers in S'' have the same sum. First, let's suppose that some subset R' of R has integers that sum to t. Then the integers in R that are not in R' must sum to $z - t$. Let's define the set S' to have all the integers in R' along with $y - t$ (so that S'' has $y - z + t$ along with all the integers in R that are not in R'). We just need to show that the integers in S' sum to y. But that's easy: the integers in R' sum to t, and adding in $y - t$ gives a sum of y.

Conversely, let's suppose that there exists a partition of S into S' and S'', both of which sum to y. I claim that the two integers we added to R when forming S ($y - t$ and $y - z + t$) can't both be in S', nor can they both be in S''. Why? If they were in the same set, then that set would sum to at least $(y - t) + (y - z + t)$, which equals $2y - z$. But remember that y is greater than z (in fact, it's greater than $2z$), and so $2y - z$ is greater than y. Therefore, if $y - t$ and $y - z + t$ were in the same set, then that set's sum would be greater than y. So we know that one of $y - t$ and $y - z + t$ is in S' and the other is in S''. It doesn't matter which set we say that $y - t$ is in, so let's say that it's in S'. Now, we know that the integers in S' sum to y, which means that the integers in S' other than $y - t$ must sum to $y - (y - t)$, or t. Since $y - z + t$ cannot also be in S', we know that all the other integers in S' came from R. Hence, there is a subset of R that sums to t.

Knapsack

In the ***knapsack problem***, we are given a set of n items, each with a weight and a value, and we ask whether there exists a subset of items whose total weight is at most a given weight W and whose total value is at least a given value V. This problem is the decision version of an optimization problem where we want to load up a knapsack with the most valuable subset of items, subject to not exceeding a weight limit. This optimization problem has obvious applications, such as deciding which items to take backpacking or what loot a burglar should choose to pilfer.

The partition problem is really just a special case of the knapsack problem, in which the value of each item equals its weight and both W and V equal half the total weight. If we could solve the knapsack problem in polynomial time, then we could solve the partition problem in polynomial time. Therefore, the knapsack problem is at least as hard as the partition problem, and we don't even need to go through the full reduction process to show that the knapsack problem is NP-complete.

General strategies

As you have probably realized by now, there is no one-size-fits-all way to reduce one problem to another in order to prove NP-hardness. Some reductions are pretty simple, such as reducing the hamiltonian-cycle problem to the traveling-salesman problem, and some are extremely complicated. Here are a few things to remember and some strategies that often help.

Go from general to specific

When reducing problem X to problem Y, you always have to start with an arbitrary input to problem X. But you are allowed to restrict the input to problem Y as much as you like. For example, when reducing from 3-CNF satisfiability to the subset-sum problem, the reduction had to be able to handle *any* 3-CNF formula as its input, but the subset-sum input it produced had a particular structure: $2n + 2k$ integers in the set, and each integer was formed in a particular way. The reduction was not able to produce *every* possible input to the subset-sum problem, but that was OK. The point is that we can solve a 3-CNF satisfiability problem by transforming the input into an input to the subset-sum problem and then using the answer to the subset-sum problem as the answer to the 3-CNF satisfiability problem.

Take note, however, that every reduction has to be of this form: transform *any* input to problem X into *some* input to problem Y, even when chaining together reductions. If you want to reduce problem X to problem Y and also problem Y to problem Z, the first reduction has to transform *any* input to X into *some* input to Y, and the second reduction has to transform *any* input to Y into *some* input to Z. It's not enough for the second reduction to transform only the types of inputs to Y that are produced by the reduction from X.

Take advantage of restrictions in the problem you're reducing from

In general, when reducing from problem X to problem Y, you may choose problem X to impose more restrictions on its input. For example, it's almost always much easier to reduce from 3-CNF satisfiability than to reduce from the Mother Problem of boolean formula satisfiability. Boolean formulas can be arbitrarily complicated, but you've seen how we can exploit the structure of 3-CNF formulas when reducing.

Likewise, it's usually more straightforward to reduce from the hamiltonian-cycle problem than from the traveling-salesman problem, even though they are so similar. That's because in the traveling-salesman problem, the edge weights can be any positive integers, not just the 0 or 1 that we required when reducing to it. The hamiltonian-cycle problem is more restricted because each edge has only one of two "values": present or absent.

Look for special cases

Several NP-complete problems are just special cases of other NP-complete problems, much as the partition problem is a special case of the knapsack problem. If you know that problem X is NP-complete and that it's a special case of problem Y, then problem Y must be NP-complete as well. That is because, as we saw for the knapsack problem, a polynomial-time solution for problem Y would automatically give a polynomial-time solution for problem X. More intuitively, problem Y, being more general than problem X, is at least as hard.

Select an appropriate problem to reduce from

It's often a good strategy to reduce from a problem in the same, or at least a related, domain as the problem you're trying to prove NP-complete. For example, we showed that the vertex-cover problem—a graph problem—was NP-complete by reducing from the clique problem—also a graph problem. From there, the NP-completeness family tree showed that we reduced to the hamiltonian-cycle, hamiltonian-path, traveling-salesman, and longest-acyclic-path problems, all of which are on graphs.

Sometimes, however, it's best to leap from one domain to another, such as when we reduced from 3-CNF satisfiability to the clique problem or to the subset-sum problem. 3-CNF satisfiability often turns out to be a good choice to reduce from when crossing domains.

Within graph problems, if you need to select a portion of the graph, without regard to ordering, then the vertex-cover problem is often a good place to start. If ordering matters, then consider starting from the hamiltonian-cycle or hamiltonian-path problem.

Make big rewards and big penalties

When we transformed the input graph G to the hamiltonian-cycle problem to the weighted graph G' as input to the traveling-salesman problem, we really wanted to encourage using edges present in G when choosing edges for the traveling-salesman tour. We did so by giving these edges a very low weight: 0. In other words, we gave a big reward for using these edges.

Alternatively, we could have given the edges in G a finite weight and given edges not in G infinite weight, thereby exacting a hefty penalty for using edges not in G. If we had taken this approach and given each edge in G a weight of W, then we would have had to set the target weight k of the entire traveling-salesman tour to nW.

Design widgets

I didn't go into widget design, because widgets can get complicated. Widgets can be useful for enforcing certain properties. The books cited in the "Further reading" section provide examples of how to construct and use widgets in reductions.

Perspective

I've painted quite a gloomy picture here, haven't I? Imagine a scenario in which you try to come up with a polynomial-time algorithm to solve a problem, and no matter how much you press, you just can't close the deal. After a while, you'd be thrilled just to find an $O(n^5)$-time algorithm, even though you know that n^5 grows awfully rapidly. Maybe this problem is close to one that you know is easily solved in polynomial time (such as 2-CNF satisfiability vs. 3-CNF, or Euler tour vs. hamiltonian cycle), and you find it incredibly frustrating that you can't adapt the polynomial-time algorithm for your problem. Eventually you suspect that maybe—just maybe—you've been banging your head against the wall to solve an NP-complete problem. And, lo and behold, you are able to reduce a known NP-complete problem to your problem, and now you know that it's NP-hard.

Is that the end of the story? There's no hope that you'll be able to solve the problem in any reasonable amount of time?

Not quite. When a problem is NP-complete, it means that *some* inputs are troublesome, but not necessarily that *all* inputs are bad. For example, finding a longest acyclic path in a directed graph is NP-complete, but if you know that the graph is acyclic, then you can find a longest acyclic path in not just polynomial time, but in $O(n + m)$ time (where the graph has n vertices and m edges). Recall that we did just that when finding a critical path in a PERT chart in Chapter 5. As another example, if you're trying to solve the partition problem and the integers in the set sum to an odd number, then you know that there's no way to partition the set so that both parts have equal sums.

The good news goes beyond such pathological special cases. From here on, let's focus on optimization problems whose decision variants are NP-complete, such as the traveling-salesman problem. Some fast methods give good, and often very good, results. The technique of **branch and bound** organizes a search for an optimal solution into a tree-like structure, and it cuts off hunks of the tree, thereby eliminating large portions of the search space, based on the simple idea that if it can determine that all the solutions emanating from one node of the search tree cannot be any better than the best solution found so far, then don't bother checking solutions within the space represented by that node or anything below it.

Another technique that often helps is ***neighborhood search***, which takes one solution and applies local operations to try to improve the solution until no further improvement occurs. Consider the traveling-salesman problem where all vertices are points in the plane and the weight of each edge is the planar distance between the points. Even with this restriction, the problem is NP-complete. In the ***2-opt*** technique, whenever two edges cross, switch them, which results in a shorter cycle:

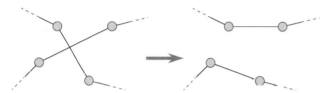

Moreover, a host of ***approximation algorithms*** give results that are guaranteed to be within a certain factor of the optimal value. For example, if the input to the traveling-salesman problem obeys the ***triangle inequality***—for all vertices u, v, and x, the weight of edge (u, v) is at most the sum of the weights of edges (u, x) and (x, v)—then there is a simple approximation algorithm that always finds a traveling-salesman tour whose total weight is at most twice that of the lowest, and this algorithm runs in time linear in the size of the input. There is an even better polynomial-time approximation algorithm for this situation, giving a tour whose total weight is at most $3/2$ times the lowest.

Strangely enough, if two NP-complete problems are closely related, the solution produced by a good approximation algorithm for one might produce a poor solution for the other. That is, a solution that is nearly optimal for one of the problems doesn't necessarily map to a solution that is anywhere nearly optimal for the other problem.

Nevertheless, in many real-world situations, a nearly optimal solution is good enough. Harking back to the discussion about the package-delivery company with brown trucks, they are happy to find nearly optimal routes for their trucks, even if the routes are not necessarily the best possible. Every dollar that they can save by planning efficient routes helps their bottom line.

Undecidable problems

Then again, if you're under the impression that NP-complete problems are the hardest in the world of algorithms, you're in for a little surprise. Theoretical computer scientists have defined a large hierarchy of complexity classes, based on how much time and other resources are necessary to solve a problem. Some problems take an amount of time that is provably exponential in the input size.

And it gets even worse. For some problems, no algorithm is possible. That is, there are problems for which it is provably impossible to create an algorithm that always gives a correct answer. We call such problems *undecidable*, and the best-known one is the *halting problem*, proven undecidable by the mathematician Alan Turing in 1937. In the halting problem, the input is a computer program A and the input x to A. The goal is to determine whether program A, running on input x, ever halts. That is, does A with input x run to completion?

Perhaps you're thinking that you could write a program—let's call it program B—that reads in program A, reads in x, and simulates A running with input x. That's fine if A on input x actually does run to completion. What if it doesn't? How would program B know when to declare that A will never halt? Couldn't B check for A getting into some sort of infinite loop? The answer is that although you could write B to check for some cases in which A doesn't halt, it is provably impossible to write program B so that *it* always halts and tells you correctly whether A on input x halts.

Because it's not possible to write a program that determines whether another program running on a particular input even halts, it's also not possible to write a program that determines whether another program meets its specification. How can one program tell whether another program gives the right answer if it can't even tell whether the program halts? So much for perfect automated software testing!

Lest you think that the only undecidable problems have to do with properties of computer programs, *Post's Correspondence Problem (PCP)* is about strings, such as we saw in Chapter 7. Suppose we have at least two characters, and we have two lists of n strings, A and B, over these characters. Let A consist of strings $A_1, A_2, A_3, \ldots, A_n$ and B consist of strings $B_1, B_2, B_3, \ldots, B_n$. The problem is to determine whether there exists a sequence of indices $i_1, i_2, i_3, \ldots, i_m$ such that $A_{i_1} A_{i_2} A_{i_3} \cdots A_{i_m}$ (that is, the strings $A_{i_1}, A_{i_2}, A_{i_3}, \ldots, A_{i_m}$ concatenated together) gives the same string as $B_{i_1} B_{i_2} B_{i_3} \cdots B_{i_m}$. For example, suppose that the characters are e, h, m, n, o, r, and y, that $n = 5$, and that

$$A_1 = \text{ey}, \qquad B_1 = \text{ym},$$
$$A_2 = \text{er}, \qquad B_2 = \text{r},$$
$$A_3 = \text{mo}, \qquad B_3 = \text{oon},$$
$$A_4 = \text{on}, \qquad B_4 = \text{e},$$
$$A_5 = \text{h}, \qquad B_5 = \text{hon}.$$

Then one solution is the index sequence $\langle 5, 4, 1, 3, 4, 2 \rangle$, since both $A_5 A_4 A_1 A_3 A_4 A_2$ and $B_5 B_4 B_1 B_3 B_4 B_2$ form honeymooner. Of course, if there's one solution, there are an infinite number of solutions, since you can just keep repeating the index sequence of a solution (giving honeymoonerhoneymooner, etc.). For PCP to be undecidable, we have to allow the strings in A and B to be used more than once, since otherwise you could just list all the possible combinations of strings.

Although Post's Correspondence Problem might not seem particularly interesting on its own, we can reduce it to other problems to show that they, too, are undecidable. It's the same basic idea as we used to show that a problem is NP-hard: given an instance of PCP, transform it into an instance of some other problem Q, such that the answer to the instance of Q gives the answer to the instance of PCP. If we could decide Q, then we could decide PCP; but since we know that we cannot decide PCP, then Q must be undecidable.

Among the undecidable problems that we can reduce PCP to are several having to do with *context-free grammars (CFGs)*, which describe the syntax of most programming languages. A CFG is a set of rules for generating a *formal language*, which is a fancy way to say "a set of strings." By reducing from PCP, we can prove that it's undecidable whether two CFGs generate the same formal language, whether two CFGs generate any strings in common, or whether a given CFG is *ambiguous*: are there two different ways to generate the same string using the rules of the CFG?

Wrap-up

We've seen quite a range of algorithms in quite a variety of domains, haven't we? We've seen an algorithm that takes sublinear time—binary search. We've seen algorithms that take linear time—linear search, counting sort, radix sort, topological sort, and finding shortest paths in a dag. We've seen algorithms that take $O(n \lg n)$ time—merge sort and quicksort (average case). We've seen algorithms that take $O(n^2)$ time—selection sort, insertion sort, and quicksort (worst case). We've seen graph algorithms that take time described by some non-linear combination of the number n of vertices and the number m of edges—Dijkstra's algorithm and the Bellman-Ford algorithm. We've seen a graph algorithm that takes $\Theta(n^3)$ time—the Floyd-Warshall algorithm. Now we've seen that for some problems, we have no idea whether a polynomial-time algorithm is even possible. And we've even seen that for some problems, no algorithm is possible, regardless of the running time.

Even with this relatively brief introduction to the world of computer algorithms,[6] you can see that the area covers a lot of ground. And this book covers only the tiniest sliver of the area. Moreover, I have restricted our analyses to a particular computational model, in which only one processor performs operations and the time to perform each operation is more or less the same, regardless of where in the computer's memory the data reside. Many alternative computational models have been proposed over the years, such as models with multiple processors, models in which the time to perform an operation depends on where its data are located, models in which the data arrive in a nonrepeatable stream, and models in which the computer is a quantum device.

And so you can see that this field of computer algorithms has plenty of unanswered questions, as well as questions yet to be asked. Take an algorithms course—you can even take one online—and help us out!

Further reading

The book on NP-completeness is by Garey and Johnson [GJ79]. If you're interested in delving into this topic, read it. CLRS [CLRS09] has a chapter on NP-completeness, which goes into more technical detail than I've gone into here, and it also has a chapter on approximation algorithms. For more on computability and complexity, and a very nice, short, understandable proof that the halting problem is undecidable, I recommend the book by Sipser [Sip06].

---

[6]Compare the size of this book with CLRS, which weighs in at 1292 pages in its third edition.

Bibliography

[AHU74]   Alfred V. Aho, John E. Hopcroft, and Jeffrey D. Ullman. *The Design and Analysis of Computer Algorithms*. Addison-Wesley, 1974.

[AMOT90]   Ravindra K. Ahuja, Kurt Mehlhorn, James B. Orlin, and Robert E. Tarjan. Faster algorithms for the shortest path problem. *Journal of the ACM*, 37(2):213–223, 1990.

[CLR90]   Thomas H. Cormen, Charles E. Leiserson, and Ronald L. Rivest. *Introduction to Algorithms*. The MIT Press, first edition, 1990.

[CLRS09]   Thomas H. Cormen, Charles E. Leiserson, Ronald L. Rivest, and Clifford Stein. *Introduction to Algorithms*. The MIT Press, third edition, 2009.

[DH76]   Whitfield Diffie and Martin E. Hellman. New directions in cryptography. *IEEE Transactions on Information Theory*, IT-22(6):644–654, 1976.

[FIP11]   Annex C: Approved random number generators for FIPS PUB 140-2, Security requirements for cryptographic modules. http://csrc.nist.gov/publications/fips/fips140-2/fips1402annexc.pdf, July 2011. Draft.

[GJ79]   Michael R. Garey and David S. Johnson. *Computers and Intractability: A Guide to the Theory of NP-Completeness*. W. H. Freeman, 1979.

[Gri81]   David Gries. *The Science of Programming*. Springer, 1981.

[KL08]   Jonathan Katz and Yehuda Lindell. *Introduction to Modern Cryptography*. Chapman & Hall/CRC, 2008.

[Knu97]   Donald E. Knuth. *The Art of Computer Programming*, Volume 1: Fundamental Algorithms. Addison-Wesley, third edition, 1997.

[Knu98a]   Donald E. Knuth. *The Art of Computer Programming*, Volume 2: Seminumeral Algorithms. Addison-Wesley, third edition, 1998.

[Knu98b]   Donald E. Knuth. *The Art of Computer Programming*, Volume 3: Sorting and Searching. Addison-Wesley, second edition, 1998.

[Knu11]   Donald E. Knuth. *The Art of Computer Programming*, Volume 4A: Combinatorial Algorithms, Part I. Addison-Wesley, 2011.

[Mac12]   John MacCormick. *Nine Algorithms That Changed the Future: The Ingenious Ideas That Drive Today's Computers*. Princeton University Press, 2012.

[Mit96]   John C. Mitchell. *Foundations for Programming Languages*. The MIT Press, 1996.

[MvOV96]   Alfred Menezes, Paul van Oorschot, and Scott Vanstone. *Handbook of Applied Cryptography*. CRC Press, 1996.

[RSA78]   Ronald L. Rivest, Adi Shamir, and Leonard M. Adleman. A method for obtaining digital signatures and public-key cryptosystems. *Communications of the ACM*, 21(2):120–126, 1978. See also U.S. Patent 4,405,829.

[Sal08]   David Salomon. *A Concise Introduction to Data Compression*. Springer, 2008.

[Sip06]   Michael Sipser. *Introduction to the Theory of Computation*. Course Technology, second edition, 2006.

[SM08]   Sean Smith and John Marchesini. *The Craft of System Security*. Addison-Wesley, 2008.

[Sto88]   James A. Storer. *Data Compression: Methods and Theory*. Computer Science Press, 1988.

[TC11]   Greg Taylor and George Cox. Digital randomness. *IEEE Spectrum*, 48(9):32–58, 2011.

Index